THE NATURE AND FUNCTION OF FAITH IN THE THEOLOGY OF JOHN CALVIN

NABPR Dissertation Series, Number 2

by
Victor A. Shepherd

MERCER UNIVERSITY PRESS, Macon, Georgia 31207

ISBN 0-86554-066-7

All books published by Mercer University Press are produced
on acid-free paper that exceeds the minimum standards set by the
National Historical Publications and Records Commission.

Shepherd, Victor A., 1944-
    The nature and function of faith in the theology of John Calvin.

    (NABPR dissertation series; no. 2)
    Bibliography: p.241
    1. Faith—History of doctrines—16th century.
2. Calvin, Jean, 1509-1564. I Title. II Series.
BT771.2.S47   1983   234'.2   82-24899
ISBN 0-86554-066-7

The Nature and Function of Faith
in the Theology of John Calvin

TABLE OF CONTENTS

DEDICATION

To Maureen

INTRODUCTION

More helpful at the outset than an apology to the reader of a study of this length will be a map indicating that what is set before him is one long continuous path and not several shorter and unconnected ones.

Calvin maintains that Jesus Christ, the living Word of God, is both the author and object of faith; he is the "living root" whose "fruit" is faith. Or, to employ another favorite metaphor of Calvin's, Christ by the Holy Spirit "embraces" us, engendering in us the faith which in turn "embraces" or "puts on" him alone. And since he is the sole pledge of the Father's love (indeed, he *is* the Father's act of mercy), faith is engendered by mercy alone and faith cleaves to that mercy. Jesus Christ, indeed, does not will to be who he is apart from the power of making people his; that is, of "engrafting" people into that mercy. Faith, then, results from the action of the exalted Christ upon men as he bestows himself upon them and binds them to himself in the power of his Spirit.

Since Jesus Christ cannot be separated from his "benefits," and his benefits cannot be separated from each other (although they can and must be distinguished) faith "justifies" only in so far as faith puts on him who alone is rightly related to the Father. Hence righteousness, the correlate of justifying faith, always remains logically prior to faith; righteousness (justification) never inheres faith. Rather, righteousness is conferred as and only as Jesus Christ, the righteous One, bestows himself upon men. Similarly, faith "sanctifies" only in so far as faith is the embracing of the sanctified One, the new Man.

Yet it must be asked precisely how faith embraces Jesus Christ. According to Calvin men *qua* sinners are dead and hence utterly incapable of responding were life offered to them; that is, they do not cooperate with God in any way in the attainment of fellowship with Jesus Christ. Life is bestowed only as God wills to bestow it gratuitously; his effectual will is sheer mercy.

Since the aim of God's mercy, the resurrecting of men to sonship, is God's *eternal* purpose, he secures the fellowship of believers with Jesus Christ against everything which sunders or could sunder that relationship. Not that faith endures in its own strength, for faith, of itself, remains weak and prone to collapse; rather, because life is God's purpose from eternity to eternity, the mercy which raises the "spiritually dead" as it creates faith will ever be the determination of that new existence, notwithstanding appearances to the contrary. The guarantee of the continuation and consummation of life is not any human alteration manifest to sight, but the promise of mercy which *is* God's inviolable will. In sum, Jesus Christ is the author and object of faith in that he is the Father's eternal decree to save.

Because fallen man is an inveterate idolater, true faith must be distinguished sharply from various pretenders to faith; for example, opinion, ideology, religion, attachment to a vague "God," as well as "implicit" faith—one's assent to Church-formulations which one does not understand. These pretenders to faith are invariably the product of the sin-vitiated creature. True faith, on the other hand, is entirely the gratuitous gift of God.

To say that faith is given is to say that Jesus Christ freely bestows himself upon men in the totality of his reality. Now Calvin insists that knowledge engendered in the creature by that bestowal is essential to faith ("blind faith" is superstition). Nonetheless, it is not to be concluded that perfect knowlege (appropriate to the totality of Christ's reality) is an invariable aspect of fellowship with the One who cannot be divided; his self-bestowal does not instantaneously supplant sheer ignorance with perfect knowledge. Rather, in achieving his eternal purpose for men God is at work in unbelievers rendering them "teachable," drawing them to himself and creating in them a longing for him (that is, an aspiration to faith) even as he remains (as yet) unknown to them. Thus there is a fluid boundary between "teachableness" and true faith. Even true faith continues to be error- and ignorance-beclouded. Nonetheless, true faith continues to advance so as to shrink, proportionately, the element of error and ignorance.

Regardless of the weakness or immaturity of faith, it is nevertheless the true or authentic determination of creaturely life; that is, Jesus Christ determines the existence of those whom he has favored, in accord with his eternal plan and purpose, with his gift of himself as the new, true Man, by drawing them into that fellowship with him which is characterized by the word "faith." This authentic humanity which he imparts to believers, however, must yet be exercised or "lived out"; while believers are wholly renewed eschatologically, that renewal must (begin to) be given "shape" or structure in the present life. Calvin maintains, then, that Jesus Christ is the substance of the law; thus the law, with respect to its chief use, is that by which Jesus Christ conforms to his authentic humanity those who have become his through faith. In other words, since Christ is the substance of the law, and since Christ does not come without his Spirit whose entire work is faith, then the purpose of the law is existence-in-faith: the law subserves the putting on of Christ and, by implication, the formation of Jesus Christ within believers. This formation occurs as believers, gratefully acknowledging the claim of that mercy which has made them what they are, submit themselves obediently to their Lord. It must be stressed that Jesus Christ does not give "shape" to the lives of believers through enjoining behavioral conformity to a code, thus effecting "moral improvement," but rather by acting *himself* upon them so as to raise them to his mature manhood.

Because faith ever needs nourishing and guiding, God has appointed the Church as that apart from which faith will surely falter. As the "treasure" "deposited" in the Church, Jesus Christ continues to mold the lives of believers by means of the ordained ministry, whose functions (preaching the Word and administering the sacraments) coincide exactly with the marks of the true Church. In other words, Jesus Christ nourishes and guides faith, through the provision of the Church, as and only as the ordained ministry continues to declare the faith-sustaining Word. The sacraments are an aspect of that declaration; as signs of the Word they assist weak faith in so far as they reflect the promise of mercy with greater clarity to imperfect faith. While the reality of the sacraments (Jesus Christ, the Word of mercy) never inheres the creaturely elements (so as to render a receiving of the elements *ipso facto* a receiving of Jesus Christ), yet the Holy Spirit acts upon the declared Word and in the hearts and minds of believers so as to offer them Jesus Christ each time the sacraments are observed.

CHAPTER 1

THE WORD AND FAITH

"It is no ordinary praise of faith to call it the cause of our salvation."
(*Commentary* Luke 8:11)

"We must realize that the whole human race is by its nature deprived of those
blessings which Christ declares we obtain by the faith of his gospel.... Thus it
follows that all are blind, because they are enlightened by faith; that all are
slaves of Satan, because they are freed from his tyranny by faith; that all are
hostile to God and liable to eternal death, because they receive the remission
of sins by faith. Accordingly, there is nothing more wretched for us than to be
without Christ and his faith." (*Commentary* Acts 26:17-18)

THE WORD AS OBJECT OF FAITH

Calvin insists that the nature of faith is determined by faith's object,
the Word of God. Faith looks to that Word alone.[1] Calvin quotes a
favorite text again and again, insisting that everything which faith
receives is contained in the Word to which faith looks: "God made him
(Jesus Christ) our wisdom, our righteousness and sanctification and
redemption." (I Cor. 1:30). This Word is that act of God which is *extra
nos* but which is always enacted *pro nobis*. As the act of God this Word is
not vague or contentless: "Jesus Christ" is not religious sentiment. While
the living Word can never be equated with the conceptual content of
doctrine, at the same time Calvin insists that doctrine is indissolubly
connected with the reality it represents; while Jesus Christ must always be
differentiated from doctrine, his personal Presence is not apprehended
apart from it. Hence faith is neither engendered nor sustained without
doctrinal teaching: "nourishing occurs only by way of Christian doctrine";[2] the "words of faith" are simply "the sum of Christian doctrine."[3]

---

[1] A discussion of Calvin's notion of the knowledge of God is beyond the province of
this work. Suffice it to say that following the Fall, the *Opera Dei* bespeak God only in the
light of the *Oracula Dei*.

[2] *Comm.* I Tim. 4:6.

[3] Ibid. For a fuller statement of the relation of Jesus Christ, doctrine and teaching, see
below on preaching.

Indeed, Calvin speaks of the content of faith as "the new and extraordinary kind of teaching by which Christ, after he became our teacher, has more clearly set forth the mercy of the Father, and has more surely testified to our salvation."[4] There is no receiving Christ without believing him, and there is belief only where there is some knowledge of doctrine: "there are many who foolishly contrive for themselves a confused faith, without any understanding of doctrine."[5]

Yet it must be stressed that in believing the *gospel* we receive in faith Jesus Christ himself who offers himself to us through the gospel; that is, that which faith apprehends is neither doctrinal abstraction nor an imprecise "Christ," but "Christ-clothed-with-his-gospel."

Calvin insists that faith never has or can have any other object, for "there is a permanent relationship between faith and the Word."[6] Indeed, the Word is the foundation of faith; faith rests upon him, never upon itself: "faith cannot be formed without hearing (Romans 10:17); that is, without understanding the Word of God; and so he bids us 'hear' before we 'come' to him. Thus, whenever faith is mentioned, let us remember that it must be joined to the Word, in which it has its foundation."[7] Word and faith are as inseparable as the sun and its rays. Without the Word it is not that "faith" merely lacks an object—as though faith were an innate human capacity or a human form, presently empty, waiting to be filled with divine content. Rather, without the Word, there is no faith: "if faith turns away even in the slightest degree from this goal toward which it should aim, it does not keep its own nature, but becomes uncertain credulity and vague error of mind."[8] Thus, while Calvin often states that there is a "mutual relation" between faith and the Word, it must ever be remembered that the Word creates in man the capacity to receive the Word; the Word does not *find* a "mutual relation" in any human capacity. Calvin is uncompromising on this point: "there is not in us any commencement of faith or any preparation for it."[9] The distinction between Israel and the surrounding nations is not that the former partake of

---

[4]*Inst.* 3.2.6: *misericordiam.* It must not be thought that for Calvin revelation is primarily ideational, and therefore faith apprehension of the information. Calvin wishes to stress here that revelation is not contentless. See below for relation of notional and extra-notional aspects of faith.

[5]*Comm.* John 1:12.

[6]*Inst.* 3.2.6.

[7]*Comm.* Isa. 55:3.

[8]*Inst.* 3.2.6: *incerta est credulitas et vagus mentis error.*

[9]*Comm.* John 6:45.

"religious genius," but rather that to Israel God has directed his "voice" (that is, his Word) as he has not to the latter.[10]

At the same time, it must be asked whether faith, upon apprehending the Word, apprehends merely something of God or God himself in his being "God-for-us." Calvin insists that the Word is God himself in his activity on our behalf: "the Word itself . . . is like a mirror in which faith may contemplate God[11] . . . God always represents himself through his Word to those whom he wills to draw to himself."[12] Similarly Calvin writes, "we ought to rely on the Word as fully as if God manifested himself to us from heaven; for he who has not this conviction [that the Word *is* God] understands nothing."[13] (It is clear that throughout his writings Calvin identifies the Word as God; subsequently Calvin's understanding of the relation between the Spirit (of the Word) and the Word will be discussed and the ramifications of this for his pneumatology and his understanding of the Trinity. In all these discussions his understanding is consistent both internally and with the best in the tradition of the Church: there is no action of God which is inconsistent with God's nature; the Word of God himself acting *pro nobis*. Yet, the consistency and even the soundness of Calvin's Trinitarian understanding with respect to the relation of election and faith will be questioned.)

However, since God unquestionably created the whole order of nature, cannot faith apprehend God's power and works apart from the Word? Calvin insists that whatever man conceives of God's power and works is salvifically ineffective without the Word;[14] a perusal of nature does not convince man of that power of God which is unto salvation, this latter being associated always with the Word. "Faith always connects the power of God with the Word, which it does not imagine to be at a distance, but, having inwardly conceived it, possesses and retains it."[15] Anything of God which is *inferred* from nature is remote, vague, and of no salvific import. Accordingly, Calvin states that he can "declare with good reason that there is no faith until God illumines it (that is, the Word)

---

[10]*Comm.* Psalm 95:7.

[11]*Inst.* 3.2.6: *sed verbum ipsum, utcumque ad nos deferatur, instar speculi esse dicimus, in quo Deum intueatur fides.* Note that the Word is both the mirror and the image.

[12]*Inst.* 3.2.6: *semper tamen iis quos ad se trahere vult, per verbum suum se repraesentat.*

[13]*Comm.* II Tim. 1:12.

[14]For a useful discussion of this point see T.H.L. Parker, *Calvin's Doctrine of the Knowledge of God.*

[15]*Comm.* II Tim. 1:12.

by the testimony of his grace."[16] In commenting upon Psalm 119 Calvin notes that the psalmist "does not simply say that he trusted in God, but that he also trusted in his Word, which is the *ground* of his trust."[17]

In speaking of the correlation of Word and faith Calvin is not suggesting that Word-begotten faith necessarily excludes error; error certainly can be mingled with faith. While such error "obscures" faith, it does not "extinguish" it.[18] There is a difference between genuine (real, true) faith's being contiguous to error and the supplanting of faith by error which occurs when something other than the Word is put forward as the object of faith.

THE WORD AS AUTHOR OF FAITH

The Word of God is not simply the object of faith, as though the movement were always from faith to faith's object; rather, it is the Word which creates faith; indeed, the Word is the "living root" which produces the real "fruit."[19] Men are not merely exhorted to "have faith in Christ"; rather, Jesus Christ exhorts men to have faith in him on the ground of his action on behalf of them. Concerning Mark 1:15 Calvin states, "First he declares that the treasures of God's mercy have been opened in himself. Then . . . he requires trust in God's promises."[20] It is the action of God bearing down on man which creates in man the faith-relationship to that action. There is no human penetration to a knowledge of God's "name"; it is not that there is a human ascent to God, at which point faith embraces the Word. Indeed, ". . . we cannot take the right road to him (that is, the Christ who has been appointed as the goal of our faith) unless the gospel goes before us."[21] *It is the Word alone which creates access to the Word.* Since the true Christ is the Christ whom the Father offers to us "clothed with his gospel",[22] therefore the gospel is the "way" to Christ. There is no

---

[16]*Inst.* 3.2.31: "illumine"—*praeluceat.* Calvin will use *illumino* almost always for "illumine" with respect to the operation of the Holy Spirit upon the Word or upon men's minds and hearts. He uses *irradio* most frequently in the context of the "light" which steals into the hearts of those of unfaith but which is not sufficient to render the Word effective for men.

[17]*Comm.* Psalm 119:42 (italics mine).

[18]*Inst.* 3.2.3. For a fuller discussion of this point see Chapter Five.

[19]Ibid.

[20]*Inst.* 3.3.19: "trust"—*fiducia,* which can mean both "trust" and "confidence".

[21]*Inst.* 3.2.26: *ita nonnisi praeeunte Evangelio recta ad eum tendemus.*

[22]Any notion of "Jesus after the flesh" Calvin maintains to pertain only to a *semblance* of faith.

human rendering of the gospel intelligible or receivable. It is not merely that men are unwilling to be spiritually perceptive, but rather that they are unable; "hence we infer that faith is not in one's own power, but is divinely conferred."[23] Similarly, "the Spirit of God, from whom the doctrine of the gospel comes, is its only true interpreter, to open it up to us."[24] The Word "makes room" for itself in men. The Word is the only fit witness to itself. Thus, when Calvin asseverates that *faith* opens access to the gospel[25] he can mean only that faith is the Word bearing witness to itself in men. Man's hearing (in faith) of the Word is his "overhearing" of the divine self-attestation. Faith is the Word, spoken to men, returning to itself.

Jesus Christ is ever the author of faith.[26] He creates that faith whose object he is. His "going before" us is ever logically prior to his being the "goal of our faith.' "

THE WORD AS PROMISE

Granted that the Word is both author and object of faith, and granted that the Word is variegated with respect to its content, one must ask whether it is the Word in its variegated entirety which effects faith, or one aspect of that Word; and if the latter, which aspect, and why? Calvin prefaces his answer to this question by specifying the cognitive content of faith's knowledge of the Word as faith's knowledge of God's will toward us: "for it is not so much our concern to know what he is in himself, as what he wills to be for us. Now, therefore, we hold faith to be a knowledge of God's will toward us, perceived from his Word."[27] The foundation of

---

[23]*Comm.* I Cor. 2:14.

[24]Ibid.

[25]*Comm.* Heb. 11:6.

[26]For a discussion of *how* he is the author of faith, see below concerning the Holy Spirit.

[27]*Inst.* 3.2.6: *iam ergo habemus fidem esse divinae erga nos voluntatis notitiam exeius verbo perceptam.* Calvin uses a variety of words for "knowledge": *agnitio* (often with the nuance of "recognition"), *cognitio, notitia* (where the context will suggest either "conception" or "acknowledgement"), *scientia* ("expert knowledge"), and *intelligentia* ("perception"). The first three are translated, almost without exception, by *la cognoissance* in French. *Scientia* is usually translated *la science*, and is used much less frequently than the first three.

this is a "preconceived conviction of God's truth."[28] That of the Word which as *fundamentum* effects faith is the mercy or benevolence of God.[29]

The Word of God includes every act and attitude of God directed *ad nos*; as such it contains exhortations, encouragements, warnings and threats—none of which properly begets faith; that is, in the foregoing faith finds nothing upon which to "lean and rest."[30] While faith should certainly hearken to every aspect of the variegated Word, it is certainly only *faith* which so hearkens, *which faith is created by the word of mercy alone*: "it is *after* we have learned that our salvation rests with God that we are attracted to seek him. This fact is confirmed for us when he declares that our salvation is his care and concern. Accordingly, we need the promise of grace, which can testify to us that the Father is merciful, since we can approach him in no other way, and upon grace alone the heart of man can rest."[31] It is not that genuine faith arises as one becomes convinced of some aspect of the Word of God; becoming convinced only of God's judgment could, for instance, drive one away from him in cowering fear: what sensible man seeks a destroyer? Therefore, merely to know God's will is insufficient to establish faith. Faith arises (from a human perspective) upon the discernment that ultimately God is *for us*; this knowledge alone brings men to faith.

Knowing that God is *true* will not help us unless he *mercifully* attracts us to himself.[32] Mercy and truth are conjoined: without the "preconceived" conviction of God's truth, unbelief continues to rule men of unfaith; without mercy as the central (and, as will be seen shortly, the determinative) truth of the Word, men would not dare to entrust themselves to God.

> This conjunction Calvin notes to be characteristic of the psalmist. In Ps. 40:10 are mentioned "righteousness," "truth," "salvation," and "mercy" in the foregoing order. Calvin comments, "If these four things should be taken in their proper order, mercy will hold the first place, as it is that by which alone God is induced to vouchsafe to regard us."[33] Elsewhere he states, "God acts in such a manner towards his people as that, in all respects, they may find from

---

[28] *Inst.* 3.2.6. "Presupposed"—*praesumpta*. *Praesumpta* in the sense that genuine (as opposed to implicit) faith presupposes understanding and conviction of truth; but never "preconceived" in the sense that man has the ability to inform himself of the truth of the Word. Also, *praesumpta* connotes a logical but not a chronological priority.

[29] Ibid.: *misericoria benevolentia*.

[30] *Inst.* 3.2.7: *nitatur et recumbat*.

[31] *Inst.* 3.2.7 (italics mine).

[32] *Inst.* 3.2.7: *quando voluntatem Dei qualemcumque nosse pro fide censendum non est*.

[33] *Comm.* Psalm 40:10.

experience that he is merciful and faithful."[34] Again, "The prophet. . .has placed his (that is, God's) mercy first in order that his faithfulness and truth, comprising an assurance of his paternal kindness, might encourage the hearts of the godly. His power and justice are equally praiseworthy, but . . . men will never cordially praise God until they are drawn by a foretaste of his goodness."[35]

Our knowledge of God's benevolence is pivotal, in that without our knowledge of that goodness we should never cast ourselves upon him.[36] Moreover, while men might offer a vast number of speculations concerning God, they will never by speculation arrive at the conclusion that he is well-disposed towards them. God himself must attest this to them, and his call of mercy must "go before" them.[37]

God attests himself as mercy only in Christ. Jesus Christ, maintains Calvin, is "the sole pledge of his love";[38] apart from Christ there are everywhere the signs of God's hatred and wrath. Accordingly, in whatever manner or proportion doubt and understanding are mixed in the man of faith, concerning the matter of Jesus Christ as the manifest pledge of God's mercy genuine faith can be in no doubt whatsoever.

In other words, while faith hearkens to the different aspects of God's word, it *rests* on the promise of mercy, for faith seeks life in God, and life is found only in the promise. Moreover, the promise must be understood as freely given, for a conditional promise merely sends us back into ourselves who need mercy, and who can never meet the prescribed conditions. Thus it is the mercy-bespeaking gospel which is the *word of faith*.

This latter affirmation is crucial, for it avers that the ever-merciful One alone determines the nature of faith; that is, any hearkening to, orientation toward, and conformity to other aspects of God's Word do not engender faith. No belief in other aspects of the Word, however sincere and however correct, is yet faith. The nature of faith is given entirely by the correlate of faith: *mercy*. Mercy, then, is always logically prior to faith. Calvin insists that the gospel (that is, mercy) ". . . offering itself at hand, kindly invites us to a fruition of itself. . . . The word of faith is to be taken for the word of promise, that is, for the gospel itself, because it bears a relation to faith."[39] Since faith is but the Word of mercy bearing

---

[34] *Comm.* Psalm 25:10.

[35] *Comm.* Psalm 117:2.

[36] *Inst.* 3.2.7: "pivotal"—*habitura* (*l'importance*); "cast"—*acquiescere* (*reposer*)

[37] *Inst.* 3.2.7: *sua invitatione praeveniat.*

[38] *Inst.* 3.2.7.

[39] *Comm.* Rom. 10:8: *quoniam relationem habet cum fide.*

fruit, there is an internal, non-contingent relation between mercy and faith. It is not that "faith" is somehow the point of contact between a word of God (which happens to be mercy, in one instance) and men; rather, mercy itself, when bestowed upon men by the Holy Spirit, "forges" faith so as to mold faith after mercy.[40] Only God's act of mercy wherein he reconciles the world to himself can establish faith.[41] In mercy God no longer counts men's trespasses against them. *That* act of God effects a faith whose nature reflects its discernment of what has been done *extra nos*. Accordingly, when Calvin speaks of the frequent correlation in St. Paul between the gospel and faith, he does not understand the correlation to be of such sort that faith is primarily a human action which goes out to meet a divine action which dovetails with it; his saying that "the gospel requires nothing else but that men *bring faith* to receive the grace of God"[42] has the force of "God attests his own activity among men." In short, the gospel determines entirely its own correlate.

Calvin insists that since the gospel effects reconciliation, "no other sufficiently firm testimony of God's benevolence to us exists, the knowledge of which faith seeks."[43] Again, this statement must be given its full weight: just because the gospel *is* that merciful act wherein God reconciles us to himself, nothing outside of this act or in addition to it can convince us of God's mercy. God alone testifies to us concerning his own action; the mercy of God must shine in its own light; nothing else can illuminate it for us or enlighten us concerning it. Mercy alone grants knowledge of mercy, as men are included in that mercy. Faith is that inclusion.

It already has been indicated that the promise of mercy is the exclusive goal of faith.[44] Calvin goes farther: the God who is mirrored in his Word and whom faith apprehends is *characterized* by mercy. Hence he avers,

> "God is bountiful and inclined to compassion, and . . . his mercy is so great as to render it impossible for him to reject any who implore his aid."[45]

> "The knowledge of his goodness is fitted both to build up our faith, and to illustrate his praises."[46]

---

[40] Hence one may put to rest the caricature of Calvin's understanding of faith as the servile submission to the omnipotent and arbitrary God.

[41] *Inst.* 3.2.19: "establish"—*stabilire*—*asseurer*. Note the nuance of the French. See below for a discussion of the relation of assurance to faith.

[42] *Comm.* Rom. 10:8 (italics mine).

[43] *Inst.* 3.2.29.

[44] *Inst.* 3.2.29: *fidei in proprium* ("characteristic," "essential," "exclusive"—all of which are more precise than Battles' "proper") *scopum*.

[45] *Comm.* Psalm 86:5.

[46] *Comm.* Psalm 103:8.

"The mercy of God extends to all his works . . . even in helping the brute creation."[47]

Nonetheless, Calvin would never deny that believers embrace the Word of God in its totality: exhortations, warnings, admonitions, as well as declarations of mercy. His critics maintain that there is an inconsistency here with respect to faith: faith is said to be left looking to the Word of God in two different respects, wherein one cannot be subsumed under the other. We have already seen that for him faith does not stand firm until a man attains to the freely given promise,[48] which faith "properly springs from promises; it is founded on them, it rests on them."[49] It is this faith which rests on the promise of mercy which "hears God in whatever he says . . . and (thus) faith alone is the teacher of obedience."[50] Calvin is here pointing to what he will state explicitly; namely, that since faith "does not reconcile us to God at all unless it joins us to Christ,"[51] and since Christ is mercy Incarnate, and since mercy (the Word) is both the "whence" and the "whither" of faith, therefore the Word of mercy must include within itself the other "words" which faith receives obediently. Indeed, Calvin states that the whole of the gospel is included under the knowledge of mercy, since all the promises of God find their "yes" in Christ: "Christ is the foundation and security of all the promises of God; it is only in Christ that God the Father is propitious to us. Now the promises are testimonies of his fatherly kindness towards us. Hence it is in him alone that they are fulfilled."[52] Similarly he adds, "if God promises anything, by it he witnesses his benevolence, so that there is no promise of his which is not a testimony of his love."[53] Because of God's merciful act in the Son, whose Father he is, his Fatherhood is the determination of his being towards us: "the designation of Son belongs truly and naturally to Christ alone; but yet he was declared to be the Son of God in the flesh, that the favour of him, whom he alone has a right to call God Father, may be also obtained for us. And thus when God presents Christ to us as Mediator, accompanied by the title Son, he declares that he is the Father of us all. . . ."[54] Calvin

---

[47] *Comm.* Psalm 145:9.

[48] *Inst.* 3.2.30.

[49] *Comm.* Heb. 11:7: *proprie quidem ex promissionibus fidem nasci, in illis esse fundatam, in illis collinare.*

[50] *Comm.* Heb. 11:7.

[51] *Inst.* 3.2.30.

[52] *Comm.* II Cor. 1:20. Christ is the *firmamentum* of all the promises of God.

[53] *Inst.* 3.2.32.

[54] *Comm.* Matt. 3:17.

is not suggesting a universalism here; he admits that ultimate loss is possible, since mercy can be spurned. He does insist, however, that in the face of God's *characteristic* will-to-mercy, ultimate loss does not arise from an aspect of the Word which mercy does not include. It arises from the rebuff which met the Word of mercy, which Word subsumes *every* other word of God. Hence ultimate loss "may be regarded as accidental, or as arising from a different cause; for they who reject the grace offered in him deserve to find him the judge and avenger of contempt so unworthy and base."[55] In the same vein he states, "now if it be the office of Christ to save what was lost, they who reject the salvation offered in him are justly suffered to remain in death."[56]

In short, the Word is ever unambiguous mercy; everything Jesus Christ intends for his people (reproof, rebuke, chastening) ultimately points to his mercy. Every word is confirmed in and testifies to the Word of mercy.[57]

Appendix I. E. A. Dowey maintains that Calvin never reconciles satisfactorily faith's looking to *the* promise (of mercy) and faith's adhering to the promises.[58] He argues that Calvin is left with faith having two different and irreconcilable objects. To be sure, Calvin does speak, rather inelegantly and rather imprecisely, of the progression from the Word at large to the Word of the gratuitous promise as a descent from genus to species: *quanquam facilior erit et aption methodus, si gradatim a genere ad speciem descendimus.* Here Dowey maintains that Calvin affirms the object of faith to comprehend less than God's total utterance; he insists that Calvin is left with a situation where the knowledge of God by the man of faith has two different contents: the promise (of mercy), and the promis*es* (or everything else that God says in Scripture). This situation reflects, says Dowey, an irremediable discrepancy between the formal principle (*sola scriptura*) and the material principle (justification by faith) of the Reformation: on the one hand, faith is directed exclusively towards Christ; on the other, faith apprehends the total Scriptural witness.

Dowey, however, misconceives the problem. He fails to see what has been indicated above concerning Calvin's implicit and explicit understanding of the relation of the Word of mercy to the variegated Word in its entirety. He fails to see that the real problem does not arise here, but

---

[55]*Comm.* John 3:17.

[56]*Comm.* John 3:36.

[57]Of course the foregoing applies to believers only, who alone participate in this mercy and therefore who have as the determination of their existence the fellowship of this mercy. Outside of Christ there is only the wrath and hatred of God.

[58]E. A. Dowey, *The Knowledge of God in Calvin's Theology,* 160f.

with the matter of election. It is obvious that for the elect every action of God upon them must subserve mercy: rebuke and reproof are ultimately taken up into and consummated in God's effectual will to save; for the elect, the promise of mercy "covers" every word addressed to them.

The problem concerning the reprobate is not really that the promises do not subserve the promise, but that for them there really is no promise. Thus Calvin escapes the discrepancy which Dowey imputes to him, but only at the price of landing in a greater problem.[59] However, it cannot be denied that with regard to the elect Calvin consistently affirms the Christogenic nature of faith: the promises subserve the promise.

> Evidence supporting the relation of promise and promises has already been adduced with respect to Psalms 25:10 and 40:10, as well as II Corinthians 1:20. There remain, nonetheless, a few references which render Dowey's thesis insupportable; for example,
>
> "It is indeed to be maintained as an axiom that all the promises of God, made to the faithful, flow from the free mercy of God, and are evidences of that paternal love and of that gratuitous adoption, on which their salvation is founded."[60]
>
> ". . . all that the Scripture anywhere says, concerning blessedness, is founded upon the free favour of God, by which he reconciles us to himself."[61]
>
> This notion was no late development with Calvin; as early as 1537 he wrote, ". . . all the promises of God are gathered together and confirmed in Christ."[62]

Calvin noted that St. Paul distinguished the gospel both from the law and from the promises; that is, the promise was distinguished from the promises which subserve it.[63] Calvin did relate them satisfactorily. Dowey saw a problem where there was none, and overlooked one which remains.

Appendix II. H. J. Forstman, in a manner very similar to Dowey, fails to appreciate the subtlety of Calvin's thought. Concerning the work of the Holy Spirit with respect to Scripture and faith he maintains, "In the one case the internal persuasion is that God is gratuitous mercy. In the other a man is persuaded that the Bible is the work of the Holy Spirit. The knowledge content of the one must always remain an inner persuasion; it can never be separated from this subjective character. With the other the persuasion confirms something which in turn opens up for the believer an almost infinite range of data which itself is *not at all related* to the internal persuasions. . . . The *erga nos* is not found in Calvin's doctrine of Scripture, nor is it mentioned in the chapter on the work of the Spirit in

---

[59]For an amplification of the difficulty see below on Election.

[60]*Comm.* Gen. 15:6.

[61]*Comm.* Psalm 32:1.

[62]*Instruction in Faith* (1537), 38.

[63]*Inst.* 3.2.29.

confirming the Scripture. No new self-understanding is involved in believing in the divine source of the Scripture."[64]

While it is beyond the province of this work to discuss Forstman's opinion of Calvin's doctrine of Scripture, it must be said that Forstman has failed, like Dowey, to see that every word of God points to and subserves the Word of mercy; accordingly, the nature of the Spirit's work with respect to Scripture cannot be of a different order from the nature of the Spirit's work of confirming the declaration of mercy.

With similar misunderstanding Forstman writes, "Obedience pervaded the whole of Calvin's theology, and it is always associated with the commands of God and thus with a legalistic understanding of the Christian faith."[65] Calvin states that St. Paul *defines* faith as "that obedience which is given to the gospel."[66] Since the gospel is nothing if not mercy, and since faith is always shaped by faith's object, legalism cannot be the response which the Word of mercy creates and elicits.

FAITH AS HIGHER KNOWLEDGE

We have seen that Jesus Christ as mercy is the author and object of faith. It must be stressed that he does not create faith in men without eliciting from them acknowledgement of him in his reality of mercy. He must be recognized. Calvin will not countenance any suggestion that there can be faith without anything being understood. Specifically, it must be *understood* that mercy *is* God's will towards us; "faith rests not on ignorance but on knowledge."[67] Calvin contrasts those who have "nothing but a confused and evanescent knowledge" with those who have "clear and full perception."[68] Faith "contains nothing but known and ascertained truth."[69] Knowledge is ever of the essence of faith. We obtain salvation not by embracing as true whatever we are told on another's supposed authority, or by relegating to someone else the task of enquiry, but rather when we "*know* that God is our merciful Father because of the reconciliation effected through Christ," and when we *know* that "Christ

---

[64]H. J. Forstman, *Word and Spirit*, 102-104 (italics mine).

[65]Ibid. p. 136.

[66]*Inst.* 3.2.6. Cf. *Comm.* Rom. 1:5: "Faith is properly that by which we obey the gospel."

[67]*Inst.* 3.2.2.

[68]*Comm.* Col. 2:2. For the same notion see *Comms.* Col. 1:9 and 3:10.

[69]*Comm.* Titus 1:1.

has been given to us as righteousness, sanctification, and life."[70] Indeed, he states that St. Paul indicates that the requisite of faith is "explicit recognition of God's goodness";[71] without such recognition there is no faith. Again, since authentic confession presupposes knowledge, St. Paul's insistence that confession is essential to salvation can mean only that without knowledge there can be only a semblance of faith.

It should be noted that Calvin does not develop his understanding of election (which, as will be seen, is the ultimate cause of faith) so as to suggest that the elect are elected irrespective of knowledge; rather, they are elected to faith in Christ. And knowledge is essential to such faith.

Calvin does not pretend that the presence of any ignorance precludes faith; indeed, it would be absurd to suggest that believers possess all knowledge. As long as believers are "in the flesh" some ignorance will remain. Nonetheless, the fact that such knowledge is somewhat obscure does not undermine its being genuine acknowledgement of mercy and the ground of the recognition and repudiation of false gods. While the knowledge of the disciples undoubtedly did increase after the Resurrection, the increase was possible only because there was first in their hearts "the seed of hidden faith" in so far as they had "reverently embraced Christ as their sole teacher."[72] They had *recognized* the merciful One as the mirror-image of God. Such recognition Calvin contrasts with "implicit faith," wherein nothing is understood, and nothing is therefore recognized, but something is affirmed "because the Church says so." One need not be able to articulate all the subtleties of the content of faith before one becomes an authentic believer; nevertheless, without the recognition that in Jesus Christ God is *for me*, "faith" is nothing more than superstition.[73]

What is the specific nature of that knowledge which is constitutive of faith? Calvin makes the obvious point that this knowledge is not "comprehension of the sort that is concerned with those things which fall under human sense perception. For faith is so far above sense that man's mind has to go beyond and rise above itself in order to attain it. Even where the mind has attained, it does not comprehend what it feels. But while it is persuaded of what it does not grasp, by the very certainty of its persuasion

---

[70]*Inst.* 3.2.2 (italics mine). Note the logical order: knowledge arises from God's prior activity.

[71]*Inst.* 3.2.2.

[72]*Inst.* 3.2.4. For a fuller discussion of this point see Chapter Five.

[73]Calvin admits that there can be a true Church from which believers must not separate even when there is some faulty doctrine present. See Chapter Seven.

it understands more than if it perceived anything human by its own capacity."[74]

This passage is crucial, for here Calvin wishes to assert several essential features of faith as knowledge:

(i) The knowledge of faith is not of the same order as sense-knowledge, and therefore the knowledge of faith is not a creaturely possibility; man does not have a natural human capacity for faith; with respect to the knowledge of God, grace does not perfect nature.

> This latter point Calvin makes in several places in the *Commentaries*. "Away now with those who idly say that men are prepared for receiving the grace of God by the movement of nature. They might as well say that the dead walk."[75]
>
> "Nothing which relates to the Holy Spirit can be learned by human reasoning; . . . he is known only by the experience of faith."[76]
>
> "The gifts of the Spirit are not the gifts of nature. Till the Lord opens them, the eyes of our heart are blind. . . . Till the Spirit of God has made it known to us by a secret revelation, the knowledge of our divine calling exceeds the capacity of our minds."[77] (Here Calvin insists that the natural mind is so far from being "on the way to faith" that it lacks even the capacity for faith. The capacity for such knowledge is a gift of the Spirit.)
>
> "No man can approach to God without being raised above himself and above the world."[78]
>
> "These words (that is, 'to whom the arm of the Lord has been revealed') refute the ignorance of those who think that faith is in the power of every person because preaching is common to all."[79]

(ii) Nonetheless, the knowledge of faith is more certain than sense-knowledge, since it does not arise from the natural human capacity for

---

[74]*Inst.* 3.2.14: *Cognitionem dum vocamus, non intelligimus* (Fr. *entondons*) *comprehensionem, qualis esse solet earum rerum quae sub humanum sensum cadunt. Adeo enim superior est, ut mentem hominis seipsam excedere et superare oporteat, quo ad illam pertingat. Neque etiam ubi pertigit, quod sentit assequitur: sed dum persuasum habet quod non capit, plus ipsa persuasionis certitudine intelligit quam si humanum aliquid sua capacitate perspiceret.*

[75]*Comm.* John 11:2S. Here I must disagree with B. Milner: ". . . the natural capacity for knowledge of God is steadily excited by the Spirit to the point of true and complete knowledge" (*Calvin's Doctrine of the Church*, 124).

[76]*Comm.* John 14:17.

[77]*Comm.* Eph. 1:17. Suffice it to say in this discussion that the Fall defaces the *Imago Dei*; were it to efface it, man, says Calvin, would no longer be human. Nonetheless, Calvin does not regard the defaced *Imago Dei* as something on which God builds knowledge of God. Fallen man is not sick, but dead—*coram Deo*.

[78]*Comm.* Eph. 3:19: *Nam hominem, ut ad Deum accedat, supra se et mundum attolli oportet.*

[79]*Comm.* Isa. 53:1.

knowledge with its weakness. The knowledge of faith is indeed *knowledge* and cannot be reduced to opinion or wishful thinking: "the word to *know* shows the certainty of faith, in order to distinguish it from opinion."[80] (iii) Since the human mind does not "comprehend what it feels" neither speculation nor rational demonstration facilitate the knowledge of faith. (Calvin's metaphysical assumption is that the spheres of divine and human being are distinct and are joined only by grace. God knows himself, and any human knowledge of him is an inclusion by grace in his self-knowing.)

(iv) Since that of which the mind is persuaded it yet does not "grasp," rational orthodoxy is ruled out. The apprehension of doctrinal content is not co-terminous with the knowledge of faith. Here Calvin distinguishes himself from the subsequent orthodox Calvinists. At the same time, of course, it is not suggested that the knowledge of faith has no relation to doctrine; while the Word of God is distinct from scripture, it is never separate from it. Here Calvin distinguishes himself from the Enthusiasts.

(v) This knowledge carries its own certainty with it; it requires nothing outside of itself to authenticate itself as knowledge to believers. In other words, this knowledge must not be confused with the human judgment of evidence; faith cannot be demonstrated, but it is knowledge nonetheless. Its not being *generated* by natural human reason does not impugn its being knowledge. Indeed, this knowledge possesses greater certainty than that which is supported by demonstrable proof. And since this knowledge is that of *faith* rather than of *sight*, Calvin concludes that "the knowledge of faith consists in assurance rather than in comprehension."[81]

(vi) This knowledge must never be confused with ratiocination or a theological abstraction:

> "We do not attain salvation by a frigid and bare knowledge of God, which all confess to be most true; for salvation comes to us by faith for this reason, because it joins us to God. And this comes not in any other way than by being united to the body of Christ, so that, living through his Spirit, we are also governed by him. There is no such thing as this in the dead image of faith."[82]

> Calvin contrasts faith with "the common knowledge of God, which can no more connect man with God than the sight of the sun carry him up to heaven."[83]

To this point, the discussion has used various related terms; for example, "God's will," "Word," "knowledge," and so forth. In his exposition of

---

[80] *Comm.* I John 3:2. For a discussion of opinion see Chapter Five.

[81] *Inst.* 3.2.14: *unde statuimus fidei notitiam certitudine magis quam apprehensione contineri.*

[82] *Comm.* James 2:14: *ex fide . . . mortu fidei simulacro.*

[83] *Comm.* James 2:19: *vulgari notitia.*

Colossians Calvin succinctly implies their relationship: "The knowledge of the divine will . . . sets aside all inventions of men, and all speculations that are at variance with the Word of God. For his will is not to be sought anywhere else than in his Word. . . . The will of God [is] the only rule of right knowledge."[84] The will of God, as we have seen, is effectual mercy; *faith* begins as a recognition of that mercy, such recognition having to be Word-facilitated. Man cannot inform himself that God is mercy.

THE HOLY SPIRIT AND FAITH

"Faith is the proper and entire work of the Holy Spirit."[85]

Fallen man's blinded mind does not perceive the will of God, nor does his wandering heart rest secure in the conviction of God's goodness. Accordingly, his mind needs illumining and his heart strengthening, that "the Word of God may obtain full faith" with him.[86] Faith, then, is "a firm and certain knowledge of God's benevolence toward us, founded upon the truth of the freely given promise in Christ, both revealed to our minds and sealed upon our hearts through the Holy Spirit."[87] So far we have dealt with the notions of benevolence, truth, promise, and knowledge. It remains for us to probe Calvin's understanding of the function of the Holy Spirit with respect to these.

The Holy Spirit does not operate in such a way as to render man capable of recognizing the truth of the Word (which is *extra nos*) even as that Word remains *extra nos*; the Holy Spirit does not operate primarily in such a way as to effect intelligibility in a reality which remains "over there." Rather, Calvin maintains that the Holy Spirit primarily effects participation in Jesus Christ who is the new Man; the elevation of the believer's mind to a discernment of the promise is a consequence of this incorporation-participation. The Holy Spirit does not first of all bestow the capacity for faith; rather, he bestows this capacity even as he "inserts" *(insero)* the believer in the new man. It is not that the Holy Spirit primarily grants acquisition of knowledge which man theretofore lacks. Thus while it is true that there is no newness of life without newness of knowlege,

---

[84] *Comm.* Col. 1:9.

[85] *Inst.* 4.14.8: *proprium ac solidum* (Fr. *propre et entière*). (See n. 44 concerning *proprium*.)

[86] *Inst.* 3.2.7.

[87] *Inst.* 3.2.7: *divinae erga nos benevolentiae firmam certamque cognitionem, quae gratuitae in Christo promissionis veritate fundata, per Spiritum sanctum et revelatur mentibus nostris et cordibus obsignatur.*

Calvin's order must be observe carefully; he insists that St. Paul speaks "not as though a simple and bare knowledge were sufficient, but . . . of the illumination of the Holy Spirit, which is lively and effectual, so as not merely to enlighten the mind by kindling it with the light of truth, *but transforming the whole man.*"[88] It is only in this sense that the Spririt is "the inner teacher by whose effor the promise of salvation penetrates into our minds."[89] The Spirit's illumination of the mind is always a consequence of man's being incorporated into the Word; knowledge of the promise is a predicate of participating in the true Humanity. Thus Calvin insists that no one can have any knowledge of the Word "without at the same time apprehending the sanctification of the Spirit."[90]

It must ever be remembered that revelation is not the dissemination of information; revelation is the act of God wherein he effects a new reality: Jesus Christ, who comes with the power to include men within his (true) Humanity. Faith, then, can be only the sharing of the total person—mind and heart—in that reality. His sharing in that reality is then the determination of his existence, which determination brings with it its own certainty.

In a word, the Holy Spirit is the bond which binds us to Christ.[91] While God certainly acts *pro nobis*, he does not act by infusing qualities of life into men, but by binding men to the One who is Life. Apart from this binding men do not share in that life. God's saving act in Christ does not of itself guarantee life for men:

> "We must understand that as long as Christ remains outside of us, and we are separated from him, all that he has suffered and done for the salvation of the human race remains useless and of no value for us."[92]

> "The death of Christ would be of no avail to us, if we did not experience its fruit and efficacy."[93]

> "The blood of Christ which has been shed will avail us nothing, except as consciences are cleansed by it . . . the Holy Spirit sprinkles our souls with the blood of Christ for the expiation of our sins."[94]

---

[88] *Comm.* Col. 3:10 (italics mine).

[89] *Inst.* 3.1.4.

[90] *Inst.* 3.2.8: *apprehendat.* The English "apprehend" suggests intellectual perception, understanding, etc. The force of the Latin *apprehendo* is to seize or take hold of. These latter meanings accord more with what Calvin intends.

[91] *Inst.* 3.1.1: *viniculum.*

[92] *Inst.* 3.1.1.

[93] *Comm.* Isa. 53:10.

[94] *Comm.* I Pet. 1:2.

"Let us now state the substance of the whole: which is, that our salvation flows from the gratuitous election of God; but that it is to be ascertained by the experience of faith, because he sanctifies us by his Spirit."[95]

"The cleansing effected by Christ and the attainment of righteousness are of no avail except to those who have been made partakers of those blessings by the power of the Spirit. . . . Christ, then, is the source of all blessings to us; from him we obtain all things; but Christ himself, with all his blessings, is communicated to us by the Spirit. For it is by faith that we receive Christ and have his graces applied to us. The author of faith is the Spirit."[96] Otherwise put, the Word "never puts forth its power except when faith gives it an entrance."[97]

While Jesus Christ *is* righteousness, sanctification, wisdom and redemption, those benefits are "made" ours only as we "put on" Christ, "clothe" ourselves with him, become "ingrafted into" him, are taken "out of" ourselves and put "in" him. This is possible only through the Holy Spirit, who is the bond "by which Christ effectually unites us to himself."[98] The Holy Spirit is the power in which the exalted Christ acts on men so as to draw them to himself, incorporate them into himself, and give them what is his. Calvin is most emphatic that Spirit-incorporation into Christ does indeed "benefit"; it is effectual. Believers, having put on Christ, "are so closely united to him that in the presence of God they bear the name and character of Christ, and are viewed in him rather than in themselves."[99] But this occurs only as in the power of the Spirit men are ingrafted into Christ. There is no sharing in Christ's benefits which the Father has prepared apart from a sharing in Christ himself. This the Holy Spirit effects through faith. Apart from the power of the Spirit the preaching of the gospel would be totally ineffective, and Christ's benefits would remain "unavailing." While *man's* (Spirit-begotten) faith does not generate life in Christ, the relation of faith to that life is so close that Calvin can speak of faith as the cause of life.[100]

---

[95] Ibid.: *sed eam simul considerandum esse fidei experientia.* . . . Note the order here: the renewal of the Holy Spirit brings about that experience. (*Experientia* can be translated "practice" or "proof." "Proof" suggests what Calvin wants to say: that the renewal of the Holy Spirit authenticates itself through faith.)

[96] *Comm.* I Cor. 6:11.

[97] *Comm.* Heb. 4:2.

[98] *Inst.* 3.1.1: *Spiritum sanctum viniculum esse, quo nos sibi efficaciter devincit Christus.*

[99] *Comm.* Gal. 3:27: *nomen ac personam. Persona* is a most important word for Calvin. The *persona* of Christ is his reality, and not merely his appearance. See Calvin's work on Scripture where he says that Scripture bears the *persona* of God; i.e., the claim which Scripture makes to authority is of the same nature as God's claim to authority: it is not authoritarian. Cf. *Inst.* 1.7.

[100] *Comm.* John 3:36: *causa* (*causa* has the force of "occasion" as well as "cause").

It should be noted that because faith admits us to Christ and thus confers upon us every gift which the Father wishes to bestow (there being nothing for God to give us in addition to what he gives us in Christ), faith is not merely the "principal" work of the Holy Spirit,[101] or the "peculiar" work[102] but the *entire* work of the Spirit.[103] The Holy Spirit has no other function than to beget faith; that is, the Holy Spirit does not grant anything from himself: his whole purpose is applying Christ-with-his-benefits to men. He is the power in which Christ confers his benefits upon men—which is to say that he creates faith. Faith is *the* gift of God.[104]

There remains an important matter which has been touched on above and which is most significant for the consistency (or inconsistency) of Calvin's understanding of the relation of Word, Spirit, election, and faith: is the Holy Spirit always and only the spirit of Christ? The material in the preceding section would seem to suggest that he is. Nonetheless, this matter should be established incontrovertibly.

Calvin insists that Christ came endowed with the Spirit; indeed, he is the bearer of the Spirit *par excellence*: God has "bestowed the whole fullness of the Spirit upon the Son to be minister and steward of his liberality."[105] This notion Calvin amplifies in a *Commentary*:

"They who separate Christ from his own Spirit make him like a dead image or carcass. . . . We become Christians through his Spirit. . . . The Spirit is, without any distinction, called sometimes the Spirit of God the Father and sometimes the Spirit of Christ; and thus called not only because his whole fullness was poured on Christ as our Mediator and head, so that from him a portion might descend on each of us, but also because he is equally the Spirit of the Father and of the Son; who have one essence, and the same eternal divinity. . . . The power of quickening is in the Spirit of Christ."[106]

Calvin maintains that the Spirit is the Spirit of Christ on the ground of who Jesus Christ is; that is, "from his character as Mediator. For he would have come to us in vain if he had not been furnished with this power."[107] Similarly, Christ as teacher would shout to no effect "if Christ himself, inner schoolmaster, did not by his Spirit draw to himself those

---

[101] *Inst.* 3.1.4: *praecipium.*

[102] *Inst.* 3.2.39: *peculiare.*

[103] *Inst.* 4.14.8.

[104] *Inst.* 3.2.33.

[105] *Inst.* 3.11.12: *penes quem omnem Spiritus sancti plenitudinem deposuit.* The same expression is used in 3.1.2.

[106] *Comm.* Rom. 8:9-10: *effuso est tota illius plenitudo . . . spiritus patris et filii communio est.*

[107] *Inst.* 3.1.2: *quia nisi hac virtute praeditus, frustra ad nos venisset.*

given to him by the Father."[108] Elsewhere Calvin can move easily from
"the Spirit dwelling in us" to "Christ dwelling in us."[109] Indeed, Calvin
estimates that the statement "He shall baptize you with the Holy Spirit"
has the same force as the statement "It is Christ alone who washes souls
with his blood," since "this very washing is performed by the power of the
Spirit."[110] The Spirit, in other words, is Christ-in-his-action bestowing
himself upon men: "We are miserable, vulnerable orphans, unless . . .
Christ govern us by his *Spirit*"; when in danger, the disciples "rely on
nothing else than the *protection of Christ*"; while "the manner in which he
dwells in his people is . . . by *the power of the Spirit*."[111] Calvin confirms
his position most emphatically when he says, "insofar as Christ is our
Mediator and Intercessor, he obtains from the Father the grace of the
Spirit; but insofar as he is God, he bestows that grace from himself."[112]
The Spirit is simply Christ reaching out effectively to men to give them
what he has for them; that is, Christ is the author of our union with him,
and he effects this union through that power of his which is the Spirit.

There is no point in adducing further evidence. Jesus Christ is the
unique bearer and bestower of the Spirit. There can be no action of the
Spirit which is not the action of Christ. There is no discrepancy in Calvin's
saying both that the Word is the author of faith and that the Holy Spirit is
the author of faith. The spirit is the *effectual* action of the exalted Christ.

ASSURANCE AND FAITH

> "Hence we may know the nature of faith to be this, that conscience has from
> the Holy Spirit a sure testimony of the goodwill of God towards it, so that,
> resting upon this, it does not hesitate to invoke God as Father."[113]

> "To have faith is to strengthen the mind with constant assurance and perfect
> confidence."[114]

The knowledge which is constitutive of faith is never surmise, opinion,
demonstration, or speculation. Rather, it is a knowledge which assures
the man of faith that Jesus Christ is the determination of his existence.

---

[108] *Inst.* 3.1.4.

[109] *Inst.* 3.2.39.

[110] *Comm.* Luke 3:16.

[111] *Comm.* John 14:18 (italics mine).

[112] *Comm.* John 14:16.

[113] *Comm.* I Cor. 2:12. For the same notion see *Comm.* II Cor. 13:5.

[114] *Inst.* 3.13.3: *constanti certitudine ac solida securitate.*

Hence, for Calvin, it is never the case that assurance is a spiritual boon granted to a privileged few; instead, where there is no assurance there is no faith: "no one can be called a son of God who does not know himself to be such."[115] The person who is not certain of his inclusion in Christ is not included: "Scripture shows that God's promises are not established unless they are grasped with the full assurance of conscience. Wherever there is doubt or uncertainty, it pronounces them void."[116]

As we could expect, the function of the Holy Spirit with respect to assurance is not somehow to bestow "assurance" in a vacuum; rather, assurance is always assurance of *my* participation in the One who never comes without his benefits; in brief, "God assures only by commending his Word to us."[117]

It was noted earlier that man has no natural capacity for faith. Then given the relation of assurance to faith, it must be the case that man has no capacity for assuring himself. And this is precisely what Calvin maintains: "as assurance of this nature is a thing that is above the capacity of the human mind, it is the part of the Holy Spirit to confirm within what God promises in his Word."[118] In the same vein Calvin adds, "The Spirit of God gives us such a testimony, that when he is our guide and teacher our spirit is made sure of the adoption of God; for our mind of itself, without the preceding testimony of the Spirit, could not convey to us this assurance."[119]

In view of the fact that assurance is necessary to true faith (and therefore to participation in Christ) it is not to be wondered at that Calvin can maintain that the "chief hinge on which faith turns" is "that we do not regard the promises of mercy that God offers as true only outside ourselves, but not at all in us; rather, we make them ours by inwardly embracing them."[120] We ought not to think of Christ as "standing afar off, and not dwelling in us."[121] Since Christ is *for me*, to contemplate him truly is to contemplate him as effecting in me what he wants to give me; that is,

---

[115]*Comm.* Rom. 8:16.

[116]*Inst.* 3.13.4: *firmas.*

[117]*Inst.* 3.2.15.

[118]*Comm.* II Cor. 1:22.

[119]*Comm.* Rom. 8:16: *praeeunte.*

[120]*Inst.* 3.2.16: *intus complectendo nostras faciamus.* (*Amplector* is far the more common word for "embrace.")

[121]*Inst.* 3.2.24: *veluti procul stantem, et non potius in nobis habitantem debeamus cogitare.*

to contemplate him as dwelling in me. "We ought not to separate Christ from ourselves or ourselves from him."[122] Since Jesus Christ is mercy, how can I regard him as mercy without at the same time regarding myself as the beneficiary of that mercy; can there even be a "mercy" which is merely "outside of" me?[123]

A true believer, then, is he who, "convinced by a firm conviction that God is a kindly and well-disposed Father toward him, promises himself all things on the basis of his generosity; who, relying upon the promises of divine benevolence towards him, lays hold on an undoubted expectation of salvation."[124] While Calvin does not say that assurance *is* faith, neither will he allow faith to be divorced from assurance; nor can assurance be regarded as related accidentally to faith: they are related as are heat and light to the sun.[125]

Calvin does not pretend that all believers have the same degree of certainty; indeed, certainty varies with the "measure of faith" granted to different persons. Nevertheless, wherever there is true faith there is always *some* assurance: "a trembling, hesitating, doubting conscience will always be a sure evidence of unbelief."[126] Assurance ever remains assurance of mercy; it is the believer's participation in this mercy which bestows assurance of mercy.

While it is relatively easy for someone to understand the meaning of "God is merciful," it is relatively difficult for the same person to be convinced that he is no longer under condemnation. Accordingly, the Spirit serves as a seal "to seal in our hearts those very promises the certainty of which it has previously impressed upon our minds, and takes the place of a guarantee to confirm and establish them."[127]

Calvin's intransigence on the necessity of assurance for faith is attested in his commentary on Hebrews: "By the term 'full assurance,' πληροφορία, the Apostle points out the nature of faith, and at the same time reminds us that the grace of Christ cannot be received except by

---

[122]*Inst.* 3.2.24.

[123]Calvin speaks frequently of the need that Christ not be viewed as "outside" us, "from afar," etc. He uses interchangeably *procul, eminus, extra nos, foris.* The fact that there cannot be a "mercy" of which men are not beneficiaries is a point which Calvin did not exploit, regrettably, in his discussion of election.

[124]*Inst.* 3.2.16. Cf. *Comm.* James 1:6: "faith is that which relies on God's promises and makes us sure of obtaining what we ask. It hence follows that it is connected with confidence (*fiducia*) and certainty (*certitudino*) as to God's love towards us."

[125]With respect to assurance and faith Calvin uses this analogy in *Comms.* Eph. 3:12 and Col. 2:2.

[126]*Comm.* Eph. 3:12.

[127]*Inst.* 3.2.36.

those who possess a fixed and unhesitating conviction."[128] If faith implies assurance, then does doubt reflect the absence of faith? On the contrary, even the most assured faith is afflicted with anxiety and unbelief. Moreover, it is not that faith doubts various "truths" of God while remaining utterly without doubt concerning mercy; rather, doubt *is* doubt about God's goodness.[129] Nonetheless, despite the severity of the attack which doubt can launch against faith, the attack is never such as to remove from believers all assurance of God's mercy (in which case, of course, they would no longer be believers); what the Word begets inevitably endures.[130] While doubt assails believers, doubt can never be determinative for them, since unbelief does not "hold sway" in them, but attacks them "from without."[131] Since Christ rules in them (as Lord the indwelling Christ must rule), doubt can only storm the fort without ever gaining entry.[132] While there is victory over the assaults only in faith, there most certainly is victory there.[133] The Word of God, effective in believers through faith, repels the attacks upon them.[134]

Unbelief is certainly sin;[135] yet Christ dwelling in believers does not allow such sin to overturn faith. In sealing the knowledge of his indwelling upon our hearts and minds by the Holy Spirit, Christ certifies that our

---

[128]*Comm.* Heb. 10:22. Cf. *Comm.* II Cor. 1:21. Calvin does speak of the *love* engendered in believers as an assurance of faith. However, he always understands such assurance to be of a subordinate sort. He views similarly such assurance as might arise from the fact that the "good tree" (believers) is now producing "good fruit." This subordinate assurance is added to the assurance born of mercy and faith, but of itself can never be the *ground* of assurance. Love is defective even in believers, and their good deeds ever remain sin-tainted. (*Comm.* I John 4:13.)

It appears evident that according to Calvin the Holy Spirit empowers the Word of mercy, which Word is attested by Scripture. However, Warfield reverses this: the Spirit primarily convinces men of the "divinity" of Scripture, and *then* they become apprised of the God of mercy; at which point assurance arises (Warfield, "Calvin's Doctrine of the Knowledge of God," in Armstrong, *Calvin and the Reformation*).

[129]*Inst.* 3.2.20.

[130]Calvin speaks of the reprobate as having a short-lived "taste" or "show" of faith which the Lord begets but not the Word. For a discussion and criticism of this notion see Chapter Five.

[131]*Inst.* 3.2.21: *non intus in cordibus piorum regnat incredulitas, sed foris oppignat.*

[132]Cf. *Inst.* 3.23.9 and *Comm.* Eph. 4:30 where Calvin speaks of the Holy Spirit *dwelling* in believers, and *Comm.* I John 3:24 where the Holy Spirit is said to *rule* believers. The Spirit is ever the Spirit of Christ.

[133]Cf. *Comm.* I John 5:4: "We are already partakers of victory."

[134]Cf. *Comm.* Eph. 6:16.

[135]Cf. *Comm.* Matt. 8:25-26 where Calvin unambiguously expounds the disciples' fear as sin.

doubt is not determinative. Christ by the Holy Spirit effects faith which possesses a firm and steady conviction, and this conviction admits of no "opposing" doubt.[136] Calvin's final word on the matter could not be plainer: "unless one knows that Christ dwells in him, he is reprobate."[137] Doubt in believers never overturns assurance.

---

[136] *Comm.* Eph. 1:13.
[137] *Inst.* 3.2.39.

CHAPTER 2

JUSTIFICATION AND FAITH

Justification: "the main hinge on which religion turns" (*Institutes* 3.11.1).

Jesus Christ is ever the believer's righteousness. The righteousness of Christ is the correlate of faith. And just as Christ, the "rightly-related Man," is *extra nos* before he is *in nobis*, so the righteousness of Christ is always logically prior to faith. Calvin's understanding of the relation of faith and righteousness is never such as to suggest that *my* faith *is* my justification; "faith" and "justification" are not logically co-terminous.

At the same time, as was seen in the discussion on the Holy Spirit, he who as our "right-relatedness to God" is prior to faith becomes ours only through faith; he must be "grasped" (apprehended) and possessed by faith.[1] We are justified only insofar as we do not see him "over there"—that is, as though Jesus Christ were who he is apart from his people—but see him in his reality as including his people: "Christ, having been made ours, makes us sharers with him in the gifts with which he has been endowed. We do not, therefore, contemplate him outside ourselves (Beveridge: 'without us') from afar in order that his righteousness may be imputed to us but because we put on Christ and are engrafted into his body—in short, because he deigns to make us one with him. For this reason we glory that we have fellowship of righteousness with him."[2]

Two things are to be noted here: as was mentioned earlier, no benefit of Christ is received apart from the receiving of Christ himself—that is, we are not given Christ's righteousness as an abstract quality, but the very One who *is* our righteousness—and thus Christ is received "before" (*prius*; Beveridge: "first") his righteousness; second, the sole function of this Christ-formed faith is to receive or "put on" Christ. Hence, while

---

[1] *Inst.* 3.11.1: *apprehendi ac possideri participatione.* (Fr. *nous recevons et possedons qu'en participant à luy.*)

[2] *Inst.* 3.11.10: *speculamur . . . consortes . . . iustitiae societatem.*

there is no justification apart from faith (apart from faith Christ who is *pro nobis* remains *extra nos* only) neither is there any justifying power inherent in faith itself: "having faith" is not intrinsically virtuous. In fact, strictly speaking, man does not "have" faith in the sense of something which he possesses. Rather, faith is the Christ- (and therefore Spirit-) formed actuality of the putting on of Christ.[3] While, in faith, man puts on Christ, man does not "possess" Christ; faith is the state of being possessed of Christ.

In speaking of faith as not having any inherent power to justify, Calvin writes: "We compare faith to a kind of vessel; for unless we come empty with the mouth of our vessel open to seek Christ's grace, we are not capable of receiving Christ."[4] Faith can be but the empty vessel which receives the treasure, never the treasure itself. "Faith" of an indeterminate object is no faith at all; exhortations to "have faith" are of themselves mere incentives to God-defiant idolatry. Faith can be only the instrument for receiving righteousness, and must not be confused ignorantly with Christ himself, who is its material cause.[5]

Again, that faith which is essential to justification is not a human product, but is produced by the Word; the preaching of the gospel (of faith) alone begets faith. Only the action of the One who alone is rightly related to the Father can create that instrument of his own reception by which instrument his right-relatedness becomes the truth and reality of the believer's existence. In other words, with respect to justification, faith must be "something merely passive, bringing nothing of ours to the recovering of God's favour but receiving from Christ that which we lack."[6] Since faith receives all from God and brings nothing except a humble confession of want,[7] the value of faith is given entirely by the value of the One whose instrument it is. For this reason Calvin says relatively little about faith in the chapter "Justification by Faith." Faith as instrument is instrument only because of its content; if faith deviated even in the slightest from being *only* instrument, then it could not be that by which believers share in Christ who is their justification; instead, justifica-

---

[3]This discussion constitutes a reiteration of the earlier discussion where it was noted that Calvin denies faith to be a natural human possibility, or a form waiting to be filled with content.

[4]*Inst.* 3.11.7.

[5]*Inst.* 3.11.7: *Inscite ergo fidem, quae instrumentum est dumtaxat percipiendae iustitiae, dico misceri cum Christo, qui materialis est causa, tantique benficii author simul et minister.*

[6]*Inst.* 3.13.5: *mere passiva fides* (lacking in French). For a discussion of the relation of preaching to the action of Jesus Christ see Chapter Seven.

[7]*Comm.* Rom. 3:27.

tion would be thought to inhere faith. If justification inhered faith our justification would be defective, for faith, from a human perspective, is always weak and sin-tainted; any justification inhering faith would have to be a partial or fragmentary righteousness. Being "partially rightly related" to God is an absurdity.

Just as Calvin insists that faith is but the instrument by which Christ is received or "put on" as our righteousness, he maintains, with utter consistency, that it is Christ who ever remains our righteousness. Since a dead man can do nothing to attain life,[8] and since believers continue to sin, and hence, *viewed in themselves*, remain dead, Jesus Christ ever remains their life. However, faith is not the instrument for receiving the Christ who then, through the "channel" of faith, gradually transfuses his righteousness into believers. Calvin rejects Osiander's opinion whereby faith is the means of the commingling of the *essence* of Christ with the essence of believers (resulting in believers becoming a hybrid). Rather, Jesus Christ ever remains the only covenant-fulfiller; he alone renders full, voluntary, perfect obedience to the Father; to him alone are addressed the words, "My beloved son, with whom I am well-pleased"; he is the eschatological (that is, true) humanity. Faith is the (Christ-granted) means whereby he includes me in his own humanity even as he remains Lord of that humanity. Faith is the means whereby the believer is presently bestowed with the eschatological reality. In other words, through the believer's faith-participation in Christ, God "looks at" him only by "looking at" Christ. God "sees" the believer only in Christ. By means of participation in Christ the righteous One, the believer is given a new standing ("set right") beyond sin which has no basis in himself. Through faith he inherits a positive eschatological destiny, and is regarded by God *definitively* as an heir to that destiny. Faith is Jesus Christ acting on the believer so as to determine the believer's existence "for Christ" (even as he remains, in himself, "against Christ").

In all this, however, faith is not the vessel by which the essence of God is received. Faith is the vessel which "receives" Christ only in the sense that Christ binds us in fellowship with himself in the power of the Spirit. Our existence is determined by this bond, but we are never deified. We are "set right" with God *as creatures*.

But what is it precisely to be determined by one's eschatological destiny? It is the remission or non-imputation of sins: "after pardon of sins has been obtained, the sinner is considered as a just man in God's sight";[9] "men are in a wretched state unless God deal mercifully with them

---

[8] *Inst.* 3.14.5.
[9] *Inst.* 3.11.3: *post impetratum peccatorum veniam, pro iusto esse coram Deo habitum.*

by not laying sins to their charge . . . [the forgiveness of sins] is the full definition of the righteousness of faith; as if the prophet had said, 'men are then only blessed when they are fully reconciled to God, and counted as righteous before him'. . . . God cannot be reconciled to those who are worthy of eternal destruction in any other way than by freely pardoning them and bestowing upon them his favour. . . . God, in lifting off or taking away sins, and likewise in covering and not imputing them, freely pardons them."[10] Calvin insists that it is only through faith that men "embrace" the remission of sins and rely upon the grace of God alone.[11] Needless to say, since faith implies assurance, those whose sins are remitted the Holy Spirit confirms in this remission; the believer *knows* that Christ is effectual Priest.

Calvin uses many expressions to refer to the great benefit which faith confers: it is to be reckoned as righteous before God and accepted on account of one's righteousness;[12] to be reckoned not in the condition of a sinner;[13] to have God affirm and witness one's (imputed) righteousness;[14] to be acquitted of guilt;[15] to be clothed with the righteousness of Christ and appear before God identified with the clothing.[16] Throughout, Calvin is concerned not with what men are in themselves, but with how God regards them: "when it is asked why God loves us and owns us as just, it is necessary that Christ should come forth as one who clothes us with his own righteousness."[17] To be "rightwised" is to embrace Christ-in-his-benefit, where that embrace is a response to and is made possible by his prior embrace of us. Through faith Christ applies to us the effectual intercession of his death.

> Most of the foregoing material on faith and righteousness Calvin summarizes in his discussion of Abraham, the prototype of the man of faith. "In the first place, the faith of Abraham is commended because by it he embraced the promise of God; it is commended in the second place, because hence Abraham obtained righteousness in the sight of God, and that by imputation. . . . And truly faith does not justify us for any other reason, than that it reconciles us to God, and that it does so, not by its own merit, but because we receive the grace offered to us in the promises, and have no doubt of eternal life, being fully persuaded that we are loved by God as sons."[18]

---

[10]*Comm.* Psalm 32:1: *levando; tollendo; tegendo; imputando.*
[11]Ibid.
[12]*Inst.* 3.11.2: *qui iudicio Dei et censetur iustus et acceptus est ob suam iustitiam.*
[13]Ibid. Calvin uses *habetur* and *censetur* synonymously.
[14]*Inst.* 3.11.2.
[15]*Inst.* 3.11.3.
[16]*Comm.* Rom. 4:3.
[17]Ibid.
[18]*Comm.* Gen. 15:6.

> In *Comm.* Romans 4:3 Calvin stresses that the righteousness of Christ is prior to Abraham's faith. "Abraham, by believing, embraced nothing but the favour offered to him. . . . Abraham laid hold of the benignity of God offered to him in the promise. . . . It is necessary in order to form an opinion of righteousness, to understand the relation between the promise and faith . . . for we cannot otherwise attain righteousness than as it is brought to us, as it were, by the promise of the gospel; and we realize its possession by faith."[19]
>
> The text to which Calvin returns again and again, however, is II Cor. 5:21; in his *Commentary* Calvin states that believers are righteous in Christ "because we are judged in connection with Christ's righteousness, which we have put on by faith, that it might become ours."[20]

While we are not pardoned on account of our faith, no one is pardoned apart from faith; not to participate in Christ and his righteousness is to be in the sphere of God's hatred and wrath: "those who do not fly to Christ and seek forgiveness in his death remain in their guilt."[21] God can "see" in Christ only those who are in Christ—by faith.

It needs to be added that the person of faith is never absorbed into Christ; his identity as person remains. The two words which Calvin most often uses in speaking of the believer's relationship to Christ— "participation" and "fellowship" (*participatio* and *societas*)—are both needed: the fellowship is not that of mere proximity, nor is the participation that of mystical absorption.[22]

Since Jesus Christ *is* one's righteousness (that is, Jesus Christ justifies), and since Christ is received only in faith, faith alone can be said to justify. Works-righteousness ever remains unrighteousness, because (i) man *qua* sinner never reflects that righteousness which God requires, and (ii) in persisting in his "working" he spurns the one righteousness which is available to him. Works-righteousness depends on the *reward* of God (which, given our sin, is never forthcoming); faith-righteousness depends on the *mercy* of God. "We are justified by faith through the mercy of God alone . . . righteousness, which is grounded on faith, depends entirely on the mercy of God."[23] Mercy and faith ever remain correlates. A free gift can be received only in faith. A man bent on works is a man satisfied with himself, and he impedes the beneficence of God.[24]

---

[19] *Comm.* Rom. 4:3.
[20] *Comm.* II Cor. 5:21.
[21] *Comm.* Acts. 13:38.
[22] Cf. *Comm.* II Pet. 1:4 where Calvin repudiates absorption.
[23] *Comm.* Rom. 1:17.
[24] *Inst.* 3.12.8.

In short, since Christ would be given us for righteousness in vain "unless there was the fruition of him by faith,"[25] faith is that instrument by which the righteousness of Christ effectually and determinatively "covers" the unrighteousness of men; and this occurs as Christ himself becomes the content of that empty vessel, which vessel was seen, earlier, to be created by Christ himself.

---

[25]*Comm.* Rom. 3:26: *nisi fruitio ex fide accederat.*

CHAPTER 3

SANCTIFICATION AND FAITH

Jesus Christ cannot be divided; no benefit of his can be separated from any other, nor can his benefits be separated from his person. He who is the believer's effectual Priest must be the believer's effectual King; he who is the believer's righteousness is the believer's sanctification. Calvin never tires of referring to I Cor. 1:30: he whom the Christian "puts on" is put on in the totality of his reality. Throughout the *Commentaries* Calvin iterates that the sum of the gospel consists in the forgiveness of sins (free reconciliation) and repentance (newness of life).[1]

Since all benefits flow from the One who is mercy, Calvin, as expected, affirms mercy to be the "whence" of repentance. In his exegesis of Matt. 3:2 he notes that John the Baptist "first brings forward the grace of God, and then exhorts men to repent. Hence it is evident that the foundation of repentance is the mercy of God, by which he restores the lost."[2] Repentance is never primarily a human action which generates or confers mercy; rather, mercy ever remains prior in order and the ground which makes repentance possible: "now, as the undeserved love of God is first in order, so it must be observed that pardon of sins is bestowed upon us in Christ, not that God may treat them with indulgence, but that he may heal us from our sins."[3] It is that prior love (mercy, Jesus Christ) which *is* the healing and restoration of the sin-vitiated man.

Christ is our sanctification. As in the case of justification this does not mean that one is sanctified through the exercise of an "ability" to "put on" Christ; the "ability" is conferred only as Jesus Christ in his power confers

---

[1] E.g., *Inst.* 3.3.1. Cf. *Comm.* Rom. 6:6 where Calvin states three times concurrently, with slight alterations in vocabulary, that the gospel consists in remission and renewal (repentance). Calvin uses "renewal," "repentance," and "sanctification" interchangeably.

[2] *Comm.* Matt. 3:2: *fundamentum.*

[3] *Comm.* Matt. 3:2.

the actuality: "for Christ gives us the *Spirit of regeneration* for this cause, that he may renew us inwardly, to the end that new life may afterward follow the newness of mind and heart . . . it is a thing as impossible for men to convert themselves as to create themselves."[4] Jesus Christ is the believer's *entire* sanctification. The man of faith does not contribute anything to the content of sanctification; nor is his faith a "contribution." Just as faith is but an "empty vessel" which can only receive the righteousness of Christ, here it is the same vessel which receives Christ's newness of life. Faith never generates sanctification, nor is faith, even as empty vessel, a creaturely possession inhering man to which sanctification is fitted. Rather, as was seen earlier, mercy determines its own correlate; the mercy which includes newness of life molds the empty vessel (in the power of the Spirit) to receive the newness.

At the same time, Calvin is eager to point out that sanctification, like justification, is not something done "over man's head" or "behind his back"; that is, there is a genuine human affirmation involved. The conversion is "voluntary."[5] What Calvin does deny is that man of himself either has or can give himself the renewed will which affirms "voluntarily" Christ's newness of life. The will can only continue to will itself; in order to will newness of life, the will itself must be created anew. This occurs only as Jesus Christ renews men by his Spirit. And faith (in Christ) is the proper and entire work of the Spirit.

With respect to the relation of faith and renewal, confusion arises as Calvin speaks ambiguously about the order of repentance and faith: is sanctification a consequence of faith (as the title of *Institutes*, Book III, Chapter 3, suggests), or is faith a consequence of a prior renewal (that is, since faith is a work of the Holy Spirit, faith can be born in us only after the work of renewal has begun)? In the 1536 *Institutes* Calvin speaks explicitly of a repentance which is *prior* to faith as well as a repentance which presupposes faith.

It must be remembered that Calvin is dealing with logical rather than temporal priority: "when we refer the origin of repentance to faith we do not imagine some space of time during which it brings it to birth; but we mean to show that a man cannot seriously apply himself to repentance without knowing himself to belong to God. But no one is truly persuaded that he belongs to God unless he has first recognized God's grace."[6] Still, the question remains: are sinners first seized by God's mercy, and then

---

[4] *Comm.* Acts 5:31 (italics mine).

[5] Ibid. Cf. *Comm.* Ez. 11:19.

[6] *Inst.* 3.3.2.

"turn to the Lord," that is, affirm who they are? Or does their awareness of the coming judgment "turn them to the Lord," in whom they then find mercy? Many texts can be culled to support both positions.

> The latter Calvin upholds in the following: "When a man is awakened with a lively sense of the judgment of God, he cannot fail to be humbled with shame and fear. Such self-dissatisfaction would not suffice, however, unless at the same time faith were added, whose office it is to raise up the hearts which were cast down with fear and to encourage them to pray for forgiveness."[7]
> ". . . fear of God is the beginning of repentance."[8]
>
> The former Calvin supports when he maintains that "repentance is a turning to God, when we frame ourselves and all our life to obey him; but faith is a receiving of the grace offered us in Christ. . . . *The beginning of repentance is a preparation unto faith.*"[9]

It would appear that Calvin speaks of repentance as preceding faith when by "repentance" he means regret, remorse, fear of the coming judgment, disgust at sin; and consequent to faith when by "repentance" he means that newness of life which Jesus Christ is. Calvin wants to avoid saying that man simply and suddenly finds himself renewed without having had any "godly sorrow," in which case renewal and therefore faith are "accomplished over his head." On the other hand, he wants to avoid saying that a man's "godly sorrow" is what effects his faith-participation in Christ, in which case renewal would be said to originate in man.

> His most balanced statement is found in *Comm.* II Cor. 7:10, where he maintains that according to St. Paul the cause and origin is sorrow according to God. (Earlier we gave an instance where Calvin stated that mercy alone could be the cause and origin of repentance.) "This is carefully to be observed, for unless the sinner be dissatisfied with himself, detest his manner of life, and be thoroughly grieved from an apprehension of sin, he will never betake himself to the Lord. On the other hand, it is impossible for a man to experience a sorrow of this kind without its giving birth to a new heart." (Note the order.) Then Calvin adds, "Paul seems to make repentance (that is, sorrow) the ground of salvation. Were it so, it would follow that we are justified by works. I answer, that we must observe what Paul here treats of, for he is not inquiring as to the ground of salvation, but simply commending repentance from the fruit which it produces; he says that it is like a way by which we arrive at salvation. Nor is it without good reason, for Christ calls us, by free favour, but it is to repentance. God, by way of free favour, pardons our sins but *only when we renounce them* . . . repentance may with fitness and propriety be represented as an introduction to salvation, but in this way of speaking of it is represented as an effect rather than as a cause. . . . While Scripture teaches us that we never obtain forgiveness of sins without repent-

---

[7] *Comm.* Psalm 130:4. For the same notion see *Comms.* Luke 26:46; Acts 11:18; Acts 17:31.

[8] *Inst.* 3.3.7.

[9] *Comm.* Acts 20:21 (italics mine).

ance, it represents, at the same time, in a variety of passages, the mercy of God alone as the ground of our obtaining it."[10]

R. S. Wallace suggests that where Scripture speaks of repentance as prior to faith, Calvin "can argue that since faith is a work of the Holy Spirit, it can only be begotten within us after the work of renewal has begun. Thus faith must flow from regeneration. But this preliminary regeneration which precedes faith is a very secret and obscure work of the Spirit. As far as human sense can investigate, faith always precedes repentance or regeneration."[11] While repentance does involve the repudiation of the "old man," Calvin insists that real repudiation is always the fruit of faith; it is the effect in us of Christ's repudiation of the "old man": "One died, therefore all have died." Any supposed mortification outside of faith is yet another form of self-assertion and hence another manifestation of concupiscence.

In a word, Calvin does not want to say that repentance (both mortification and vivification) is not something applied to me in such a way as not to pertain to my existence; neither does he want to say that repentance is a natural human possibility. The mercy of God ever remains the ground and, as empowered by the Spirit, the "whence" of our sanctification; Christ-with-his-benefit-of-newness remains its content. Faith is the Christ-engendered means of Christ "forming himself" in man.

It should be added that while Christ really is the believer's sanctification (that is, *coram Deo* the man of faith is a new creature and is advancing in holiness) he must ever remain such. While sin no longer rules believers (that is, determines their existence), sin does continue to dwell in them; δουλοι of Jesus Christ, they are no longer in bondage to sin;[12] yet, while sin's guilt has been abolished, its "very substance" has not.[13] A man is newly constituted by his Lord, and this means that sin no longer "lords" it over him; yet sin is not absent from him.[14] In short, until the day of the Lord the believer remains *totus peccator* as well as, by virtue of faith, *totus sanctus*. Faith, then, is not a channel by which Christ's holiness is transfused into believers until a point of sufficiency is reached. Faith is, rather, that fellowship with Christ in which the believer is given such an anticipation of the full renewal of the day of the Lord that he is moved presently to aspire zealously after it.

---

[10]*Comm.* II Cor. 7:10 (italics mine).

[11]R. S. Wallace, *Calvin's Doctrine of the Christian Life,* 96.

[12]*Inst.* 3.3.10: *a peccati servitute.*

[13]Ibid.: *at reatum potius referimus quam ad ipsam peccati materiam* (Fr. *l'imputation du péché plustost qu'à la matière*). (*materia* connotes "occasion" as well as "substance." Both meanings reflect the subtlety of Calvin's thought.)

[14]*Comm.* Rom. 8:9.

CHAPTER 4

PREDESTINATION AND FAITH

"Predestination, rightly understood, brings no shaking of faith but rather its best confirmation." (*Institutes*, 3.24.9.)

In theological discussion the very mention of Calvin's doctrine of predestination (election and reprobation) is usually sufficient to call forth vehement criticism and denunciation, for Calvin is considered to have articulated precisely that for which his opponents excoriated him: the imputing to God "a cruelty quite alien to his nature."[1] However, Calvin should be allowed to unfold his doctrine and explicate its positive significance for faith before he is so sharply contradicted.

Undoubtedly Calvin is convinced that since predestination is a fact, the doctrine must be heard in the Church; God is not honoured, nor his cause among men advanced, by the Church's silence here on the grounds that the doctrine is too awesome for Christians to apprehend and find profitable. Rather, that which reflects the being and activity of God must be heard and understood if believers are to find nourished, developed, and guaranteed their faith which they would not have apart from that predestinating activity. Nor is God honoured by those who hear and receive the doctrine but account it a scar on the face of God: "whoever, then, heaps odium upon the doctrine of predestination openly reproaches God, as if he had unadvisedly let slip something hurtful to the Church."[2] Indeed, to hesitate in this matter is to second-guess God himself: the Holy Spirit (who instructs us in the "school" of scripture) teaches us nothing but what is in our best interest to know. Accordingly, faith's knowledge of the doctrine cannot fail to be *useful*, as long as the doctrine is not sought

---

[1] *De Aet. Dei Praed.* 59.

[2] *Inst.* 3.21.4

or made a ground for speculation outside the Word of God.[3] We turn now to an appreciation of that usefulness.

MERCY

> "What mean the preachers of free-will, unless it be to tell us that by our own endeavours we have, from being sons of Adam, become the sons of God?"[4]

Calvin insists that the doctrine of predestination forces upon believers as nothing else can the recognition that their salvation is *entirely* of God's free mercy: "whatever excellence there is in men is not implanted by nature, so that it can be attributed to nature or heredity, nor is it *procured by our own free will so as to put God under our control*, but it flows from his mercy which is pure and free."[5] It is not the case that men come to faith (and thus put on Christ-with-his-benefits) because they have a spiritual sensitivity or perceptivity superior to those who remain in unfaith; it is not the case that they have a superior *natural* capacity for discerning the ways and works of God; it is not the case that their judgment excels that of unbelievers who continue to spurn life when it is offered. They are persons who come to faith *solely* by the action of God upon them, for "it is the calling of God and not the perception of our minds that is the effective cause of faith."[6] To suggest anything else is to pretend that a human decision and action is ultimately determinative (with respect to the engendering of faith); this in turn is to suggest that God is subject to human control and to render his mercy entirely superfluous. Mercy (whereby God brings men to faith) is his definitive action upon them. To say that mercy brings men to faith, however, is to say that men are incapable of granting themselves faith.

The fact that the same mercy is necessary to bestow faith in all manner of men means that Calvin repudiates any suggestion that some men are more deeply mired in sin than others, or that some are more obstinate,[7] or

---

[3]*Comm.* Rom. 9:14 and *De. Aet. Dei Praed.* 77 where Calvin stresses both the necessity of becoming apprised of the doctrine and its usefulness. The French text of the latter work adds the warning that to deal with the work outside the Word of God, however, "will plunge us into darkness instead of instructing us." Calvin insists in many places that since predestination is mentioned *passim* in scripture, believers cannot doubt that God wishes the doctrine expounded and appreciated.

[4]*Comm.* Psalm 103:3.

[5]*Comm.* I Cor. 4:7 (italics mine). For same see *Inst.* 3.21.1.

[6]*Comm.* II Pet. 1:3.

[7]Pighius maintains that opposition to God is found only among the refractory and proud. Calvin says that all men are refractory and proud (*De Aet. Dei Praed.* 87).

that the ravages of sin are greater in some men: "all are equally unworthy and the nature of all equally corrupt."[8] Indeed, what degrees of concupiscence can there be when all men possess a will which can be said to be only *in se curvatus*? What degrees of blindness and of death? Of course, in this context Calvin's question is never far away: what can a dead man do to attain life? Given that human inability which is appropriate for a corpse, Calvin not surprisingly maintains it to be "the most crass stupidity not to acknowledge that the eyes of our mind are opened by God."[9] Only that man whose eyes remain firmly shut is so deluded as to think he can open them by himself. There is no operation sin-riddled man can perform on himself to extricate himself from his predicament; dead men "do not yield obedience to God at their own motion."[10] The deadliness of the human predicament is such that the Father must draw us to the One who is life, for "neither the beginning of faith *nor any preparation for it* lies in us."[11] Men simply have no propensity for loving God.[12] Since the wages of sin are but death, it can be deduced with utter certainty that salvation is "wholly of the grace and pure kindness of God."[13]

Calvin maintains that since the bestowal of faith depends not upon man's will or exertion but upon God's mercy,[14] it becomes impossible to affirm eternal life to be a gift and deny predestination to salvation to be a fact. St. Paul concludes incontrovertibly, in Calvin's opinion, that "our election is to be attributed neither to our diligence, zeal, nor efforts, but is to be ascribed entirely to the counsel of God."[15] The elect differ from the damned *only* in the fact of their utterly gratuitous deliverance from the same gulf of destruction.[16]

As was noted earlier Calvin denies that men possess any rudiment of faith or any preparation for faith. Thus Calvin disavows any suggestion that "election" is a pronouncement God makes over any orientation towards him, that is, over some pre-reflective inclination towards him.

---

[8] *De Aet. Dei Praed.* 81.

[9] Ibid., 50.

[10] *Comm.* John 6:44.

[11] *Comm.* John 6:45. See *Comm.* John 11.25—"Away with those who say that the movement of nature prepares the way for grace. They might as well say that the dead walk."

[12] *De Aet. Dei Praed.* 70: "propensity"—*propensio.*

[13] *Comm.* Rom. 6:23.

[14] *Comm.* Rom. 9:16.

[15] Ibid.

[16] Ibid.

Election is not the bringing to full consciousness any primordial obedience (as Pighius and his disciples maintain); it is not the final empower-
ing of a "flexible will" which happens to "flex" in the direction of God. In
a word, the elect and the non-elect can never be distinguished on the basis
of the *faith* of the elect. Calvin is careful to state that even that which
characterizes the elect in contradistinction to the non-elect is not the basis
of that distinction. God distinguishes the elect "*not by faith* . . . but by
pure grace."[17] Since the redeemed are distinguished from the lost by grace
alone,[18] no man is permitted to think that *his* faith is what renders him
non-reprobate. Election is not divine ratification of a human discernment
and decision. It is never the case that grace is God's alighting upon human
apprehension of God, which, while vague or obscure, is yet veridical.
There is no such veridicality prior to the bestowal of mercy: "when they
(the Galatians) were at the furthest possible remove from thinking about
him, God prevented them with his mercy."[19] Of course, it must not be
thought, on the strength of the foregoing, that men do not think about
God; they do, and think "religiously." In the wake of the Fall, however,
such thinking is defective.

> "For St. Paul teaches that it is due not only to the stubborn pride of the
> human will, but also to the impotence of the mind, that man cannot by
> himself attain to the things of the Spirit. He would have been saying no more
> than the truth if he had said that men do not wish to be wise, but he goes
> further and says that they do not even have the power. From this we conclude
> that faith is not something that depends on our decision, but is something
> given by God. . . . Because of that there is even less ground for tolerating the
> ignorance of those who think that the gospel is offered to men universally in
> such a way that it is free to all without distinction to lay hold of salvation by
> faith."[20]

In other words, the gospel is not a "free-floating" reality which man must
himself reach out for and grasp, however implicit the grasping might be.
Nor is it a "content" which is inserted into a "form" of faith which man
retains. A form/content discussion simply does not pertain to a corpse.
Rather, man's coming to faith (participation in Christ) ever remains the
entire prerogative of God, who in his sovereignty chooses to show mercy.
One can only stand amazed that God chose to show mercy on him.
Mercy, never faith as a human affirmation and act, distinguishes believer
from unbeliever.

---

[17]*Comm.* John 17:6 (italics mine).

[18]*De Aet. Dei Praed.* 80.

[19]*Comm.* Gal. 4:9.

[20]*Comm.* I Cor. 2:14: *ne posse fidem . . . non in arbitrio cuiusque esse fidem sed
divinitus conferri . . . ut promiscue liberum sit in omnibus salutem fide amplecti.*

Similarly, Calvin repudiates any suggestion that man cooperates with God in achieving union with him. It is not the case that the elect are those who "open their eyes to see God when he appears to them."[21] Changing the metaphor, Calvin insists that either election to salvation (gratuitous, free mercy) is upheld or a synergism is declared wherein "the willing and running do avail, but that because by themselves they are not sufficient, the palm has to be awarded to the grace of God."[22] There can be no concurrence between mercy (grace) and the human will.[23] Grace does not *help* the will; man does not go to meet God (albeit only part way) at all.

> "St. Paul does not say that we are assisted by God. He does not say that the will is prepared, and has then to proceed in its own strength. He does not say that the power of choosing aright is bestowed upon us and that we have afterwards to make our own choice. That is what those who would weaken God's grace (so far as they can) are accustomed to babble. But he says that we are God's work, and that everything good in us is his creation. By which he means that the whole man is formed by his hand to become good. . . . St. Paul means to prove that man does not *in any way* procure salvation for himself, but obtains it freely from God. The proof is that man is nothing but by divine grace."[24]

> "All have obtained salvation by mere grace, because they have been freely adopted according to eternal election."[25]

> "The word *mercy* is emphatic. It means that God is bound to none and saves all freely, since all are equally lost."[26]

In the light of what was stated earlier concerning the place of works with respect to justification, it is not unexpected that Calvin, for whom election is the sole cause of faith, understands election to rule out any notion that God's mercy is called down by our works or is granted as reward for them. Works and election (with respect to the bestowal of grace) are mutually exclusive: "we did not possess works that might have enabled us to *take the initiative out of God's hand*, so that our salvation depends *entirely* on his gracious purpose and election. . . . Although St. Paul usually uses the word 'purpose' to mean God's secret decree which depends on himself alone, he chose to add 'grace' to make his point more explicit and completely exclude all reference to works. . . . *there is no*

---

[21] *De Aet. Dei Praed.* 79.

[22] Ibid., 83.

[23] This is not to deny the place of human affirmation in both election and reprobation. See below.

[24] *Comm.* Eph. 2:10 (italics mine).

[25] *Comm.* Eph. 1:11.

[26] *Comm.* Rom. 11:32 (italics his).

place for works where God's grace reigns."27

Just as election proclaims that faith is not granted to us on account of works, so it proclaims that faith does not spring from a residual goodness in men, for the fact of a divine priority (which election certainly is) renders irrelevant a discussion of some alleged 'residual goodness.' Faith is granted for no other reason than God's determination within himself to be merciful. In face of our wretchedness, then, election can only magnify God's kindness inestimably: "how incomparable is God's goodness towards us, because he sanctified us who are by nature polluted. He has chosen us when he could find nothing in us but evil and vileness; he makes us his peculiar possession when of ourselves we are worthless dregs. . . . we must learn from this what man's condition is before he is translated into the Kingdom of God."28 Election forces upon faith the recognition that the engendering of faith is sheer miracle: dead men do not resurrect themselves.

In insisting that God's decree of election precedes even his decree to create (that is, the elect are such even before they are born; see *Institutes* 3.22.2) Calvin emphasizes the utter disregard God has for the creature's merit. In expounding Ephesians 1:4 ("elect before the foundation of the world") Calvin notes that it is logically impossible for merit to consist in anything prior to the creation. The proclamation of election heightens the understanding of the freedom of God's gratuitous mercy.

It must be stressed at this point, although it has been implied through-out this section, that the *expression* of God's freedom and sovereignty is the expression of his love. Popular caricatures or one-sided understand-ings of Calvin suggest that God hovers above mankind, and then sud-denly (and inexplicably) seizes some here and some there as he "injects" them with faith, as though his activity were sheer arbitrariness. It cannot be stated with sufficient emphasis that that sovereign act of God which brings men to faith and thus secures their salvation is an act of love: "it proceeds from the fountain of God's gracious electing love that we are accounted the people of God."29 We are not saved by God's power in such a way that his effective action is logically unrelated to his own nature; election, his action upon men, is simply his movement of himself *in his own nature* towards men and in them.30 (It should be acknowledged that in an unguarded moment Calvin can suggest that faith is granted only

---

27*Comm.* II Tim. 1:9 (italics mine).

28*Comm.* I Pet. 2:9.

29*Comm.* Psalm 33:12.

30See below where Calvin is noted to state unambiguously that God's nature *is* love.

because God wills to save, where such willing appears unrelated to God's nature; for example, "those whom God has chosen without any regard to merit are saved by his power."[31])

Since it is the same God who acts upon all men, both elect and reprobate, and since his action is his movement, in his own nature, upon men, then all men must be the beneficiaries of his love. Any doubt concerning this matter Calvin dispels with an incontrovertible line: "God is love; that is, his nature is to love men."[32] This can only mean that even upon the reprobate God acts in love. (How consistent Calvin will be in developing this theme of God's love with respect to the reprobate is, of course, a matter requiring fuller explication.) In any case, this truth must be allowed its full weight. Love is not arbitrary or tyrannical. Men are not compelled by the decree of election (love concretizing itself in effectual calling); instead, they are wooed by his loving-kindness, the effectiveness of which wooing the decree of election is intended to declare. "God chooses to invite his people by kindness. . . ."[33] God brings men to faith in a manner consonant with his own nature.

There remains for this section only the reminder that since God's sovereignty *is* his freedom, the bestowal of faith through election reflects the sheer freedom of God. As there is nothing in men to necessitate the outpouring of God's mercy, so there is nothing in God—apart from his own nature. He grants faith (that is, acts to save) in utter freedom: "His is the right to be free in the dispensation of his grace; for in his sovereignty he says that he will be merciful to whomsoever he will."[34]

In sum, Calvin's understanding of the consequences of sin renders impossible any suggestion that there is anything at all about men which elicits God's salvific activity or which can facilitate a movement towards God, or that there is a human activity which God's parallel or complementary activity completes. Man is dead. He can be resurrected only by the action of God. The doctrine of election reminds men of faith that they owe their salvation to God's sovereign will and power. And since his sovereign will *is* grace (Calvin insists that even reprobation does not contradict mercy—*Institutes* 3.23.11), his action upon men is unambiguous kindness. In this activity he is subject to no constraint. Thus the doctrine of election upholds the truth that God's faith-engendering activity is utterly gratuitous. Men do not, of themselves, will themselves to

---

[31]*Comm.* Rom. 11:2.

[32]*Comm.* I John 4:8.

[33]*Comm.* Deut. 7:9.

[34]*Comm.* Ex. 33:19.

faith or unfaith; their destiny (with respect to faith) is not in men's hands. Nor do men stumble on faith: "faith is not at men's disposal, so that this man or that may believe indiscriminately or fortuitously."[35] Faith is sheer gift. Life rests with the sovereign decision of God himself. And since the sole will of fallen man is a sinful will, the doctrine of election points to the triumph of God's eternal will.[36] The doctrine of election "is simply the Lord's clear declaration that he finds in men themselves no reason to bless them but takes it from his mercy alone; therefore, the salvation of his own is his own work."[37]

GLORY

The second great benefit of the doctrine of predestination[38] is a consequent of the first; an action of God which is sheer mercy poured upon the dead redounds to the praise of his glory. "Being nothing of ourselves, and by his grace only the vessels of his mercy, his glory cannot fail to shine in us."[39] Were we to cooperate with God in any way in the securing of our salvation, or were we to require only assistance (rather than a *gift* of life), or were the gift to be reward in part, God's glory would be diminished to the extent that some credit for the revivified corpse would be due us. Having no glory ourselves, our very existence as men of faith magnifies God's glory.

Moreover, while the glory of God is manifested by the free bestowal of mercy, it must not be thought that God is content with an incidental accrual: one of the purposes of election is precisely that his name be esteemed: "the elect are instruments or organs by whom God exercises his mercy *for the purpose* of glorifying his name among them."[40] As rightly jealous, God insists on being acknowledged and exalted as the giver of life. St. Peter points out, Calvin reminds us, that the *end* of our calling is that we be stimulated to give glory to God.[41] Calvin exhorts believers to

---

[35]*Comm.* John 6:37.

[36]*De Aet. Dei Praed.* 69.

[37]*Inst.* 3.22.6.

[38]Calvin speaks of the three principal benefits as the extolling of God's mercy, his glory, and believers' humility.

[39]*Comm.* Eph. 1:11.

[40]*Comm.* Rom. 9:23 (italics mine).

[41]*Comm.* I Pet. 2:9.

reflect daily on the fact of their election, in order that they might daily proclaim God's glory.[42]

Failure to render to God the praise of his glory is surreptitiously to arrogate to oneself at least a part of one's salvation. A creature either glorifies God or it boasts. Undeniably it is St. Paul's concern to eliminate all boasting and allow to shine in its own splendor that grace which exposes boasting as the pitiful imposture that it is. The praise of God's glory is that exposure.[43] In other words, "grace" and "glory" imply each other. Insofar as glory is withheld, grace (mercy) is demeaned; as mercy is exalted, glory is rendered. Calvin insists not only that God is the sole testator of his inheritance (faith and the benefits which faith receives), but also that God wills to be recognized as such.

HUMILITY

Since the doctrine of election indicates that faith lives by mercy alone and that in acknowledging this, faith glorifies God, it must also indicate that faith has no reason for not remaining humble before its God. Indeed, Calvin maintains, if the doctrine of election is not set forth undisguised, then "humility is torn up by the very roots . . . for neither will anything else suffice to make us humble as we ought to be, nor shall we otherwise sincerely feel how much we are obliged to God."[44] Nothing of our newness-of-life in faith is attributable to us in any way. Admittedly, faith's God-ordained repudiation of the "old man" can produce pride where such repudiation appears to meet with success; indeed, any fulfillment of God's command can, and in fact, does tend to engender pride. The antidote is the recalling to mind that everything about us which suggests life is to be traced only to that decree whereby we were granted life. Faith, *qua* gift, is not something we have given ourselves through inordinate ability or resources; and even as gift (as will be explicated more fully later) it is not something which we continue to possess or retain in virtue of our own strength or capacity. Indeed, "since no man has anything in his own resources to make him superior . . . the true basis of Christian humility is, on the one hand, not to be self-satisfied, for we know that we have no good in ourselves at all; and, on the other hand, if God has implanted any good in us, to be, for that reason, all the more

---

[42]Ibid.

[43]Cf. "Paul wishes to lay low all glorying in the flesh, so that we may know that no one will be saved except whom God saves by his pure grace" (*De Aet. Dei Praed.* 100).

[44]*Inst.* 3.21.1.

indebted to his grace."[45] Whatever "good work" appears in us is the product of God's willing and working his good pleasure.

Just as it is God's eternal decree which when known elicits a constant ascription of praise, it is the same decree which when known ought to render faith ceaselessly humble, for apart from that decree of grace faith will instantly collapse. Our sober knowledge of this latter fact should train us to modesty and fear as nothing else can.[46] Faith's awareness of how it became such should stop all bragging, for "there is no residue wherein we can take pride in ourselves when it is by the grace of God we are what we are."[47]

PERSEVERANCE

> "The Church has been gathered together from the beginning and in all ages
> by the pure grace and goodness of God; for never have men been found to
> possess any intrinsic meritorious claims to his regard, and the Church is too
> precious to be left to depend upon the powers of men."[48]

Once it is acknowledged that faith becomes such only by the free, gratuitous mercy of God, it must then be asked whether faith is cast upon its own resources to maintain itself. If it is, is it not virtually certain that at some point the assault of temptation and tribulation will overturn it? Calvin counters any such suggestion with his insistence that the eternal decree of election guarantees faith's perseverance; and, moreover, *only* that decree can guarantee such. Most succinctly he states, "through the same grace which has once been imparted to us we continue safe and unimpaired until the end."[49] "The same grace" is the one grace of God reflecting his eternal purpose for his people. It is the grace which embraced us when we, as dead, were not capable of embracing anything. Now that God's embrace has enabled us to embrace him in return,[50] our continuing in faith, however, has not come to depend on the strength of our embrace. The latter, however strong it becomes, ever remains weak, and of itself weak enough to be ineffectual. To say that perseverance depends on faith itself is to say that faith is going to collapse. Grace never

---

[45]*Comm.* 1 Cor. 4:7: . . . *verum est fundamentum christianiae . . . nos bonorum omnium inanes esse vacuus . . . nihil reliquum fieri gloriae nostrae.*

[46]*Comm.* Phil. 2:13.

[47]*Comm.* 1 Cor. 4:7.

[48]*Comm.* Psalm 78:68.

[49]*Comm.* Psalm 100:3.

[50]Again see below where the aspect of human affirmation in faith is considered.

equips faith so as to enable faith to stand in its own power.

It should be noted that Calvin never suggests there is the slightest ground for perseverance apart from election; those who challenge his doctrine of election, he insists, will find their doctrine of perseverance but wishful thinking; once it is denied that God elects faith from all eternity *to* all eternity, then it should be admitted that faith will never stand until the final day. Election *alone* guarantees perseverance. Thus Calvin writes unashamedly, "it is the incomparable fruit of faith that Christ bids us be sure and untroubled when we are brought by faith into his fold. But we must also see what basis this assurance rests on. It is that he will be the faithful guardian of our salvation, for he says that it is *in his hand.* And as if this were not enough, he says that they will be safely protected by his Father's power. This is a remarkable passage, teaching us that the salvation of the elect is as certain as God's power is invincible."[51] Similarly, he notes that "the mere fact that believers will persevere he (that is, Jesus) ascribes to their election. For the frail strength of men would sway before every breeze and would be collapsed by the lightest movement did not the Lord uphold it by his hand."[52] God's determination that we be his people cannot fail to find fullfilment; otherwise put, "as the divine goodness is everlasting, the weakness and frailty of the faithful does not prevent them from boasting of eternal salvation to the close of life, and even in death itself."[53]

The force of such God-ordained perseverance is not to render believers complacent; it is to free them from anxiety about the outcome of the life of faith in the face of their own weakness. Since the salvation of the elect is, by virtue of God's election, in his hands, the elect are not responsible for its safe-keeping. They are responsible for looking ever to him whose purpose for them anticipated their birth and will most certainly succeed their death.[54]

No doubt the question is raised concerning those persons who have "lost" their faith. Are they not a living contradiction to what Calvin is expounding here? He admits there to be many persons who at some point profess the gospel and at a subsequent point do not. He admits that they lack stability—and that precisely because they never did come to faith. What they "lost" is what they mistakenly thought to be faith. The elect, on the other hand, never fail to have "the living root of faith and carry a

---

[51]*Comm.* John 10:28 (italics his).

[52]*Comm.* John 13:18.

[53]*Comm.* Psalm 103:17.

[54]*Comm.* II Tim. 1:12.

testimony of their adoption firmly fixed in their hearts . . . it is impossible for them to be alienated from the Church."[55] Calvin knows that it is not merely likely that weak, sin-riddled faith will collapse apart from an eternal decree of election; its collapse is veritably certain. The only stay of the elect is that they were chosen to be "in Christ" from eternity to eternity. Thus his final word on this matter is unambiguous, and in his mind at least, unarguable: "where God's calling is effectual, perseverance will be certain."[56]

ASSURANCE

> ". . . that sure establishment of election which I bid believers seek from the word of the gospel."[57]

Earlier in this study it was stated that assurance is a concomitant of faith; faith implies assurance. The person who lacks assurance simply lacks faith: "no-one can be called a son of God who does not know himself to be such."[58] There it was seen that believers are not assured *in vacuuo*, but are assured of participation in Christ as Christ so acts upon them, in the power of his Spirit, as to convince them that he has become theirs and they have become his. Calvin now relates his earlier (that is, earlier in the *Institutes*) work on this subject to election. While believers are granted assurance of life in Christ as and only as they are granted that life itself, Christ, in fact, becomes theirs only in virtue of the decree whereby God determined to resurrect them. Assurance, Calvin now insists, is impossible apart from election. Unless the man of faith knows that Christ's-becoming-his is *eternally* ordained of God, his faith is always turned back on itself to ascertain whether indeed Christ has become his, whether Christ is at this moment and will be at the next moment, and so forth. Without the decree of election, "assurance" is faith's informing itself on the basis of a "quality" it thinks it can see in itself.

It is important that notice be taken of a point which will be crucial in the discussion of the adequacy of Calvin's understanding of predestination: viz., his insistence that the Holy Spirit does not seal upon faith's mind and heart assurance concerning the doctrine of election *nudus*; it is not the case that the issue here has become one of intelligibility, and that

---

[55] *Comm.* 1 John 2:19: *alienari.*

[56] Ibid.

[57] *Inst.* 3.24.7.

[58] *Comm.* Rom. 8:16.

the believers receive assurance first of all because they understand the doctrine. Rather, assurance of eternal life is borne in upon faith as it betakes itself to the Word and ceases to think of Christ as "standing afar off";[59] that is, the Holy Spirit seals upon mind and heart the presence and power of Jesus Christ, which presence and power are realized by faith to be synonymous with God's eternal purposes. Jesus Christ attests the eternal purpose of God in awakening faith; apart from faith's (God-empowered) discernment that what faith knows and enjoys now *is* God's *eternal* purpose, assurance would be impossible: "assurance" with respect to the present moment only is no assurance at all. Calvin, in his discussion of election, fills in some *lacunae* present in his treatment of faith which appears at the beginning of Book III of the *Institutes*; viz., that no inward work of the Holy Spirit, however vivid, can ultimately impart assurance, unless that work brings with it the assurance that what is presently borne in upon faith is identical with the *eternal* purpose of God for faith.

But of course there can be no assurance with respect to God's eternal purpose unless there is first that purpose: the decree of election. It is this decree alone which can ground assurance. (Again, whether Calvin can ultimately ground assurance in the decree of election when there is another decree alongside the first is a matter to be explored shortly.)

SECURITY

"Before the foundation of the world we were both ordained to faith and also elected to the inheritance of eternal life. Hence arises an impregnable security."[60]

"There is no consideration more apt for the building up of faith than that we should listen to this election which the Spirit of God testifies in our hearts to stand in the eternal and inflexible goodwill of God, invulnerable to all storms of the world, all assaults of Satan and all vacillation of the flesh . . . since we find its cause in the heart of God." (Fr. "in his will which never alters.")[61]

"The fact that everything happens to the saints for their salvation depends on the free adoption of God as the first cause."[62]

With respect to perseverance Calvin insisted that faith, though of itself always weak, would endure to the end by the foreordination of God. He now deals with a related (and perhaps subsidiary) matter: the fact that the

---

[59] *Inst.* 3.2.24: *veluti procul stantem, et non potius in nobis habitantem debeamus cogitare.*

[60] *De Aet. Dei Praed.* 56. For same see *Inst.* 3.22.1U and 3.24.6.

[61] Ibid.

[62] *Comm.* Rom. 8:28. For same see *Comm.* Rom. 11:2.

tribulations and upheavals which come from without cannot overturn God's purposes for believers, and the comfort they can take from such knowledge. Before, he was dealing chiefly with the weakness of faith itself and what God's decree meant with respect to it; here, he is dealing with the life-in-faith which is tormented by the vicissitudes of life.

In his opening paragraphs on predestination in the *Institutes,* Calvin remarks that election "is our *only* ground for firmness and confidence; in order to free us of all fear and render us victorious amid so many dangers, snares and mortal struggles, Jesus promises that whatever the Father has entrusted into his keeping will be kept safe."[63] Calvin is aware that believers are being given up to death every day: "while our life is hidden, we are like dead men. For how do believers differ from the ungodly, but that they are overwhelmed with miseries and, like sheep appointed for the slaughter, always have one foot in the grave? Yes indeed, and are never far from being swallowed up by death?"[64]

Aware that difficulties can becloud faith's sense of God's presence and faith's confidence that God can still be "reached," Calvin insists, in the context of his discussion of a passage which he regards as undeniably predestinarian ("All that the Father gives me will come to me"—John 6:37) that the words, "And him who comes to me I will never cast out" are "added for the consolation of the godly, that they may be fully persuaded they have clear access to Christ by faith."[65] No tribulation, however intense, no work of the evil one, however devastating, can impede the believer's approach to God. The only ground of this fact and therefore of confidence in this fact is God's determination to safeguard his own from every assault.

Nor is it the case that God simply brings believers through myriad difficulties, "bloody but unbowed"; rather, the very difficulties become, in the context of his decree to elect, that by which he fashions believers after his Son. It is not merely the case that the negative circumstances of life are deprived of their power to impair the life of believers; instead, the very difficulties themselves become the material which God uses to perfect his people. Once more Calvin insists that this use of the vicissitudes is not facilitated by anything about the difficulties themselves or by a non-specific benevolence on the part of God; only the eternal decree of election can transmute the instruments of death into the instruments of renewal: "St. Paul shows . . . by the very order of election that all the

---

[63]*Inst.* 3.21.1.

[64]*Comm.* Heb. 2:13.

[65]*Comm.* John 6:37: *aditum.*

afflictions of believers are simply the means by which they are conformed to Christ. . . . Affliction, therefore, is no reason why we should be grieved, bitter, or burdened, unless we also disapprove of the election of the Lord, by which we have been foreordained to life, and are unwilling to bear in our persons the image of the Son of God, by which we are prepared for the glory of heaven."[66] Similarly, ". . . though believers see that almost the whole of the world is carried to destruction as in a wild storm, their condition in life continues peaceful and steadfast by the hand of God. . . . this, then, is the true heaven of our security, that God, who has chosen us of old, will rescue us from all the distresses that threaten us."[67]

Again, Calvin insists that this security does not arise as God grants assistance to faith's striving in the midst of tribulation or from God's recompensing a noble human endeavour: it arises entirely from God's "good pleasure"; faith is secure in the knowledge that the whole course of its life is directed according to the "benevolent attitude" of God himself.[68]

Again, how are believers guaranteed security in life? Calvin does not pretend that tribulation is an unfortunate contingency; rather, as surely as the elect are blessed in the gratuitous mercy of God, they are appointed to bear the cross.[69] Their master was appointed to cross-bearing before them. In the midst of affliction, then, believers, *qua* believers, have fellowship with the One who was borne through that affliction. *He* is the pioneer and perfecter of faith; he has "blazed the way" for life-in-faith. This is a point which Calvin says little about, but which is nonetheless significant. Believers are not granted "safe-conduct" as though led by One who is himself remote from the upheavals of life. Rather, believers are not to doubt that Jesus Christ is "in it with us as if he were distressed along with us."[70] Accordingly, Calvin writes most tellingly, "Who will be afraid under *the faith* and guardianship of Christ? Who, relying on such a protector, will not totally disregard all dangers? . . . This teaching provides a unique support for our faith."[71] Moreover, since it was through his suffering that Jesus Christ learned obedience, it is through the God-ordained cross-bearing that believers learn affliction to be for their

---

[66]*Comm.* Rom. 8:29.

[67]*Comm.* II Thess. 2:13.

[68]*Comm.* Phil. 2:13: *benevolum affectum.*

[69]Cf. *Comm.* Rom. 8:29 where Calvin speaks, oddly, of cross-bearing as "this other decree," where he is certainly not speaking of the decree of reprobation. The decree of election and that of cross-bearing belong together.

[70]*Comm.* Heb. 2:17.

[71]*Comm.* Heb. 2:13 (italics mine).

greater good. God-ordained suffering does not mean that God has become satanic, for believers are not appointed to anything to which God did not appoint himself in his Son. The decree of election guarantees that the affliction believers bear will be the means of realizing God's intention for them.[72] This fact overturns that attitude toward affliction maintained by those who do not know of God's eternal purpose.

At every moment believers are in the hands of the living God (contrary to all appearances) whose only intention for them, "in Christ," is life. That theology which fails to include a doctrine of election Calvin maintains to be "unfortunate," for believers are then deprived of God's final word concerning their affliction.[73] Indeed, "those who rightly and duly examine the doctrine of predestination as it is contained in his Word reap the inestimable fruit of comfort."[74]

WITNESS

> "We draw from it (that is, election) this highly useful doctrine; namely, that teachers and ministers of the Word ought constantly to persevere in discharging their office, though it may seem that all men revolt and give no evidence of anything but obstinacy and rebellion."[75]

Calvin does not countenance any suggestion that the doctrine of election facilitates human complacency with respect to witness. Nor does he tolerate the Church's becoming cavalier concerning the indifference to the gospel which witness appears to encounter. In fact, the spurning of the gospel should remain a horror to those who know it to be life. In view of those who do not believe the Church's report Calvin maintains that believers should "groan and complain along with the prophet, and let us be distressed with grief when we see that our labour is unprofitable, and let us complain before God; for godly ministers must be deeply affected if they wish to perform their work faithfully."[76]

Yet, while concern for evident lack of response is appropriate, anxiety is not; it is inappropriate in so far as believers know that in virtue of the decree to elect, witness faithfully borne to Jesus Christ cannot fail to be

---

[72]Cf. Calvin's interpretation of Job's suffering (*De Aet. Dei Praed.* 51), and Calvin's frequently iterated remark, following Augustine, that God allows evil because he can use it for our greater good.

[73]*De Aet. Dei Praed.* 52.

[74]*Inst.* 3.24.4. For same see *Comm.* John 10:29.

[75]*Comm.* Isa. 8:16.

[76]*Comm.* Isa. 53:1.

used of God in the resurrecting of others. It is the eternal decree *alone*, insists Calvin, which counters the paralyzing discouragement believers will otherwise undergo. It is only as believers remember the *effectual* decree of God in their bearing witness to men who are blind, deaf, and even dead (and as such utterly incapable of even making preparation for a resurrection *ab extra*: "neither the beginning of faith nor any preparation for it lies in us"—*Comm*. John 6:45) that the same believers will be spared anxiety, anger, and abandonment of their witness. Since those whom God has ordained to life he will invariably resurrect, any human ignoring of or trifling with or obstinacy to the gospel believers can confidently endure, knowing that through their witness God can raise up sons to Abraham from cold, lifeless stones.

> "The Lord, therefore, merely forewarns Isaiah that he will have to do with obstinate men, on whom he will produce little effect; but that so unusual an occurrence must not lead him to take offence and lose courage or yield to the rebellion of men; that, on the contrary, he must proceed with unshaken firmness and rise superior to temptation of this nature. For God gives him due warning beforehand . . . 'You will indeed teach without any good effect; but do not regret your teaching for I enjoin it upon you; and do not refrain from teaching because it yields no advantage; only obey me, and leave to my disposal all the consequences of your labours.' "[77]

Indeed, just as the determinative reality in the twelve's becoming disciples was Jesus' choosing them (rather than their choosing him), so the Son, in concert with the Father, continues to choose whom he will, where his choice is what determines their coming to faith (and therein appropriating the "benefits" which the Son bestows). In the certainty that Jesus Christ will not fail to choose men, godly teachers "must do their utmost to bring the whole world into Christ's fold; but when they do not succeed as they would wish, they must be satisfied with the single thought that those who are sheep will be collected together by their work."[78] For Calvin the coming-to-faith of men is always in the hands of God. To affirm this, however, is simply to affirm election. Accordingly, apart from the fact and knowledge of election the Church's confidence concerning the prosecution of the Christian mission is groundless.

It must be noted that Calvin repudiates one kind of interpretation of this argument: that those who are not presently of faith will never come to faith because they are not of the elect. This notion, Calvin maintains, is "imprecation rather than doctrine."[79] In other words, the force of the

---

[77] *Comm*. Isa. 6:9.

[78] *Comm*. John 10:27.

[79] *De Aet. Dei Praed.* 138.

doctrine of election, in the context of Christian witness, is always positive; the doctrine is to be considered that which obviates numbing discouragement, and not that which enables believers to ascertain just who is elect and who is not. Believers are never to survey the apparent indifference which greets their witness and then conclude that the evident results are scanty because God has, in fact, decided not to elect the recipients of their witness. Rather, the use which believers are to make of the doctrine is always positive.

> "Since the conversion of a man is in God's hands, who knows whether those who today seem unteachable may be suddenly changed by God's power into different men? Thus when we remember that repentance is God's gift and work, we shall hope the more earnestly and, encouraged by this assurance, will give more labour and care to the instruction of rebels. We should consider it our duty to sow and to water and, while we do that, we should expect God to give the increase. Thus our endeavours and labours are by themselves useless, and yet by God's favour they are not fruitless."[80]

It is important to realize that while the decree of election guarantees the efficacy of witness, it is the promulgation of the gospel through which men are brought to faith. Christian witness, therefore, is to concern itself with the declaration of the gospel, and not with attempts at arguing, cajoling, or persuading men towards "faith": "*let it suffice* that the gospel will always have the power to gather the elect to salvation."[81] It is only the Word of Life which engenders faith; election is the guarantee that witness is not fruitless; that is, that faith will be engendered. Predestination, so far from being something *horrible*, serves *only* as encouragement: "this (doctrine) also is a comfort to ministers of the gospel, if their labour is not profitable to all."[82]

APOSTASY

> "For it does more to upset the weak when anyone among us who professes the true faith falls away than when a thousand outsiders conspire against us."[83]

Related to the matter discussed in the foregoing section is the baleful influence of apostates and pseudo-believers upon those of authentic faith. Calvin maintains that while discouragement concerning the slow progress of the gospel among men is serious, that created by men who jettison

---

[80]*Comm.* II Tim. 2:25. For same see *Comm.* John 15:6.

[81]*Comm.* John 6:39 (italics mine).

[82]*Comm.* John 10:26.

[83]*Comm.* I John 2:19.

the faith is critical, especially where such men are persons of standing in the Church. In the face of this, what comfort is pressed upon believers? Again, Calvin returns to his conviction that only the decree of election can sustain believers as those whose "faith" was thought to be invincible drop away.

> "There is no reason for godly men to lose heart even if they see falling those whom they thought firm in the faith. To console them, St. Paul points out that men's fickleness or unfaithfulness cannot prevent God from preserving his Church to the end. First he reminds us of God's eternal election which he calls figuratively a foundation, meaning by this word its firm and enduring constancy. All this tends to prove the certainty of our salvation, provided that we belong to God's elect. It is as if he had said, 'God's elect do not depend upon changing events, but rest upon a solid and immovable foundation, for their salvation is in God's hands. Just as "every plant which the Heavenly Father has not planted must be rooted up," so the root which his hand has fixed cannot be injured by winds or storms.' Let us remember first, therefore, that in spite of this weakness of the flesh the elect are nevertheless not in danger, *for they do not stand in their own power but are founded on God.*"[84]

Similarly, Calvin insists that one of St. Paul's aims in writing to the Ephesians was to equip them lest they be shaken by the false apostles. In supporting these persons the apostle tells them "that the full certainty of salvation consists in the fact that through the gospel God reveals his love to us in Christ. But to confirm the matter more fully he recalls them to the first cause, to the fountain, the eternal election of God, by which before we are born, we are adopted as sons."[85] Only God's decree of election can sustain faith as those of apparent faith forsake the way of life.

There are several considerations in the above paragraph which invite comment. It should be noted that in the face of doubt augmented by the "falling away" of those of seeming faith, Calvin insists that the "full certainty" of salvation is enlivened by the *gospel*; that is, there can be no greater certainty than that which the gospel produces, where the gospel is the declaration of God's love in Christ. It is not the case that while the gospel grants life, it cannot impart assurance of that life: the assurance of what the gospel brings is the gospel itself. The gospel is not authenticated by anything lying behind it. Admittedly, Calvin then adds, "But to confirm the matter more fully he recalls them to the first cause . . .", as though greater confirmation were needed than the "full certainty" imparted by the gospel. It must be asked, then, what Calvin is trying to impress upon his readers through his somewhat convoluted thought.

---

[84]*Comm.* II Tim. 2:19 (italics mine): . . .*fundamentum . . . certitudinem . . . non stent propria virtute, sed in Deo sint fundati.*

[85]*Comm.* Eph. 1:3.

Since there can be no greater assurance than "full" certainty, the reference to eternal election does not increase certainty; it does, however, indicate that what certainty the gospel produces is an accurate reflection upon and discernment of God's *eternal* intention for men, which intention is that he, in his love, wills sons for himself. In other words, "God's love to us in Christ" *is* the eternal election of God, the fountain, the first cause. Otherwise put, election and gospel can be equated. The gospel declared and received is the eternal decree manifesting itself in time. The content of "election" and "gospel" are identical. This understanding must be allowed its full weight in any subsequent probing of Calvin's doctrine of predestination.

In brief, then, the uncertainty created by apostasy is countered, ultimately, by the decree of election, which decree simply is the gospel through which God reveals his love to us. "Full certainty" comes through faith's betaking itself again and again to the gospel.

EXHORTATION

"If election has as its goal holiness of life, it ought to arouse and goad us
eagerly to set our mind upon it than to serve as a pretext for doing nothing."[86]

When Calvin deals with election in the *Institutes* he devotes no little space to his refutation of the notion that the doctrine of election renders all admonitions meaningless. He does not treat the matter primarily by an explication of how election and godly living are related, but simply by indicating that St. Paul juxtaposed both the doctrine and exhortation. In the *Commentaries*, however, he does explicate the inner logic of the juxtaposition and does state why the doctrine of election is the only context in which the exhortations are meaningful.[87]

It cannot be denied, given the believer's continuing propensity to sin, that exhortations to godly living must seem as futile as urging a corpse to walk. However, it must not be forgotten that for Calvin, election is the inception of the life of faith, that by which faith is sustained amid the attacks which beat upon it, and the guarantee that God will complete the good work he has begun in believers. Their awareness of having been made alive by God's will and determination, when as dead men they could do nothing to attain life, should move them to "become what they are." Indeed, "the more we owe the Lord, the more fervent we should be in

---

[86]*Inst.* 3.21.12.

[87]As far as I know this point is not dealt with anywhere in the literature.

performing the duties he demands of us. Otherwise we cannot escape the charge of base ingratitude. It is therefore clear that there is nothing which should more keenly kindle in us a striving for holy and godly living than when we acknowledge that we owe everything to God and that we have nothing of our own, that both the beginning of our salvation and all the parts which follow from it flow from his free mercy."[88]

While the *awareness* of what believers owe to the God who gratuitously granted them mercy no doubt is an incentive to godly living, Calvin ultimately asseverates that the relation between them is more than merely psychological. It is not the mere awareness of mercy that engenders godly living, but that mercy itself. Accordingly, Calvin, following St. John, ascribes the beginning of godliness to election.[89] Exhortations to godliness become effectual only in the context of that decree which imparts and sustains life in the midst of an otherwise-victorious deadliness. The integral connection between election and godly living Calvin could not state any more precisely than, "it is the gift of divine election when, having embraced the teaching of Christ by faith, we also follow it in our life."[90]

Appendix. Having stated that election engenders godly living, Calvin then maintains that godly living is in turn evidence of election: "The purity of life is rightly regarded as the illustration and evidence of election, whereby the faithful not only show to others that they are the sons of God, but also confirm themselves in this faith, but in such a way that they place their sure foundations elsewhere."[91] It should be noted that while Calvin is flirting here with something that he will denounce elsewhere (viz., the notion that there is a manifest quality to human existence which enables onlookers to distinguish elect and reprobate), he is careful to state that the confirmatory significance of election-engendered godly living does *not* lead believers to regard their conformity to Christ (of whatever degree) as the *fundamentum* of their life-in-faith, but rather points them back to the decree itself: effectual mercy.

All the more surprising, then, is Calvin's comment on the same verse, "the sons of God are distinguished from the reprobate by this mark, that they live holy and godly lives." Earlier it was noted in this study that while faith is *the* difference between elect and reprobate, that difference is not *grounded* in the faith of the elect. Calvin's point there was that it is God's

---

[88]*Comm.* John 15:16.

[89]*Comm.* John 13:8.

[90]Ibid.

[91]*Comm.* II Pet. 1:10.

decision and action which constitute the Christian man, rather than something predicated of that man himself. Is Calvin not in danger here of retracting what he has said heretofore? When he expounds his doctrine of the Church and the necessity of maintaining unity with her, Calvin criticizes the Anabaptist notion that the discernment of the slightest taint gives one excuse for leaving her. In this connection Calvin says of those who think they can distinguish "upright" from "prone" by the quality of life: "Let them ponder that in a great multitude there are many men, truly holy and innocent in the Lord's sight, who escape their notice. Let them ponder that among those who seemed diseased there are many who in no wise are pleased with, or flatter themselves in, their faults, but aroused again and again by a profound fear of the Lord, aspire to a more upright life. Let them ponder that a man is not to be judged for one deed, inasmuch as the holiest sometimes undergo a most grievous fall. . . ."[92] In the light of the foregoing Calvin's insistence that the love they have for the brethren *proves* the indwelling of God with respect to believers appears to be a surd element.[93] How surd it remains in the exposition of the double decree, however, is a moot point: can such "secondary" indicators of election remain secondary once Jesus Christ is no longer to be identified with the totality of God's ways and works?

PRESUMPTUOUSNESS

Because men's coming-to-faith is in the hands of God, and because God can always be trusted to bring to faith those whom he has from all eternity marked out for life, and because who the elect are is known ultimately only to God, believers could only most inappropriately become "spiritual sleuths" attempting to find clues as to who is of faith and who of none. Spiritual snobbery, or pretension to a heightened perceptivity that can distinguish elect from reprobate simply contradicts one's supposed confidence that God elects as he wills, and therefore persons of faith are not to concern themselves with appying such criteria as will satisfy them that others have come to faith.

Moreover, since the gift of faith ever remains the prerogative of the Giver, it is never appropriate for believers to regard anyone as "hopeless"; after all, what authentic believer can say that his case, of itself, was at one time something other than hopeless: is there anything more "hopeless"

---

[92] *Inst.* 4.1.16.

[93] *Comm.* I John 4:13: "prove"—*probabimus.*

than a corpse? *Any* man may yet become the beneficiary of God's will. Hence Calvin insists that "we ought to pray that this and that and every man may be saved and so embrace the whole human race, because we cannot yet distinguish the elect from the reprobate."[94] It is simply not faith's responsibility to detect apparent faith.

To be sure, for purposes of Church membership, Church offices, ordination, and so forth, some recognition of and confession of the gospel is required. And it will no doubt be true that some persons who are regarded as of faith in virtue of their confession will fall away—that is, were never more than pseudo-believers. Nonetheless, it is not the Church's responsibility to cull out beforehand those who will fall away. Just *because* God knows who are his, "it is the judgment of charity and not of faith to consider as elect all those in whom the mark of divine adoption occurs . . . as everyone is made sure of his own election by the testimony of the Spirit, so he can know nothing certain about that of others."[95] Indeed, "the salvation of the elect is in God's secret keeping, like a signet ring, for the scripture declares that they are 'written in the book of life.' Both the word 'seal' (*sigillum*) and the clause that follows ('the Lord knows those who are his') remind us that we are not to judge according to our own opinion whether the number of the elect is great or small. For what God has sealed he intends to be as it were a closed book to us; also, if it belongs to God to *know who are his*, it is not surprising that often a great number of them are unknown to us and that we should make mistakes as to who they are."[96]

In virtue of the decree whereby God knows who are his, believers are spared the anxiety and the arrogance of thinking that part of their obedience-in-faith is that *they* must know, or that their work and witness presuppose their being able to know.

Appendix. Although the fact and knowledge of election render inappropriate any pretension on the part of believers that they must distinguish the elect from the reprobate or that they even have the capacity for such differentiation, it must not be thought that therein all spiritual discernment is thought to be inappropriate or even impossible. Indeed, faith must be able to distinguish truth from falsehood, the gospel from idolatry, light from darkness, sheep from wolves; "this is the spirit of discernment, by which the elect discriminate between the truth of God

---

[94] *Comm.* John 17:9.

[95] *Comm.* I Pet. 1:1.

[96] *Comm.* II Tim. 2:19 (italics his).

and men's false inventions."[97] Again, it is a capability for which men of faith can take no credit, for it arises entirely from God's will-to-mercy: "I own, indeed, that it is by faith that we distinguish the true God from idols; but this principle is always to be held fast, that we have no interest in him at all unless he prevent us by his grace."[98]

GOD'S PURPOSE IS FROM ETERNITY TO ETERNITY

While Calvin's whole discussion up to this point is intended to provide measureless comfort and encouragement to believers, he anchors that comfort and encouragement in the fact that the purpose God has for his people is not something he happened upon after the Fall had disrupted his plans. Instead, human "integrity" has always been his intention. Before his gracious purpose was declared in Jesus Christ and rendered effectual by the Holy Spirit, he had determined with himself that there be a people for himself; that is, grace becomes effective in us only because God's intention for us has always been grace: "Often God is said to give us this grace only at the time when it begins to work effectively in us. But here Paul is dealing with what God determined with himself from the beginning."[99] Can it be otherwise and God's entire activity *pro nobis* not become, at best, a species of contingency plan, and at worst, a mere afterthought? Calvin's remark, then, is entirely appropriate: "What foundation would our faith have if we believed that a remedy for mankind had suddenly occurred to God at last after some thousands of years?... In this (that is, God's eternal intention) there shines forth more clearly the incomparable goodness of God, in that he anticipated our disease by the remedy of his grace, and provided a restoration to life before the first man had fallen into death."[100] (It should be noted here that again Calvin uses *fundamentum*—"foundation" to speak of God's eternal will that men live before him. It is not an abstract decree to elect which engenders faith, but his mercy becoming effectual.) A people who "live before him" is his eternal purpose; to be sure, a subsequent Fall necessitates a peculiar intervention of God; but the intervention is only that which facilitates the realization of the eternal purpose. Those persons who presently constitute that people are "saved not by an accidental or unforeseen occurrence

---

[97]*Comm.* John 10:4.

[98]*Comm.* Psalm 33:12.

[99]*Comm.* II Tim. 1:9.

[100]*Comm.* I Pet. 1:20: . . . *incomparabilis bonitas . . . anteverterit.* . . .

but by the eternal and unchangeable decree of God."[101]

The continuity of God's eternal purpose and peculiar intervention is clear, since Jesus Christ, who *is* God's decree to elect, is the express image of God's eternal purpose, the eternal wisdom and will of God who always was life and the eternal Word of God, for no other reason than he *is* himself the eternal God.[102] Accordingly, in contemplating Jesus Christ faith does not see One who discloses part of God's intention, even the brighter part, thus allowing a darker dimension of that intention to remain in the background; nor is the faith which contemplates Christ made *partially* privy to the divine wisdom; nor is such faith engendered, according to *Comm.* John 1:1, by an activity of God which only partially reflects his being. Jesus Christ is not *a* word from God, but the Word and Truth because he *is* himself the eternal God. Therefore, God cannot speak otherwise or act otherwise than he does in the eternal Son.

This latter point, again, must be allowed its full weight. While Calvin, to be sure, will subsequently complicate and obscure his doctrine of predestination as it becomes a-christological, the christological determination of that doctrine as adumbrated in the above-mentioned commentaries must not be overlooked in any haste to criticize Calvin's understanding.

In view of the fact that election is determined by the One who can spell only life, and in view of the encouragement, clarity and effectiveness to the life of faith which the doctrine lends, it is little wonder that Calvin can speak of it as "bearing very sweet fruit,"[103] and can insist as well that "no doctrine is more useful, provided it be handled properly and soberly."[104]

THE DOCTRINE ITSELF

The fact and the knowledge of election bring many benefits to those of faith. It must now be asked precisely how Calvin develops this doctrine whose fruit is so very sweet; and subsequently it will have to be asked whether Calvin's articulation of this doctrine is consistent with what he has said elsewhere about the relations of the Word, the Son, with the Holy Spirit and the Father.

"We call predestination God's eternal decree, by which he compacted

---

[101] *Comm.* Eph. 1:3.

[102] *Comm.* John 1:1; I John 1:1.

[103] *Inst.* 3.21.1.

[104] *Comm.* Eph. 1:4.

with himself what he willed to become of each man."[105] Calvin maintains
that God has destined each individual either to faith or unbelief according
to his "good pleasure" alone; that is, there is no consideration apart from
God's "secret" decision which is a factor in the destiny of men. Indeed,
there can be no other consideration, since all men, equally blind, corrupt
and dead, are of themselves utterly incapable of receiving grace. (This
latter point does not mean that fallen man ceases to be *imago dei* or that
he must become "extra-human" in order to receive grace; it does mean
that when grace is offered men cannot put out a hand or "open themselves" to receive it. Calvin is eager to retain both truths: a corpse can do
nothing to attain life; yet the corpse remains a *human* corpse.)

Since the hidden decree is indeed a "secret," it will not disclose itself to
human probing; Calvin rebukes those who attempt to leave no secret to
God, for attempting to seize what he has willed to be hid in himself.[106]
Any attempted penetration will land the speculator in a "labyrinth"
(Calvin's favorite word for that confusing, distressing, exit-less maze
wherein those who will not be contented with what God has revealed in
his Word find themselves). We are not to second-guess God; he has
revealed the fact of predestination to us, which revelation is the "unfold-
ing of his sublimest wisdom"[107] and which we are to revere but which we
were never meant to understand.[108] With respect to predestination we
shall have to content ourselves with a "learned ignorance" which is unlike
the "brutish ignorance" of those who prefer to know less about predestination than God intends for us to know, for such "brutish ignorance" is
sheer ingratitude to God for the help he provides through our knowledge
of the doctrine.[109] Deliberately to remain ignorant of the doctrine is
nothing more than disobedience.

We are left suspended between two poles: predestination must be
acknowledged and expounded; predestination cannot be understood
(that is, with respect to its division into election and reprobation). Any
attempt to go behind what God discloses explicitly in his Word (viz., that
he elects solely in accord with his *hidden* good pleasure) does not honor
God. Calvin leaves us in no doubt concerning the utter impropriety of
attempting to peer behind doors which God has willed to remain closed.
Assurance of election (that is, assurance of faith) is not to be gained

---

[105]*Inst.* 3.21.5: *se constitutum habuit* (Fr. *il a déterminé*).

[106]*Inst.* 3.21.1.

[107]Ibid.

[108]Then is this an instance of implicit faith?

[109]*Inst.* 3.22.2.

through an attempt to unlock the secret: "There is nothing more dangerous or more absurd than to overlook our calling and to seek for the
certainty of our election in the hidden foreknowledge of God, which is a
very deep labyrinth."[110] "Where the Lord stops his holy mouth, let us stop
our minds from going further."[111] "Whoever is not satisfied with Christ
but enquires curiously about eternal predestination desires, as far as in
him lies, to be saved contrary to God's purpose."[112] At the same time, it
must not be thought that that act by which God brings men to faith (or
fixes them in unbelief) is mere whim; God never acts capriciously. While
the "reason" for his action (his "eternal purpose") is not known to us, he
does not act unreasonably.[113] Yet, since Calvin cannot state the reason, he
can only ask himself and us to be content with affirming that God does
nothing without *his* reason, for he does not "do what he does in blind
temerity."[114]

Nonetheless, Calvin has no little difficulty rendering this notion credi-
ble. When he asserts that "such honour is rightly ascribed to God's will
that it constitutes sufficient reason, since it is the origin and rule of all
righteousness,"[115] he is affirming not that God's will is in fact reasonable
(that is, not logically contradictory and not whimsical; Calvin, of course,
is not suggesting that God's action is amenable to the categories of
rationalism), but that whatever God wills constitutes "reason." His
rejoinder that our insistence on an explication of God's "good pleasure" is
but a reflection of our pride does not help.[116]

To be sure, there is a dimension to election so stunning that Calvin is
correct to insist that our clamoring for a reason is irreverent: it is the sheer
amazement that overtakes any sinner when he realizes that *he* was
granted mercy, indeed, that anyone is granted mercy; that God should
will a people for himself when he is subject to no constraint whatsoever in
this regard. Of course, there is no "reason" why God should do anything
with sinners besides visit them with the condemnation they deserve. Here
Calvin's effusiveness is entirely in order: "You ask a reason. I stand in awe
before the height and the depth. You ratiocinate, I admire. You dispute, I
believe. I see the height, but I do not comprehend the depth. Paul rests

---

[110]*Comm.* I Pet. 1:2.

[111]*Comm.* Rom. 9:14.

[112]*Comm.* John 6:40.

[113]*De Aet. Dei Praed.* 114, 118; *Inst.* 3.23.4.

[114]*De Aet. Dei Praed.* 119.

[115]*De Aet. Dei Praed.* 118.

[116]Ibid.

quietly because he found wonder."[117]

However, the "reason" for which any reader of Calvin asks and which will not be forthcoming is not why God shows mercy at all, but why he determined within himself to make only *some* men the beneficiaries of his mercy (that is, bring them to faith) when all alike are undeserving. Surely the request for a reason suggests not pride but bewilderment. Calvin does attempt to ease the problem by saying that God's eternal purpose (= reason) is that he may declare the glory of his name.[118] He immediately adds that he has not contradicted himself by giving a reason where he said none could be given, since the declaration of God's glory is the "reason" for all of God's works, and therefore to posit it as the reason for a special election in no way violates the "secret." But neither does it shed any light on why the God whose nature *is* mercy should bring only some to faith ("election is the cause and beginning of faith"[119]). Calvin cannot, as he thinks, strengthen his case by reminding his reader that Paul proclaims God's reason for raising up Pharaoh was the manifestation of his name, while at the same time proclaiming that God's election is inscrutable; for Calvin was mistaken in thinking that Paul was here concerned with the election and reprobation of individuals rather than salvation history.

Ultimately, Calvin is left saying that while it is hidden from us why God brings only some to faith, God is not arbitrary or tyrannical in doing so; he has his reason, although he has not made us privy to it.

HUMAN RESPONSIBILITY

"The fault of our damnation resides entirely in ourselves."[120]

"Christ . . . reproaches them with having refused his grace in every age."[121]

"We should contemplate the evident cause of condemnation in the corrupt nature of humanity—which is closer to us—rather than seek a hidden and utterly incomprehensible cause in God's predestination."[122]

Despite a recurrent contradictory counter-theme in his doctrine of repro-

---

[117] 118.

[118] 119.

[119] 70.

[120] 113.

[121] *Inst.* 3.24.17.

[122] *Inst.* 3.23.8: *Quare in corrupta potius humani generis natura evidentem damnationis causam, quae nobis propinquior est, contemplemur, quam absconditam ac penitus incomprehensibilem inquiramus in Dei praedestinatione.*

bation, Calvin insists everywhere that those on whom God does not bestow faith are *justly* condemned. They have been abandoned to that destiny which as sinners they deserve from the righteous God. Sin is always hateful to God; he is not the author of it. Indeed, "the proper and genuine cause of sin is not God's hidden counsel but the evident will of man."[123] God is entirely just towards the reprobate, since the cause and occasion of sin is found in themselves.[124] While men sin "of necessity" they yet sin "voluntarily." They know this; and their hearts tell them that their condemnation is just.[125]

Accordingly, "if all whom the Lord predestines to death are by condition of nature subject to the judgment of death, of what injustice towards themselves may they complain?"[126] While God is not the author of sin, he *is* the author of condemnation—which condemnation they deserve; God judiciously abandons them to the consequences of their own sin: "their ruin and condemnation stem from the fact of their having been forsaken by God."[127]

> It should be noted that this note of human responsibility Calvin sounds over and over again in the *Commentaries*. There he insists that no man can say that in virtue of a divine decision concerning him he was foreordained to sin and hence not accountable. Despite the contradictory counter-theme mentioned above (and which will be explicated shortly) the greater weight by far in his understanding of how it is the reprobate are condemned Calvin attaches to their hard-hearted, God-defiant, disobedient unbelief—for which they are fully responsible.
>
> "Men are so unbelieving as to reject their salvation."[128]
>
> "On account of their ingratitude and insolence the Lord rejects them as unworthy."[129]

In response to the question, "Does the cause of unbelief lie in God?"

---

[123] *De Aet. Dei Praed.* 122: *Neque enim propria genuinaque peccati est arcanum Dei consilium: sed aperta hominis voluntas.*

[124] *Inst.* 3.23.3.

[125] *De Aet. Dei Praed.* 101. Men acknowledge their condemnation to be just in that they cannot deny that they sin "willingly"—i.e., they are not constrained *ab extra* to act in the way they do. Hence they must bear full responsibility for their freely-willed activity.

While there is no impediment to their acting in accordance with their own nature, that nature has been corrupted by the Fall, and they are powerless to renew it. Since their every act is and will be a manifestation of *that* nature, they sin "necessarily": a concupiscent nature gives rise to a concupiscent act. Men cannot fail to be sinners; they are not free to will righteousness. Yet they are free to continue to will sin.

[126] *Inst.* 3.23.3.

[127] *Comm.* Rom. 11:7. See also *Inst.* 3.23.3.

[128] *Comm.* Isa. 53:1.

[129] *Comm.* Isa. 65:2 (italics mine).

Calvin states, "He is free from all blame, for it is *only* by their voluntary malice that men reject his grace. God does everything necessary to bring about faith in himself, but wild beasts will never be tamed until they are changed into 'sheep' by God's Spirit."[130]

> "It is their own fault if God does not wish to convert them, for they were the authors of their own hopelessness."[131]
>
> "There follows the reproach that they (the Jews) are rejecting so great a favour by their own free-will."[132]
>
> "Paul does not mean that God blinds all men in such a way that their unbelief is to be *imputed to him*, but that he has so disposed things by his providence that all men are guilty."[133]
>
> "The gospel is preached unto salvation, for that is its essential purpose, but only believers share in this salvation; for unbelievers it is an occasion of condemnation, but *it is they who make it so*."[134]
>
> "For in the reprobate we see as in a mirror a reflection of how detestable a man's state is if he refuses to serve God from the heart."[135]
>
> "Man's mind is blinded for as long as he stubbornly holds out against God and his doctrine."[136]
>
> "It is a consistent mark of God that he prosecutes his course of benevolence right to the end, unless we ourselves interrupt it by our faithlessness."[137]

While God gratuitously chooses for faith some not yet born, he leaves others to that destruction which all men "by nature equally deserve."[138] Calvin's final word is his succinct statement, "God cut off the greater part of men on account of their unbelief."[139]

THE COUNTER-THEME

". . . reprobate by the secret counsel of God before they were born."[140]

---

[130] *Comm.* John 10:26 (italics mine): *voluntaria malitia . . . reiciunt.*

[131] *Comm.* John 12:40.

[132] *Comm.* Acts 15:46.

[133] *Comm.* Rom. 11:32 (italics mine).

[134] *Comm.* II Cor. 2:15 (italics mine): *. . . id esse illius proprium.*

[135] *Comm.* II Tim. 2:21.

[136] *Comm.* II Tim. 2:25.

[137] *Comm.* II Pet. 1:3.

[138] *De Aet. Dei Praed.* 88.

[139] *Comm.* Isa. 41:9.

[140] *De Aet. Dei Praed.* 94.

". . . Esau was raised up to be a reprobate."[141]

"It is utterly inconsistent to transfer the preparation for destruction to anything but God's secret plan."[142]

The counter-theme, of course, is that God ordains reprobation in a sense prior to his just condemnation of sinners who are inexcusably guilty. At his starkest Calvin speaks of men who are "predestined to eternal death solely by his decision, apart from their own merit."[143] For some reason known only to him Calvin insists that there is a necessary complementarity to election and reprobation: "there is a mutual relation between the elect and the reprobate, so that the elect spoken of here cannot stand unless we confess that God separated out from others certain men as seemed good to him."[144] So "mutual" is the relation that Calvin cannot see election as standing except as set over against reprobation.[145] As God determined with himself to bring some men to faith, irrespective of merit, so he determined to condemn others *irrespective of merit*; that is, here, men are *not* condemned on account of their sin.

It must be remembered that for Calvin foreknowledge equals foreordination; to say, then, that God foreknew the ruin of men is to say that he effected it. Thus he repudiates the notion that election and reprobation are grounded in God's "pre-information" of who will or will not come to faith. Rather, God's foreknowledge determines who will come to faith.[146] Jacob is not elect because God foresaw faith and obedience; rather, Jacob and Esau go to their destinies by God's appointment.[147] Calvin notes that Christ was given up to death by the foreknowledge of God (foreordination of God), otherwise "God sits idle in heaven."[148] God does not merely "pass over" those who, in accord with his good pleasure, he prefers not to elect—that is, leaving them to the fate they deserve. Those who are to be condemned have been reproved by a decree which exactly parallels that of election. Here Calvin obviously leaves behind what he was so concerned to uphold in other contexts; viz., that some men reject the life that is

---

[141]*Inst.* 3.22.11.

[142]*Inst.* 3.23.1.

[143]*Inst.* 3.23.2.

[144]*De Aet. Dei Praed.* 68.

[145]*Inst.* 3.23.1.

[146]*De Aet. Dei Praed.* 71.

[147]Ibid., 78.

[148]*Comm.* Acts. 2:23. Cf. "For as it pertains to wisdom to foreknow everything that is to happen, so it pertains to his might to rule and control everything by his hand" (*Inst.* 3.22.7).

offered to them or stubbornly hold out against God and thus are condemned on account of their disobedience. Instead, such men reject and
hold out *because* God has decreed them to belong to that class which was
foreordained to death even before there were any members of it (and that
for the same reason as the elect were foreordained to life: that God's glory
might be enhanced). God *is*, ultimately, the cause of both faith and
unfaith. *Why* God has effectually relegated some men to unfaith remains
hidden in him. Calvin admits that the decree is *horrible*. No one will
disagree with him, since he claims for God, in accord with his reading of
St. Paul, "the right and the power to harden and have mercy as he will."[149]

The catena of quotations in the preceding sub-section was adduced to
indicate the weight Calvin places upon human responsibility. Virtually all
the critical studies concerned with this issue in Calvin's theology treat
reprobation chiefly, indeed almost only, as a decree parallel to that of
election; that is, the two decrees are weighed equally. Admittedly, Calvin
does say that the decrees are parallel, and are essential to each other.
Nonetheless, vastly greater weight is given to the notion that while the
elect are such through mercy, the reprobate are such deservedly: they are
abandoned to the destiny they merit. It is to be noted that rarely, if at all
significantly, does Calvin speak of the decrees as parallel in the *Commentaries*. Most certainly he does in the *Institutes*; yet even here the notion of
the negative decree is overshadowed by his attempt to point out the just
condemnation of disobedient unbelief.

In view of this imbalance with respect to the reprobate, is there any
hint as to why Calvin thought it necessary to posit the parallel structure of
the decrees? To be sure, Calvin likely felt that the logic of his theology
required a parallel decree and did not see how election, by itself, would be
other than a glaring inconsistency in it. Nevertheless, frequently in the
Commentaries but not in the *Institutes* Calvin indicates that reprobation
sets the limit to human unbelief as a creaturely attitude and action over
against God. Calvin will not tolerate the notion that man's wilful, deliberate unbelief constitutes an effective defiance of God's sovereignty.
Indeed, can God be almighty and the last word with respect to faith/un-
faith (obedience/disobedience) be left with men? Can the almighty God
allow his light-shedding purposes to be thwarted by men who prefer to
remain in darkness? Is the creature going to be allowed *finally* to determine himself in opposition to the Creator's intention? (Whether Calvin's
understanding here adequately and accurately reflects the Biblical witness to God's sovereignty, and indeed what the precise content of "sover-

---

[149] *De Aet. Dei Praed.* 85.

eignty" is, will have to be probed.) Calvin brings forward the doctrine of reprobation as that which estops any boasting that even his condemnation man ultimately controls. He has no power *at all* over the sovereign God. The doctrine reminds that those who are tempted to think that they can resist God finally are deluded, and that their very "resistance," although unknown to them, arises from his free decision concerning them. (Again, whether God can "decide" anything with respect to men apart from mercy is an issue for subsequent discussion.) God does not abdicate his royal rule; least of all concerning those who think that their being disobedient subjects of the king arises from their self-determination. The ultimate reason for unbelief is God's decree of reprobation: "we must notice Christ's aim. Since they boasted that they were the Church of God, he affirms that believing is a special gift, lest their unbelief should detract at all from the gospel."[150] Unless it is God who blinds the reprobate there is the intolerable situation of the creature conclusively defying the Creator. This God cannot allow without compromising his own deity.

> ". . . all whom the Spirit of God does not subdue to the obedience of faith are fierce and untameable beasts. So much the more intolerable and unreasonable is it that the authority of the gospel *should depend on the assent of men*."[151]

> "John here distinguishes between the elect and the reprobate, so that the authority of Christ's teaching may stand firm even though many do not believe it."[152]

The decree of reprobation ensures unbelief's having no "rights" alongside the gospel, no power to detract from the gospel, and no implication that even in his perversity man can thwart God's eternal purposes. The clay, even that clay which constitutes a vessel of dishonor and wrath, does not defy the potter. The reprobated do indeed proceed from the secret fountain of God's providence.[153] There is *no* situation in which God is powerless. Calvin notes that while men *do* refuse the proffered grace, "it does not follow from this that God's plan was made void by men's evil intent."[154]

---

[150]*Comm.* John 10:26: *incredulitas evangelio deroget.*

[151]Ibid. (italics mine): "assent"—*fide.*

[152]*Comm.* John 6:37.

[153]*Comm.* Rom. 9:17.

[154]*Inst.* 3.24.17.

ELECTION: THE ONE DECREE OF FATHER AND SON

Although Calvin indubitably reduces the emphasis on the decree of reprobation by speaking of the just condemnation of unfaith, and although he then develops the theological significance of that decree in order to remove from human pretention any claim to effective power, nonetheless it must be admitted that the decree remains. Then does God speak with *eternal* ambiguity? Is Jesus Christ the image of the Father *simpliciter* or the image of part of the Father? Does he do *the* will of his Father or merely *a* will? Does (can) God "say" something other than, even contradictory to, what he says in Christ? Is faith engendered by God himself acting in the totality of his being, or by *an* act inscrutably rooted in his "good pleasure"? Does the use God makes of both his right and left hands point to an eternal ambidexterity? Before Calvin is criticized for what he says concerning reprobation he must be heard and heeded. And it cannot be doubted that throughout the *Commentaries* Calvin speaks of Jesus Christ as the sole, definitive Word and Act of God; that to seek a word or act outside of Jesus Christ or parallel to him is both ridiculous and futile. Hence he avers, "Christ is a perfection to which nothing can be added . . . the whole God is found in him, so that he who is not satisfied with Christ alone desires something better and more excellent than God. The sum is that God has manifested himself to us fully and perfectly in Christ. . . . In Christ God communicates himself to us wholly . . . in Christ he has appeared to us essentially."[155] Similarly Calvin states, "for Christ would not truly represent God if he were not the essential word of God."[156] If God appears to us "wholly" and "essentially" in Christ, what can he say behind or beyond what he says in his Son? Calvin states unqualifiedly that since in the Son are hid all the treasures and the wisdom of God, therefore ". . . we are perfect in wisdom if we truly know Christ, so that it is madness to wish to know anything besides him. For since the Father has manifested himself wholly in him, that man wills to be wise apart from God who is not content with Christ alone . . . no knowledge, erudition, learning, wisdom, can be found elsewhere."[157] "We cannot advance further when he have come to him."[158] (Not even to the *fact* of reprobation?) Furthermore, the term χαρακτηρ "reminds us that

---

[155]*Comm.* Col. 2:9: . . . *plene atque in solidum . . . totum . . . essentialiter. . . .*

[156]*Comm.* Col. 1:15: *Neque enim Deum vere Christus repraesentaret, nisi verbum esset essentiale.*

[157]*Comm.* Col. 2:3: *Nam quum pater totum se in illo patefecerit.*

[158]*Comm.* Heb. 13:8.

God is known *truly* and firmly *only in Christ*. His likeness is an express image which represents God himself. . . . Indeed, the apostle goes even further and says that the substance of the Father is in some way engraven on Christ. . . . God is reaveled to us *in no other way* than in Christ."[159] God is known truly only in Christ; God reveals himself in no other way than in Christ. And it was noted earlier that Jesus Christ is always and only the Father's *effectual* will-to-mercy, since Jesus Christ never comes to us without his Spirit; that is, without his power to include us in himself. In other words, there can be no other knowledge of God and no other revelation apart from the God whose presence can mean, ultimately, blessing only. Moreover, on Calvin's presuppositions it cannot be the case that Jesus Christ is merely provision for blessing, or that his coming to us suspends us mid-way between blessing and curse. As the effectual mercy of the Father, in whom alone God is truly known, his presence can be only life-giving. Moreover, since God is truly known only in his manifest and unambiguous will-to-save, any affirmation concerning God which is contrary to that will *must* be false. In addition, it is to be noted that in the *Comm.* Heb. 1:3 referred to above Calvin is careful to point out that *substantia* ("the substance of the Father . . . is engraven upon Christ") here has the force simply of *persona*. *Persona* is, of course, a most significant term in Calvin's vocabulary. Scripture bears the *persona* of God; that is, scripture makes no claim and no claim can be made for its authority, which is not of the order of God's authority; the authority grounded in pure mercy. To say, then, that God can have no other *persona* than Christ is to say that there can be no attitude or act of God other than the "appearance" of Jesus Christ—which appearance is mercy. Indeed, it cannot be surprising that God can have no other *persona* than Christ, since Christ *is* God lowly in aspect.[160]

Nor is it the case that God's attitude and act even towards unfaith are other than what is disclosed in Jesus Christ: "in Christ's *persona* we have a mirror which represents for us the universal providence of God, which extends throughout the whole world, and yet shines especially upon ourselves who are members of Christ."[161]

As was noted earlier, Calvin insists that Jesus Christ *is* the effectual mercy of God. It must now be asked, even in light of the preceding paragraphs, whether at bottom Calvin wants to say that that mercy is an aspect of God's being, or that being itself; does God merely act mercifully,

---

[159] *Comm.* Heb. 1:3 (italics mine).

[160] *Comm.* John 14:1.

[161] *Comm.* Acts 2:23.

or is his very being mercy-in-act? Is God's call a call *to* mercy, or mercy "advertising" itself so compellingly as to press itself upon men? Does God merely love (with the implication that he can, if he so wills, do something else), or *is* he love, his "hatred" then being a word from him which ever subserves his definitive Word of love? The material adduced in this sub-section, wherein Jesus Christ is said to be *the* Word and Act of God, leaves no room for doubt. Nonetheless, Calvin confirms our conclusion: "God is love; that is, his nature is to love men."[162] And what is the scope of this love? "Christ brought life because the heavenly Father does not wish *the human race that he loves* to perish."[163] Similarly, "God demonstrates his undeserved love, by which he embraced us all in his only begotten Son."[164] In principle Calvin dispels all doubt when he writes, with respect to "God does not desire the death of a sinner, but that he should turn from his wickedness and live," that "God desires nothing more earnestly than that those who were perishing and rushing to destruction should return into the way of safety. And for this reason not only is the gospel spread abroad in the world, but God wished to bear witness through all ages how inclined he is to pity."[165] Elsewhere Calvin concisely states not that men are called *to* the gospel, but are called *by* the gospel. Election *is* the gospel declaring itself;[166] that is, Jesus Christ, behind whom there is not another act of God because he is the sole act of God, calls men to himself: every act of God is an act of mercy.

The foregoing need not imply universalism; but it does imply that the one Word of God which is Jesus Christ comprehends God's speaking and doing: he *intends* life for all men. Accordingly, "the proper function of the gospel is always to be distinguished from what we may call its accidental function"[167] "for it is accidental to the Word of God to blind man."[168] Jesus Christ, insists Calvin, was foreordained before the foundation of the world to wash away the sins *of the world*.[169] All men are the beneficiaries of his action; and behind his action or alongside it there can be no other activity of God, for Jesus Christ *is* the eternal God himself.[170]

---

[162] *Comm.* I John 4:8.

[163] *Comm.* John 3:16 (italics mine).

[164] *Comm.* Isa. 42:1.

[165] *Comm.* Ez. 18:23.

[166] *De Aet. Dei Praed.* 69.

[167] *Comm.* II Cor. 2:15: *proprium officium . . . ab accidentali.*

[168] *Comm.* John 12:40: *accidentale esse verbo Dei.*

[169] *De Aet. Dei Praed.* 70. (Italics mine.)

[170] *Comm.* John 1:1.

The fact that election is the one eternal decree of Father and Son is fraught with significance for faith. Indeed, in view of the identification of Jesus Christ with the *totality* of the Father's act and attitude, faith must ever look only to Christ in order to gain assurance. Doubt, persecution, temptation and death, all of which sorely try believers, can be dealt with only as faith looks to Jesus Christ and realizes that *there* it is contemplating God's definitive attitude and act. Calvin never wearies of reminding believers that faith's looking in upon itself for assurance is not only useless but deleterious. Faith must ever look to the mirror (*speculum*) in which it sees reflected mercy alone; it is in Jesus Christ that faith can see "without deception" God's love.[171] Throughout the literature Calvin comes back to this matter again and again: "Christ is more than a thousand testimonies to me."[172] "The Saviour and Son of God himself is the most excellent luminary of grace and predestination."[173] "Life is set before us in Christ, who not only makes himself known in the gospel but also presents himself to be enjoyed. Let the eye of faith look fixedly in this mirror. . . . Since this is the right way, let the sons of God walk in it."[174] Most important of all, however, is Calvin's contention that it is the gospel which *establishes* election.[175] The order here is crucial. Were election to establish the gospel, then one would suspect an activity of God behind the gospel. Calvin indicates here that such is a logical impossibility. Indeed, he states that just because the gospel establishes election (that is, at bottom election is nothing other than the gospel) we are to have a "quiet reliance" upon the promise. If election were something other than just the gospel, then a quiet reliance upon the promise would be impossible. Calvin's logic is unimpeachable.

THE CONTRADICTION

"But I hold the grace of God to be so universal that I make the distinction to consist in this; not all are called according to God's purpose."[176]

Upon reading the above one, immediately wants to ask what *is* the relation between purpose and grace, since God's purpose can apparently

---

[171]*Inst.* 3.24.5.

[172]*De Aet. Dei Praed.* 130.

[173]Ibid., 64.

[174]Ibid., 80. For same see ibid., 13, 127, and *Inst.* 3.24.5.

[175]*Inst.* 3.24.7.

[176]*De Aet. Dei Praed.* 148.

no longer be identified with grace. When Calvin states, "God stretches out his hand to all alike, but grasps only those (in such a way as to lead to himself) whom he has chosen before the foundation of the world,"[177] the questions multiply. When Calvin speaks of the Word of God being "held out indiscriminately to all"[178] one has to wonder if the out-stretched hand is more than a piece of poor theatre. Suspicion increases when Calvin states, "Christ has been manifested to the world to confirm what the Father has decreed on our salvation."[179] Does Jesus Christ merely *confirm* a decree? Did not Calvin indicate earlier that Christ is the author of that decree which he is?

Calvin, throughout his work, maintains that Jesus Christ *is* Mercy, which *is* the gospel; the gospel is "brought" to men *via* preaching, which he calls "outward calling," and which points, as nothing else does, to the universality of grace.[180] Now he informs us that the secret election of God overrules the outward calling,[181] the outward calling being the announcement of grace. But by definition, what can overrule grace, when Jesus Christ (who is mercy) *is* the eternal God? At this point it must be wondered whether there is anything more than a contingent relationship between outward calling and election, and worse still, between election and gospel; that is, are men elect in the power of something other than the gospel?

Whereas formerly Calvin insisted that God has only one will, and that a will-to-mercy (that is, a will-to-bestow-faith) now he maintains that we must ever bear in mind the distinction between the secret counsel of God and his will revealed in scripture; to the latter faith has access; to the former no man has access.[182] Is a distinction between God's counsel and his will theologically defensible, especially when that counsel is something other than the manifest will of God, in fact a counsel veiled in the recesses of his own life? While Calvin did insist that all creatures were created through Christ whom he understands to be the substance or foundation of all things,[183] it must be asked whether he really holds that the reprobate were made through him; indeed, whether they could have been. When Calvin distinguishes between God's "fatherly love" and his

---

[177]*Comm.* II Pet. 3:9.

[178]*Comm.* Isa. 8:16.

[179]*Comm.* John 6:38.

[180]E.g., *De Aet. Dei Praed.* 103.

[181]*Comm.* Rom. 9:17.

[182]*Comm.* Rom. 1:34.

[183]*Comm.* Col. 1:15.

"common beneficence" (where the former expression refers to his dealings in Christ) our suspicion is heightened.[184]

In his exegesis of Heb. 4:16 this ambiguity in Calvin's thought can scarcely be missed. He asserts that "the way is open for all who trust the mediation of Christ and come to him. Indeed, he (the author of Hebrews) encourages those who believe to be bold in presenting themselves before God without any hesitation. This is the outstanding fruit of spiritual teaching; namely, the sure confidence of calling on God, just as on the other hand all religion falls and perishes when this certainty is taken away from men's consciences. . . . Indeed, if we were so persuaded that Christ was holding out his hand to us, who would not seize the full boldness of approaching?. . . The basis of this confidence is that the throne of God is not marked by a naked majesty which overpowers us, but is adorned with a new name, that of grace."[185] The ambiguity concerning God's holding out his hand has already been noted. And has not Calvin in fact supplanted *grace* as the name of the throne of God with that naked majesty which undermines confidence? Is not the secret counsel that naked majesty?

THE ATTEMPTED ACQUITTAL

Calvin attempts to acquit God of the accusation of unrighteousness with respect to election *and* reprobation by averring that the human category of "righteousness" cannot comprehend the divine will. God's ways are not man's: what he wills *is* righteous, for no other reason than that he wills it.[186] Those who suggest that God acts unrighteously by becoming angry at the reprobate, that is, at "his creatures who have not provoked him by any previous offense," judging that for God, to determine for destruction whomever he pleases is more like the caprice of a tyrant than the lawful sentence of a judge, are those who are "seeking something greater and higher than God's will, which cannot be found."[187]

However, the vocabulary Calvin uses indicates his uneasiness. Earlier it was noted that "will of God" is always Jesus Christ; that is, God's will to save, while "secret counsel" embraces God's decision to elect and reprobate. Now, in expounding predestination, Calvin maintains that St. Paul

---

[184]*Comm.* Psalm 47:4.

[185]*Comm.* Heb. 4:16.

[186]*Inst.* 3.23.2.

[187]Ibid.

"advances no higher cause than the will of God."[188] Similarly, St. Paul "claims for God the right and the power to harden and have mercy according to his will."[189] Why does Calvin now posit the will of God as the seat of the decrees rather than the hidden counsel? Moreover, why has Calvin begun using *arbitrio* for "will"? In *Inst.* 3.2.6, where Calvin spoke of faith as "a knowledge of God's will towards us," he used *voluntas* (*fidem esse divinae ergo nos voluntatis notitiam*). The reader is somewhat stunned to hear Calvin say that while election is grounded in the gratuitous volition of God, reprobation is grounded in his mere will.[190] God has both *arbitrio* and *voluntas*; Calvin moves back and forth between the two expressions. Presumably, when "secret counsel" gives way to "will," Calvin has *arbitrio* in mind. And that is precisely the problem. Surely what he said with respect to Father and Son and the one decree of election must imply that the secret counsel could be only *voluntas*. But this is precisely what Calvin will not state. With rigorous consistency Calvin maintains that God is said to will life in that he wills repentance; he manifests that will in so far as "he invites all to it by his word." This, Calvin insists, does not contradict his secret counsel, wherein he brings only some to life. As lawgiver God illuminates all with the external doctrine of life, "in this first sense calling all men to life. But in the other sense he brings to life whom he will. . . ."[191] Throughout this passage Calvin uses *volo* only of God's bestowing faith, and contrasts this with his secret counsel. Calvin employs *arbitrio* to convey what he normally means by "secret counsel." The shift in vocabulary indicates that he recognizes something of the problem. But the shift will not extricate him.

Ultimately, Calvin can only state, not explicate, the fact that God's secret counsel is righteous; for example, "St. Paul shows that as far as God's predestination manifests itself, it reveals true righteousness."[192] Yet he never says how. Similarly, we are not helped when he contends that

---

[188] *Comm.* Rom. 9:20: *superiorem causam atque arbitrio Dei.*

[189] *De Aet. Dei Praed.* 85: *hoc iuris et postetatis Deo vindicat, ut suo arbitrio induret vel misereatur.*

[190] Ibid., 65: *Quemadmodum vero electionis initium ex gratuita Dei voluntate deducens, reprobationem in mero eius arbitrio statuit.*

[191] Ibid., 106: *Vitam ergo velle dicitur Deus qualiter et poenitentiam. Hanc autem vult, quia verbo suo omnes ad eam invitat. Caeterum, id cum arcano ipsius consilio non pugnat, quo nonnisi suos electos, convertere decrevit. Neque propterea varium censeri fas est, quia tanquam legislator omnes externa vitae doctrina; illuminet ad vitam omnes priore modo vocet: hoc autem altero quos vult adducat.* Calvin regularly uses *illuminatio* only for the work of the Spirit. Then what does he mean by saying that men are illumined by the external doctrine of life? Is it a matter of intelligibility?

[192] *Comm.* Rom. 9:22.

"God's unimpeachable equity is to be seen as clearly in the destruction of the reprobate as in the salvation of the elect."[193]

Calvin does his best to indicate that reprobation subserves election, in that in viewing the reprobate the elect are all the more amazed and grateful, as they perceive the extent and gratuitousness of God's mercy. Whereupon Calvin asks, "Is there anything reprehensible with this dispensation?"[194] Surely we are constrained to say "yes," for this consideration of the usefulness of the reprobate does nothing to explain how God's secret counsel is compatible with his *voluntas ad misericordiam*. Similarly, Calvin's statement that God does not make us privy to the secret counsel because he pities our weakness does not enlighten us.[195] While Calvin is correct in saying that our comprehension of God's works should elicit astonishment, his attempted justification of the secret counsel on the grounds that it can elicit *only* astonishment *because* it is not understandable is not helpful. Is reverence owed an obscurity? Calvin continues by adding the consideration that the inscrutable judgment of God is greater than men can penetrate.[196] But is the problem human inability to penetrate, or an obscurity which remains impenetrable in principle, and hence absurd? In his attempted exoneration Calvin blurs two considerations: (i) is it not presumptuous for us to claim to be able to comprehend all the ways and works of God? (ii) is there no justice in God except what we can conceive?[197] However, these considerations are not the same. Of course the first claim is presumptuous; all that is asked is that what is not known is not implied to be inconsistent with what is known: that is, that while there may be unfathomable depths to God there are no unillumined areas. With respect to the second consideration: why use the word "justice" when the meaning in this context has no relation to that of normal usage?

Calvin reiterates tirelessly that the reprobate are visited with judgment and the elect with mercy. St. Paul maintains, however, that God is *both* just and justifier—and that for all men, not for two different classes of men. In the cross judgment is executed upon all, and mercy is conferred upon all. Calvin puts asunder what Paul proclaims God has joined together. Calvin tends to use "justice" ambiguously; for example, "predestination is nothing but the meting out of divine justice—secret, indeed, but blameless. . . . Where you hear God's glory mentioned, think of

---

[193]*Comm.* Rom. 9:20: *inculpatam aequitatem.*

[194]*Comm.* Rom. 9:22.

[195]*Comm.* Rom. 9:20. For same see *Comm.* Rom. 11:33.

[196]E.g., *De Aet. Dei Praed.* 58.

[197]E.g., ibid.

justice."[198] How is "justice" done in the face of the same culpability when that justice issues in two disparate destinies? Calvin seems to think that either God is allowed to elect whom he will, or he is not allowed to judge any at all. Why cannot God judge all and elect all?

The major problem with respect to the secret counsel is, of course, the place of Christ. Is he *the* elect one, in whose election, as representative humanity, all men are elect; or is he the instrument of one decree? There are places where Calvin does suggest the former; for example, "Christ is said to manifest the name of the Father to us because by his Spirit he seals on our hearts the knowledge of our election testified to us by the voice of his gospel."[199] However, more often than not Calvin falls back into his peculiar refuge: the secret counsel. His attempts at vindicating the righteousness of God's secret activity are, at bottom, the assertion that he always acts rightly.[200] He defends his understanding of Rom. 9:20—"God does what he does"—by arguing that any man, "wishing to rid himself of the censures of others, would say, 'I will go whither I will go, or I will do what I will do.' "[201]

At the end of the day Calvin's attempts at making "secret counsel" conform with "will of God," where that will everywhere else means only *mercy*, are found wanting. The Almighty has not been acquitted.

FAITH AS GIFT

If the ravages of sin are as Calvin describes—to wit, that man *qua* sinner is dead and not merely ill, then his insistence that faith is sheer gift is surely correct. A corpse is incapable of doing anything, of making any response, of anticipating grace in any way, of orienting itself toward God however unthematically or uncategorically. God can act upon such a man; he cannot cooperate with God in any way. The action God can perform upon a corpse is either burial or resurrection. Those whom God chooses to raise he raises to *life*; he does not raise to a state mid-way between life and death: his action upon men does not suspend them between blessing and curse. Moreover, to say that grace is sheer mercy is to say that it can only be *given*; "mercy" is never earned. Once Calvin has stated that mercy becomes effectual only through faith (". . . as there is no

---

[198]*Inst.* 3.22.11.

[199]*De Aet. Dei Praed.* 127.

[200]*Comm.* Rom. 9:21.

[201]*Comm.* Ex. 33:19.

other gate into the kingdom of heaven than faith in Christ contained in the promises of the gospel . . ."[202]) he must state as well that faith itself is sheer gift. Bestowal for the mere possibility of faith or the mere capacity of faith will not suffice; what is a corpse to do with the capacity for faith? The self-bestowal of Jesus Christ (which, as has been seen, is what faith is) does not suspend men between life and death; it does not plunge them into indeterminism.

Calvin realizes that the will, *in se curvatus*, can will only continued concupiscence unless it is wholly supplanted by a renewed will. The will, of course, is powerless to grant itself such. God's original intention for man was not suspension between life and death, nor is the result of his redemptive activity that suspension. That choice which the renewed will makes is not the choice between faith and unfaith. Therefore, the faith-determination of any man cannot be, even in part, a product of his own choosing. Faith itself must be bestowed. Accordingly, Calvin's remark, "faith is fitly joined to election, provided it takes second place" manifests the consistency in his thought.[203] Since neither sin-determined nor grace-determined man lives *sub specie aeternitatis* where he can survey both faith and unfaith beneath him, he "sees" only by that reality which constitutes his true life: sin (unbelief) or grace (faith). The latter will constitute his life only as it is bestowed. Sin-blinded man has lost not only sight, but even the capacity for sight; the capacity is restored only as light (sight) itself is given.

It should be indicated that if the gift (mercy) were prior to faith but *not* faith's entire source, then the gift and the faith which receives it would be related contingently; that is, there would be no logical relation between mercy and faith. Again, if only the capacity for faith is given, then is it not left to man to supply the content? This, of course, is that semi-pelagianism Calvin sought to exterminate. He speaks against it explicitly when he opposes Pighius' notion wherein God gives men a "flexible heart," the difference between elect and reprobate being the direction in which each chooses to flex his heart.[204] Calvin's question is, "Whence the flexing?" In order for God's activity to be blessing, faith must be gift—life; not the possibility of life, and not the capacity for life.

---

[202] *De Aet. Dei Praed.* 50.

[203] *Inst.* 3.22.10.

[204] *De Aet. Dei Praed.* 103: *flexibile cor datum est.*

FAITH AS HUMAN AFFIRMATION

Calvin insists that the action of mercy upon men restores them to their true humanity; it does not render them automatons. Hence there is a human activity (affirmation) which is engendered by the sovereign action of God upon men, which is appropriate for men as volitional creatures and which is, in fact, essential to faith's being "faith." Thus Calvin writes, "no one comes (to Christ) *unless* he will. Hence in wonderful ways men are drawn so that they will by him who knows how to work inwardly on the hearts of men, not that they may unwillingly believe, *which is impossible*, but that from being unwilling they may be made willing."[205] To be sure, God must first grant repentance; once he has done so, however, man must then "repent": that is, affirm what has been granted.[206] While it is true, maintains Calvin, that our hearts are not simply turned or stirred up, or that the weakness of a good will is helped, but rather that a good will is *wholly* the work of God,[207] the recipient of the good will must still not "reject" the gift.[208]

The relation between divine determination and human affirmation is indicated by Calvin's saying that "we should be most careful lest we fall from faith. Yet we must believe that God keeps his elect by a secret bridle, that they may not fall to their destruction."[209] In the same vein he writes, "it is true that this mercy is offered to all without exception, but they must have sought it by faith";[210] indeed, they must "lay hold" of it.[211]

The foregoing references to faith as human affirmation should occasion no surprise, for Calvin's work is filled with suggestions concerning this human activity: his insistence that Christ be "put on" or "embraced"; his urging believers of little faith to "shake off that fault";[212] his exhortation to anxious believers to struggle with their weakness and press towards faith; his proclamation that men need to "open the door" *of*

---

[205] Ibid., 108 (italics mine): *Nemo tamen venit, nisi trahitur ergo miris modis ut velit, ab iblo qui novit intus in ipsis hominum cordibus operari, non ut nolentes credant, quod fieri non potest: sed ut volentes ex nolentibus fiant.* (For same see ibid., 138.)

[206] *Inst.* 3.24.15.

[207] *Comm.* Phil. 2:13.

[208] *De Aet. Dei Praed.* 143.

[209] *Comm.* John 28:20.

[210] *Comm.* Rom. 11:32.

[211] *De Aet. Dei Praed.* 56.

[212] *Inst.* 3.2.17.

themselves by faith;[213] his insistence that people can refuse grace and reject the testimony of God's love.

The widest possible scope for human affirmation, however, is allowed in Calvin's discussion of the unpardonable sin. People who commit it are those who "strive" against the illumination of the Holy Spirit; having been enlightened, they join unbelief to knowledge and are thus without excuse.[214] They endeavour to extinguish the Spirit who shines "evidently" (*palam*) before them; and therein show utter disdain for God. The fact that the unpardonable sin is even possible Calvin regards as confirmation of the place of human affirmation in faith.

While the Spirit draws men in such a way as to "form" their hearts to obey him,[215] Calvin notes that this obedience of faith is nothing if not a human activity.[216] Moreover, to separate faith from trust (as human act) would be like attempting to separate heat and light from the sun.[217]

While Calvin does, of course, maintain that Christ's "choice" of the elect is prior to any affirmation they make concerning him, he maintains as well that believers do "choose" Christ.[218] While election is of mercy rather than of him who runs, the election of God is nonetheless "assented to by the subsequent running of men."[219] Faith, indeed, is that gift by which the election of God is ratified.[220]

FAITH AND THE TWO DECREES

"It is the Spirit of Satan that is separable from the Word, to which the Spirit of God is continually joined."[221]

"God works or produces faith in us."[222]

It has been shown that Calvin wishes to preserve at all costs the fact that our salvation flows from God's mercy alone. It has also been shown that,

---

[213]*Inst.* 3.7.17.

[214]*Comm.* Matt. 12:31 and *Inst.* 3.3.22.

[215]*Comm.* John 6:44.

[216]*Comm.* Rom. 1:5.

[217]*Comm.* Eph. 3:17.

[218]*De Aet. Dei Praed.* 69.

[219]Ibid., 84: *videmus ergo sic Dei electionem approbari subsequenti hominum cursu. . .*

[220]Ibid., 104: *speciale donum est fides, quorata fit Dei electio.*

[221]*Comm.* Isa. 59:21.

[222]*Comm.* I Thess. 1:11: *operatur vel efficit.*

according to him, faith is integral to that salvation. Accordingly, faith too must be a work of God. When he asks why the preaching of the gospel is not met with the same acceptance either constantly or in equal degree,[223] he is certain of the answer: faith is God's work and through granting or withholding that by which life is received God determines within himself what he wills to become of each man.[224]

It must be asked what is the place of the Word in this scheme, since the Word, in the power of the Spirit, was heretofore posited as the author of faith. It is precisely at this point that difficulties accumulate. It was noted that "will of God" is synonymous with "mercy." Were Calvin consistent he would have to continue to say that that will of God is the Word of mercy. However, in developing his doctrine of election and reprobation he posits a will of God which is wider than mercy, and which indeed is ambiguous with respect to mercy.

This ambiguity is reflected time and again in his *Commentaries*; for example, on the one hand Calvin maintains that "since by his Word God calls all men indiscriminately to salvation, and since the end of preaching is that all should betake themselves to his guardianship and protection, it may justly be said that he wills to gather all men to himself." On the other hand, "if it is objected that it is obscure to suppose the existence of two wills in God, I reply that we fully believe his will to be simple and one; but as our minds do not fathom the deep abyss of secret election, in accommodation to the capacity of our weakness the will of God is exhibited to us in two ways."[225] In this same passage Calvin distinguishes the will of God and his "secret purpose" (*arcanum consilium*). Then what is the relation of "secret purpose" to will? A few lines later he does state that the "nature of the Word" manifests God's will. However, this does not help; what is the relation of "secret purpose" to Word? Early in the *Institutes* the will of God was identified with Jesus Christ in his mercy. Now there is a "manifest" will and a "secret" will.[226]

What does Calvin do with the texts which seem to point unambiguously to the universality of God's will to save, for example, I Timothy 2:4? He begins well:

---

[223]*Inst.* 3.21.1.

[224]*Inst.* 3.21.5.

[225]*Comm.* Matt. 23:37.

[226]B. B. Warfield implies this too when he argues that "the whole objective revelation of God lies in the Word. But the whole subjective capacitating for the reception of the Word lies in the *will* of the Spirit" (*Calvin and the Reformation*, 178—italics mine).

"For what could be more reasonable than that all our prayers should be
conformed to this decree of God? In conclusion St. Paul is showing that God
has at heart (*cordi*) the salvation of all men, for he calls all men to acknowledge his truth. This is an argument from an observed effect back to its cause.
For if 'the gospel is the power of God unto salvation for every one that
believeth' it is certain that all those to whom the gospel is preached are invited
to the hope of eternal life."

Then, with shocking abruptness, Calvin insists that "all" in this context
refers not to all individual men but to all classes of men; that is, no race or
nation as such is excluded. A few lines earlier Calvin indicated that even if
"all" did refer to individuals rather than classes, the "all" would still be
consistent with predestination: "for although the will of God ought not to
be judged from his secret decrees (*occultis iudiciis*) when he reveals them
to us by outward signs, yet it does not therefore follow that he has not
determined with himself what he intends to do with every individual
man."[227] Here Calvin maintains that both the will of God ("God intends
all men to be saved") and the "secret decrees" (election of some) can be
affirmed without contradiction. The difficulty is manifest. The same
difficulty is reflected in the *Institutes* where Calvin affirms God to declare
that he *wills* the salvation of all, and therefore directs exhortations to all
in common; yet "whomsoever God wills to snatch from death, he
quickens by the Spirit of regeneration."[228] "Will" is not being used
univocally.

His exegesis of I Timothy 4:10 is similarly weak. God is the "savior" of
all men only insofar as God defends and preserves; Paul means no more
here than that the kindness of God extends to all men. Those who come to
faith are those who "feel the goodness of God towards them even more
than the ungodly."

Calvin's characteristic word concerning those passages wherein the
promises invite all men to salvation is this: "they do not simply and
positively declare what God has decreed in his secret counsel, but what he
is prepared to do for all who are brought to faith and repentance."[229]
Regrettably, God's secret counsel is not that by which he "simply and
positively" grants repentance and faith to all men; the secret counsel and
the promises do not have the same content. In the face of this, his
assertion that mercy is offered to all indiscriminately (*indifferenter*) is
simply not true, since mercy has to do with the promises only, and the

---

[227] *Comm.* I Tim. 2:4.

[228] *Inst.* 3.3.21: *quoscunque eripere vult Deus ab interitu, hos Spiritu regenerationis
vivifacat.*

[229] *De Aet. Dei Praed.* 106: *non simpliciter naec praecise.*

promises do not pertain to all men.[230]

It was noted earlier that the Holy Spirit is the Spirit of Christ. Calvin insists on this in the face of the Anabaptist vagaries concerning the Spirit. However, if Christ is always the Word of mercy, while the Holy Spirit seals the fate of both elect and reprobate, then the Holy Spirit is not the Spirit of Christ but the Spirit of a decree(s) which, unlike mercy, is double-edged. If God determines *within himself* what he wills to become of each man, then God obviously intends something other than participation in Christ for some men. In other words, God the Father decrees the eternal destiny of each man, and the Holy Spirit applies or implements that decree. In the case of the elect, the Holy Spirit applies it in such a way as to include men in Christ (herein resides their salvation); in the case of the reprobate, the Spirit applies that decree which stands outside of and beyond Christ. The Holy Spirit, then, is really the Spirit of God (and therefore of a decree) but not of Christ. The Spirit is no longer the Spirit of the gospel (that is, the gospel-in-its-power) but rather *a* power which happens to apply the gospel. The problems raised here are enormous. It is evident that the Spirit is no longer *only* the power by which Christ binds us to himself; no longer is the Spirit *only* Christ-in-his-power creating faith in himself. And of course faith ceases to become the proper and *entire* work of the Holy Spirit.

In turn problems arise concerning Calvin's understanding of the Trinity. Indeed, Calvin is always in danger, on the strength of what he says about predestination, of sundering the unity of the Godhead. He states that God inwardly addresses his disciples by his Spirit in order that he may deliver them into the possession of Christ.[231] What has happened to the notion of Jesus Christ as *the* act of God pouring forth his own Spirit so as to possess all men himself? The Godhead seems now not to act in concert for the salvation of men. Indeed, Calvin asseverates explicitly that the Son wanted to call all men to God, but only among the elect was his call efficacious;[232] is he suggesting that the Son was willing but the Father was not? Later he writes, "faith flows from the outward predestination of God; it is not given indiscriminately to all, because not all belong to Christ." This is a most clear statement that faith flows *not* from mercy (the Son in his action as the One in whom the *fullness* of the Godhead dwells) but from the decree of the Father which the Son happens to implement. The weakness with respect to the doctrine of the

---

[230] *Comm.* Rom. 11:32.

[231] *De Aet. Dei Praed.* 73.

[232] *Comm.* John 17:6.

Trinity implies that with respect to Incarnation: no longer is the Incarnation what tradition has affirmed it to be; that is, the full revelation of God. This is not to say that there are no unfathomable depths to God, but rather that there are no "dark" areas of God which can contradict the light of the Incarnation. Jesus Christ ceases to *be* the presence and power of God (recall Calvin's exegesis of John 1:1 where he said that Jesus Christ *is* the eternal God) and is instead the instrument of one decree of God which cannot bespeak God unambiguously.

Calvin states several times that there is a universal, outward call by which God invites all men equally to himself through the preaching of the Word, and a particular call consisting of the Word illumined and sealed by the Holy Spirit, which creates faith.[233] At first sight Calvin could be understood as saying simply that faith is created by the preached Word shining upon men and illumining them. However, in view of God's foreordination of some to damnation, the outward call cannot be that by which God invites all men equally to himself. His assertion that "the hidden election of God overrules the outward calling"[234] is of greater weight than his grounding of Christ's invitation to all men in the universal human need for Christ.[235] God's "voice" may indeed urge all men to repentance; but the fact that he draws only the elect to himself by the secret moving of his Spirit means that the effectual call is not the preaching of that Word which shines in its own brightness to illumine men unto faith.[236] But then there must be a preaching of the Word which God does not positively honor and empower by his Spirit. Word and Spirit are sundered once more. (And confidence in preaching is scarcely augmented.) God is not concerned to have all men come to faith. Faith is not the grateful embracing of the God whose sole act is mercy; faith is the means God must use to implement his decree to save, once he has ordained that salvation be through faith. In view of the prior decrees of election *and* reprobation, Calvin's saying that while the promise is made to all it is effective only in the elect means that the promise is not made sincerely to all.[237] God is not to be trusted; his "voice" does not reflect his intention, and his voice (*vox evangelii*) and the "rare gift of faith" are not

---

[233] *Inst.* 3.24.8: *universalis* ("universal" is better than Battles' "general"); *specialis* ("individual" or "particular" is better than Battles' "special").

[234] *Comm.* Rom. 9:7.

[235] *Comm.* Isa. 55:9.

[236] *Inst.* 3.24.2: *motu secrete.* For same see *Comm.* Matt. 15:13.

[237] *Inst.* 3.24.17: *efficaces* (Fr. *vallables*).

internally related.[238]

Calvin repeatedly excoriates that irreverent, human curiosity which leaves no "secret" to God. However, it is not so much curiosity as bewilderment which arises when it becomes evident that this "secret" of God contradicts the Word of God. One is rendered all the more bewildered upon realizing that the secret decrees are logically prior to the Word; for example, "if, to make us fit to receive the glory of the life to come, election *precedes* this grace of God. . . ."[239] If election is prior to grace (mercy), then grace does not elect but merely implements what does elect. For Calvin, then, there can be an act of God concerning men which is not of grace. Then who is the actor? Can it be the God who is Father of the One who *is* grace? Moreover, according to scripture is "grace" grace if it merely implements one of two decrees? Does not the logic of Calvin's position entail his saying that since the decree is prior to the Word, then faith must be logically prior to the Word—that is, prior to the Word of mercy, which Word, so far from creating faith, merely confirms that faith which is logically independent of the Word of mercy? Calvin does attempt to extricate himself from affirming the decree to be prior to Christ by insisting that "although Christ interposes himself as mediator, he claims for himself, in common with the Father, the right to choose."[240] However, this assertion raises yet more difficulties: is even *Christ himself* now an ambiguity? (Before, the ambiguity was in God's will, while Christ was his unambiguous will to mercy.) If Christ claims the "right to choose," why should not *reprobation* (as well as election) be discussed "in Christ"? (The latter would, of course, collapse entirely Christ as Word of mercy, God's benevolence—unless Calvin moved to the position where Christ is not the instrument of both decrees, but is both decrees, one died, therefore all died; one is raised, therefore all are raised. Alas, he does not.)

Bewilderment is magnified when Calvin insists that men do not ratify their election by their consent (here he contradicts in the *Institutes* what was quoted earlier from the *Commentaries*), for this would indicate their will to be superior to God's.[241] Faith is not a gift which men *exercise*, but simply receive; men do not confirm (render effectual) their election through faith. Rather, election occurs before they have embraced the gospel. Coming to faith *seals* election but does not actualize it.[242] By the

---

[238] *Inst.* 3.22.10.

[239] *Inst.* 3.22.1: *praecedit* (italics mine).

[240] *Inst.* 3.22.7.

[241] *Inst.* 3.24.3.

[242] *Inst.* 3.21.7: *signat.*

call God does not actualize but rather "manifests" the decree he otherwise holds hidden within himself.[243]

In the light of the foregoing it must be asked how genuine is the human affirmation in faith. Surely this understanding of the effective operation of the decrees casts a shadow of unreality over virtually everything he says about human affirmation. Calvin often expounds a scriptural text so as to reflect the human affirmation suggested by it, only to conclude his exposition with a counter-thesis about predestination. This shadow reflects, of course, Calvin's insistence that the capacity for faith is not a natural, human capacity; man does not contribute anything to his faith. Semi-pelagianism of any hue must be avoided.

It appears that the only possibilities Calvin could envisage were double predestination or works-righteousness.[244] Whether the denial of semi-pelagianism necessarily implies double predestination of the sort which renders faith without any human activity is a matter to be discussed.

As is evident by now, Calvin's difficulties concerning predestination arise from his understanding of God's will and his refusal—in the context of his doctrine of predestination—to allow mercy to *be* that will. He speaks of omnipotence as the power whereby God "regulates all things according to his secret plan, which depends solely on itself."[245] Despite the glorious line in *De Aet. Dei Praed.* where Calvin speaks of God's "omnipotent goodness"[246]—that is, the all-powerful *mercy* of God— "omnipotence" is not presented as an aspect of God's goodness; more precisely, the content of "omnipotence," whether "good" or not, is something whose content is other than Jesus Christ. Omnipotence is simply God's ability to do whatever he wills. However, since God wills according to a secret plan, his will is always ambiguous, if at all discernible. Similarly, Calvin's insistence (noted earlier) that God's will is righteous simply because God wills it does not extricate Calvin. Surely, in scripture, omnipotence is his unimpeded action in accord with his resolve to "right-wise" men; that is, he remains faithful to himself in his will and acts to show

---

[243]*Inst.* 3.24.1: *manifestat.* In the light of this statement one must understand his subsequent (and, at first sight, better) statement that while God has already adopted the elect, they enter upon possession (*possessionem*) of it only when they are called. However, as elect, how can they fail to be called effectually? Then have they not really "taken possession" of it already?

[244]E. Doumergue, *Jean Calvin*, IV, 368.

[245]*Inst.* 3.23.7: *secundum arcanum consilium, quod aliunde non pendet, omnia moderatur.*

[246]*De Aet. Dei Praed.* 67: *omnipotente bono.*

mercy. In a word, nothing inhibits God from acting in accord with his own nature. Once Calvin understands God's freedom to be his ability to act in accord with his secret plan, declaring the plan "just" simply because it is God's plan, then the content of "omnipotence" is simply the two decrees, which two are related symmetrically: the one bespeaks God as much as the other. (Jesus Christ as *the* eternal God has been removed from consideration.) Mercy then becomes not *the* action of God which effects faith in that act, but an act of a God who favors some with it (mercy) but not others, although all alike are undeserving. What understanding of both "mercy" and "freedom" is indicated by the action of that God who is free to select some men and not others? Calvin has confused freedom with arbitrariness when he maintains that *because* God's mercy is gratuitous it can turn wherever it pleases.[247] At this point faith has become that which the unknowable God infuses in those whom he favors; faith has been begotten by a will of God which is other than the will of God which Calvin in other contexts proclaims as God's characteristic will: Jesus Christ as God's will to mercy. While faith's object is mercy, faith's subject is not. Thus Calvin can say, "as salvation depends solely on the election of God, the reprobate must perish. . . . The first origin of our salvation flows from that grace by which God elected us before we were created."[248] That is, faith flows from the "Father's giving believers to Christ. . . . If the origin of faith is this act of giving, and if election comes before it in order *and time*, what remains but that we acknowledge that those whom God wishes to be saved out of the world are elected by free grace?"[249] The origin of faith is not mercy, but the Father's determination to give some men to the Son.

FAITH AND INTERIORITY

"Now among the elect we regard the call as a testimony of election."[250]

". . . calling is proof of secret election."[251]

In the face of the Anabaptist exhortation to ascertain one's standing-in-faith through psycho-spiritual introspection Calvin insists that such

---

[247]*Comm.* Rom. 9:15: *misericordiam Dei, quia gratuita est, non esse adstrictam, sed inclinare quo libuerit.*

[248]*Comm.* Matt. 15:13.

[249]*Comm.* John 17:9 (italics mine). For same see *Comm.* John 6:37-39.

[250]*Inst.* 3.21.7: "call"—*vocatione.*

[251]*Comm.* I Tim. 2:4.

standing is to be ascertained by one's looking *away* from oneself to Jesus Christ. He, it must be remembered, never comes to us without the power to include us in himself; accordingly, any "contemplation" of him *must* include a contemplation of ourselves in him; he is not who he is apart from his making us his. Jesus Christ *is* the promise, and "when we hear the promises of God we ought to consider what is his design in them, so that when he promises the free pardon of our sins, we may be fully assured that we are reconciled through Christ."[252]

Moreover, it must not be forgotten that Calvin eschews the Anabaptist outlook, since it forces attention upon the quality of the believer's faith; faith as a human occurrence then becomes the focus of attention rather than a determinative, divine action, which action is not called into question by the weakness of faith. From a human standpoint faith will always be defective (although nonetheless real). That which is defective is not strengthened by viewing itself. In addition, since faith is engendered and sustained by Jesus Christ in the power of his Spirit, faith is drawn to gaze upon him rather than upon oneself. All of the foregoing was discussed in the section dealing with Jesus Christ as the mirror of election.

However, once mercy is no longer synonymous with God's will, and once Jesus Christ is no longer the *sole*, definitive action of God wherein *all* of God's acts *ad extra* are comprehended, then a looking towards Jesus Christ cannot assure the looker that in him he is contemplating the only action (and the only possible action) of God upon men. There is little point in insisting that Jesus Christ is the *speculum* of the Father's will and determination when Jesus Christ reflects only part of that will and determination. Simply put, it cannot be maintained that in the mirror we apprehend all God's ways and works; no amount of gazing *at* Christ can yield assurance of election when *behind* Christ there is a "hidden" will of God. In gazing at Christ how is one to know that one is viewing God's definitive attitude and action towards oneself? His comment to the effect that since it is in Christ that God loves us, then "all who inquire, apart from Christ, what is settled respecting them in God's secret counsel are mad to their own ruin"[253] would have point were it not for the fact that there *are* vast numbers of persons for whom God's secret counsel has sealed a fate other than Jesus Christ. These latter, in inquiring apart from Christ as to their fate, may indeed be mad to their own ruin; but they are not acting illogically.

Calvin's position is weakened still further when he insists that God

---

[252] *Comm.* Isa. 55:11.

[253] *Comm.* I John 4:10. For same see *Comm.* John 14:9.

sometimes illumines people for a short time and then withdraws his Spirit because of their ungratefulness. If God does indeed do this, then how can faith ever be assured through looking at the Word? How is one certain that God will not withdraw his Spirit? The same notion is reflected in his contention that the reprobates can have "signs of a call" similar to those of the elect, but not that "sure establishment of election" which believers are to seek from the Word.[254] Given the double decree and the "taste of faith" which the reprobate can have, the pledge (*pignus*) of our salvation becomes not Christ (the Word *extra nos*) but the "inner call."[255]

At bottom Calvin knows this. For this reason his frequent exhortations to look only at the mirror and not in upon oneself and the quality of one's faith and the extent of one's spiritual progress gradually give way to attestations of faith which Calvin finds defective when urged by the Anabaptists. Calvin is left urging believers to introspect. Calling becomes *evidence* of election to faith.[256] Believers are turned back in on themselves; *they* are the arbiters of the veridicality of their calling. As an aspect of faith, however, does not one's "sense" of calling fluctuate as faith appears weaker or stronger, more adequate or less adequate?

Calvin is on equally dangerous ground when he states that one's experience of newness of life attests one's election to faith. With respect to this sanctification which is a "sign" or "token" of election he writes, ". . . we find *in ourselves* an appropriate proving of whether he has sanctified us by his Spirit and enlightened us to faith in his gospel."[257] Admittedly, he does say as well, in the next line, that the gospel is a testimony to one's adoption. His argument would have been uncriticisable if he had said simply that the gospel itself *is the* testimony of adoption; that in discerning the One whose very being always includes me there is provided all the "proof" of election needed (or possible). However, as soon as he says (or implies) that something is needed in addition to the gospel—which he has to say in the light of the double decree—his argument is gravely weakened. It is not surprising that he says, "St. Paul makes our calling the sure seal of our salvation";[258] but it is regrettable. And such statements are not uncommon throughout his treatment of predestination; for example, in

---

[254] *Inst.* 3.24.7. Here Calvin is close to suggesting that the Word is that which confirms the election of believers, whose faith is *prior* to the Word. Unbelievers can look to the Word and not be "established," since they are among the non-elect.

[255] *Inst.* 3.24.2.

[256] "Our calling should be evidence of eternal grace" (*Comm.* I Thess. 5:24).

[257] *Comm.* II Thess. 2:13 (italics mine): *in nobis reperiemus legitiman probationem.*

[258] *Comm.* II Tim. 1:9 (italics mine): *salutis obsignationem ponit in vocatione.*

urging believers not to speculate about the hidden foreknowledge ("a very deep labyrinth") he maintains that St. Peter ". . . recalls us to the *effect* by which he sets forth and bears witness to our election. That effect is the sanctification of the Spirit; that is, effectual calling, when faith which is born of the inward operation of the Spirit is added to the outward preaching of the gospel."[259] Should believers not be urged instead to gaze at the Sanctifier himself? Why does Calvin keep referring to the fact that the seal which the Holy Spirit empowers upon men's consciences cannot be obliterated?[260] Is it not because, in view of the two decrees, the gospel cannot be the attestation of how any man is regarded by God? Now believers are urged to appeal to their consciences in order to gain assurance of their election and faith.

In several places in the *Commentaries* where he discusses election Calvin appears to begin his discussion in a way which is consonant with the rest of his theology, setting forth the relations among gospel, election and Holy Spirit; but, at the conclusion of each discussion he adds whatever is necessary to avoid implying that God has only one will towards mankind; for example, ". . . since the election of God carries his calling with it by an inseparable bond, so when God has effectually called us to faith in Christ it should have as much force with us as if he confirmed his decree concerning our salvation with an engraven seal. For the testimony of the Spirit is nothing but the sealing of our adoption. Therefore *every man's faith is an abundant witness to the eternal predestination of God.*"[261] How can faith attest faith, when it is precisely faith in its imperfection and weakness which requires attestation? Faith as the witness of faith is precisely that understanding for which Calvin criticizes the Anabaptists and which he wants to avoid himself. Yet he is driven to it. In view of all he says about the *speculum,* we expect him to be consistent in his insistence that Christ is a "singular pledge" of the Father's love; his use of the "secret counsel," however, drives him to say that *faith* is such a pledge.[262] The "secret counsel," of course, means that election is not in Christ but in the Father. Christ as attestation of election is then eliminated; faith must assure faith.

Calvin is aware of the difficulty into which he has plunged himself. He knows what faith's introspection yields: "if anyone should regard himself,

---

[259]*Comm.* I Pet. 1:2 (italics mine).

[260]*Comm.* I John 2:19 *et al.*

[261]*Comm.* John 6:40 (italics mine).

[262]*Inst.* 3.22.10.

what can he do but tremble?"[263] Elsewhere he can say, "confidence of salvation is founded upon Christ and rests on the promises of the gospel,"[264] without making any reference to interiority or one's experience of sanctification. Here he is utterly consistent with what he says in general (that is, outside the explicit context of predestination) about that mercy which *alone* begets faith.

Ultimately, Calvin wants to affirm both Jesus Christ as *the* Word, will and wisdom of the Father, and double predestination as an incontestable scriptural fact. He attempts to preserve both in the conclusion of his treatment of predestination in the *Institutes*: "since he is the eternal wisdom of the Father, his unchangeable truth, his firm counsel, we ought not to be afraid of what he tells us in his Word varying in the slightest from that will of the Father which we seek."[265] However, Calvin also says in his conclusion that Jesus Christ discloses only one will of the Father, while scripture speaks of two. Jesus Christ, then, cannot be God's definitive Word.

Calvin regarded as most unsettling, even diabolical, the question which Anabaptists put to Reformed Christians: "what revelation have you of your election?"[266] Alas, he raises that question himself.

FAITH AND EMPIRICAL OBSERVATION

"If all men in general bowed the knee to Christ, election would be general; now, in the fewness of believers, a manifest diversity appears."[267]

Calvin appears to have been led to formulate his understanding of predestination largely by what he saw around him, and the interpretation he placed upon what he saw. "Why is it that when the covenant of life is preached it does not gain the same acceptance either constantly or in equal degree?"[268] appears to be the question his doctrine sought to answer. It demanded answer, Calvin thought, for the faithlessness which confronted most preaching could be *seen*.[269] Similarly, he insisted that *experience* taught that the Spirit is not bestowed upon all,[270] and expe-

---

[263] *De Aet. Dei Praed.* 75.

[264] Ibid., 56.

[265] *Inst.* 3.24.5.

[266] *Inst.* 3.24.4.

[267] *Inst.* 3.22.7. For same see *Inst.* 3.22.1.

[268] *Inst.* 3.21.1.

[269] *Inst.* 3.22.2.

[270] *De Aet. Dei Praed.* 104.

rience demonstrated that faith is not given promiscuously to all.[271]

In Calvin's estimation it is impossible that God have mercy ineffectually. Therefore, where there is no faith, mercy cannot have been offered (it being impossible for anyone to spurn mercy; God's will is not thwarted). He maintained that if it were pretended that the beneficence of God were extended to all "promiscuously," then that beneficence would be demeaned. God's grace is not rightly exalted where an attempt is made at covering over the awesome disparity between life and death. If believers lose sight of the deadliness all around them, do they not cease to be properly grateful for the life they have been granted?

Yet it must be asked if Calvin was not misled by what he thought he could observe. Is not sin present in believers? Is not one's true life *hid* with Christ in God? Is faith in any way empirically discernible? (Again, faith and confession are to be distinguished; a distinction Calvin would want, since unbelievers may "confess" Jesus Christ.) Is Calvin not drawing near a species of pharisaism when he speaks of the "evident" deadliness surrounding believers and the "evident" life in believers? Is not his understanding of election given an impetus in the wrong direction and severely warped by his attempted empirical assessment?

CONCLUDING REMARKS

The most distressing feature of Calvin's understanding of election is that it is not an implication of his Christology; it is a surd. Calvin did maintain that the Holy Spirit is the Spirit of Christ, and therefore of mercy; that Christ is who he is only in his power to include men in himself; that since Jesus Christ *is* eternal God, there can be no attitude or act of God behind or alongside Christ simply because there is no God behind or alongside Christ; that the bestowal of faith is precisely what renders a genuine human affirmation both possible and necessary.

He appears to have developed the surd elements under the stimulus of his empirical observation and his conviction that God's sovereignty (omnipotence) must be protected against the "detraction" of human unbelief. Concerning the matter of empirical assessment with respect to faith something has already been said. Concerning omnipotence it must be said that Calvin was too eager to "protect" God. Of course, a theology which has room for human affirmation in faith should have room for a negative affirmation. Calvin could not countenance this. But could God not be sufficiently powerful to allow the creature to be creature over against him, the creature being empowered by God's gift to negate (or

---

[271]Ibid., 74.

exercise) the gift itself? Is God's deity threatened by the creature's negative affirmation, when it is only by God's free bestowal that that negative situation is even possible?

One wonders how Calvin could move from the Christocentric determination of this theology to his candid acknowledgement that election is founded not on Christ but on the hidden counsel of God.[272] How could he move from the Word's being God's will (that is, effectual mercy) to his insistence on the distinction between the Word and the secrets of God's will?[273]

Again, surely Calvin's understanding of the substitutionary aspect of Christ's work implies that Christ *is* reprobate—for us. And surely Calvin's understanding of Christ as true humanity necessitates his being such for all men; Christ is representative man. While Pighius no doubt was a weaker theologian than Calvin, he was not weaker when he maintained that "the whole human race is chosen in Christ, so that whoever should lay hold of him by faith may obtain salvation."[274] Indeed, this statement is implied by Calvin's Christology—but contradicted by his understanding of election. In short, the slightest adjustment in Calvin's theology; viz., a consistent exploitation of his Christology, remedies the difficulties.

Doumergue maintains, in defence of Calvin, that predestination (not "election") and Christ are inseparable.[275] The tragedy is that they are not. Because predestination and Christ are not inseparable, the knowledge of God's act (that is, the knowledge that in Jesus Christ God is *pro nobis*) is not an implication of that act itself, but rather must be added to the act; it is not the case that *all* men, in contemplating Jesus Christ, know themselves to be elect (and this is surely a telling criticism in view of scripture's understanding of the relations between divine activity and revelation); while election is *known* only in Christ, predestination cannot *be* in Christ, since one aspect of predestination is (absurdly) reprobation.

---

[272]Ibid., 161.

[273]*Inst.* 3.24.1.

[274]*De Aet. Dei Praed.* 68.

[275]E. Doumergue, *Jean Calvin*, IV, 358. In arguing that predestination and Christ are inseparable Doumergue has collapsed predestination into election; in "predestination" he has in mind only God's decree to save. Undeniably, when Calvin is consistent he maintains that mercy is *the* decree of God; men are called *by* the gospel; Jesus Christ is the mirror of what God wills for men; there is no "Word" of God other than the Word of mercy; in short, Jesus Christ is the electing God (cf. *Comm.* John 1:1). However, predestination can never be said to be "in Christ." So far from predestination's not being separable from Christ, it *must* be separated from him.

CHAPTER 5

PRETENDERS TO FAITH, PREPARATORY FAITH, AND THE GROWTH OF FAITH

FAITH AS KNOWLEDGE

Calvin never wearies of iterating that knowledge is essential to faith. "Unless there is knowledge present it is not God that we worship but a spectre or a ghost. Hence all so-called good intentions are struck by this thunderbolt, which tells us that men can do nothing but err when they are guided by their own opinion without the word or command of God."[1] Salvation is from the Jews, who do not "worship some unknown deity but only the God who revealed himself to them . . . they were separated from the rest of the nations on the condition that the pure knowledge of God should in the end flow out from them to the whole world."[2] It is not human credulity as such or cultic participation which constitutes the veracity of faith. Men are not to be congratulated because they "believe" or "worship," for "no matter how pleased credulous men are with themselves, no religion is either pleasing to God or ought to be regarded as holy and legitimate if it lacks knowledge and truth. . . . God cannot be worshipped in a proper and devout manner until he has been made known."[3]

As was seen in Chapter One, the knowledge of God, for Calvin, must be knowledge of his will.[4] The will of God is effectual mercy, which mercy

---

[1] *Comm.* John 4:22.

[2] Ibid.

[3] *Comm.* Acts 17:22-23.

[4] *Inst.* 3.2.2: *non Dei modo, sed divinae voluntatis.*

in turn is Christ. Accordingly, knowledge of God *is* knowledge of Jesus Christ. Calvin is intransigent on this matter: "outside of Christ there is *not even a spark of true light*,"[5] which, amplified, means, "if any man turns aside from Christ he can do nothing but go astray. If any man does not rest on him, he will feed elsewhere on nothing but wind and vanity. If any man aims beyond him, he will find death instead of life. . . . For Christ proves that he is the life, inasmuch as God, with whom he is the fountain of life, can be possessed in no other way than in him."[6] Indeed, Calvin leaves instances of this insistence scattered throughout the *Commentaries*:

> "God is known only in the face of Jesus Christ, who is the living and express image. . . . God is known by the intervention of the Mediator."[7]
>
> "God . . . is to be known only in so far as he reveals himself in Christ."[8]
>
> "Faith is not conceived but . . . by the hearing of the Word. It follows from that that men cannot be brought to the saving knowledge of God except by the direction of the Word."[9]

The Word incarnate "benefits" men only as it is proclaimed; accordingly, righteousness is obtained only as men embrace the goodness of God offered in the gospel.[10] And the gospel is properly known only through the illumination of the Spirit.[11] The Spirit enables men to perceive and embrace the Son who is proclaimed; the Son makes known the Father. Indeed, the Father *must* be sought "solely in this image."[12] The Spirit, of course, is none other than Jesus Christ in his power pressing and "impressing" himself upon men as he creates faith in them. In other words faith, and therefore the knowledge requisite for faith, arises from the action of Jesus Christ exclusively; he is both the object which is that knowledge and, from a human perspective, the condition for the assimilation of that knowledge. Calvin insists, in this regard, that Jesus Christ is both man's destination and the means of reaching that destination; he alone "puts us on the road" which he is; yet to be on the road is also to be

---

[5] *Comm.* John 8:12 (italics mine).

[6] *Comm.* John 14:6.

[7] *Comm.* John 17:3.

[8] *Comm.* II Cor. 4:6.

[9] *Comm.* Acts 14:17: *nisi verbi directione ad salvificam Dei notitiam homines adduci.*

[10] *Comm.* Rom. 10:10.

[11] *Comm.* Heb. 6:4: *non aliter rite cognosci.*

[12] *Inst.* 3.2.1: *ita vicissum monendi sumus invisibilem partem non alibi, quam in hac imagine quaerendum esse.*

at the destination.[13] To know him is simply to know God.

OPINION

In order to render more precise our understanding of the *sort* of knowledge necessary for faith Calvin states briefly what does not qualify as "knowledge." He insists that this knowledge of the divine mercy is not the intensification of a persuasion or opinion "however strong."[14] That knowledge which is integral to faith is qualitatively different from opinion.[15] Opinion, Calvin maintains, is always of the order of probability, and faith can never remain satisfied with this: what man can live with the awareness that his salvation is but *likely*? Probability and certitude of truth are mutually exclusive.

More must be said than this, however. Earlier it was noted that Jesus Christ is the author as well as the object of faith; he "forges" in men the capacity for faith as he bestows faith itself. Opinion, on the other hand, is *not* created by its object but rather arises from a purely creaturely assessment of some aspect of the creation; the "soundness" of the opinion depends on the acuity and perceptivity of the subject. In principle, opinion is always open to revision.

Faith, it must be noted, does not depend in any way upon a *natural* human acuity or perceptivity. This is not to suggest that there is not a genuinely *human* discernment in faith; it is to deny that such a discernment men possess as fallen creatures, and therefore to deny, of course, that faith presupposes such. Apart from the illumination of the Spirit, Calvin everywhere insists, men are blind and hence are without any *spiritual* discernment. (Calvin never denies that unregenerate man is capable of a natural perception of and control of the creation.) Again, faith, unlike opinion, is not open to revision despite its being a genuine discernment and decision. No believer—that is, one who affirms Jesus Christ only because Christ-in-his-power has created *ex nihilo* an understanding of himself as the word and work of God as a consequence of his being the believer's only and entire blessing—could say that he might, some day, prefer a religious (or irreligious) alternative. It is ludicrous to pretend

---

[13]*Inst.* 3.2.6. For same see *Comm.* John 14:6.

[14]*Inst.* 3.2.1: *non quamlibet opinionem aut etiam persuasionem parem esse constat.* Battles' "mere" for *quamlibet* moves in the wrong direction. The root meaning of *quamlibet* is "however much," not "mere." Calvin wishes to distinguish faith from even the *strongest* opinion.

[15]See *Comm.* Titus 1:1.

anything else. That reality which never fails to authenticate itself *as* reality could never be exchanged for a probability. And since as reality authenticates itself faith is authenticated as well, faith can never be of the order of opinion, "however strong."

IDEOLOGY

Neither is faith of the order of ideology. Calvin rules out faith as a "common assent to the gospel history."[16] Ideology is always of the order of a philosophical or historical judgment. Again, the judgment that the events indicated in the gospels did in fact occur is a purely creaturely assessment; moreover, the content of such a judgment is not Jesus Christ as the work and word of God but the veracity of historical narrative. Calvin succinctly states, "let us note that the seat of faith is not in the head but in the heart . . . and since the word *heart* generally means a sincere and serious affection, I maintain that faith is a firm and effectual confidence and not just a bare idea."[17] There *is* a notional element to faith, of course; but faith cannot be reduced to the ideational: "with an *unfeeling* and *bare* understanding of God we shall by no means attain to salvation . . . our salvation comes from faith, which ties us to God; and the only pathway is our insertion into the Body of Christ, to live by his Spirit, and also to be ruled by him. That *dead representation of faith* shows us none of this, and so it is no wonder if James refuses its effectiveness for salvation."[18]

Additionally, while the ideational is understood, reflected upon, even cherished, it is never *confessed.* Faith, on the contrary, must be confessed in order to be faith: "no one can believe in the heart without confessing with the mouth. It is quite nonsensical to insist that there is fire when there is neither flame nor heat."[19] That "faith" which does not reflect a man's believing unto righteousness with his *heart* is but a human invention and a "cold quality" as well.[20]

Calvin maintains that ideological reflection is not the same as life; a bare idea of who God is and what he does is not the same as a life bestowed, oriented and ordered through fellowship with the living God. That "unformed" faith which is mere ideology is the property of those

---

[16]*Inst.* 3.2.1.

[17]*Comm.* Rom. 10:10.

[18]*Comm.* James 2:14 (italics mine): *nos frigida et nuda Dei notitia salutem minime consequi.*

[19]*Comm.* Rom. 10:10.

[20]*Inst.* 3.2.8.

persons "who are touched by no fear of God, no sense of piety, (yet who) nevertheless believe whatever it is necessary to know for salvation."[21] In other words, there is among men a credence of the doctrinal truths pertaining to salvation where the content of that credence is accurate and adequate; yet such credence must not be confused with that incorporation of the *person* into Jesus Christ, which constitutes faith. The mere credence Calvin contrasts with the latter reality: "as if the Holy Spirit, by illumining our hearts unto faith, were not the witness to us of our adoption. And yet they presumptuously dignify that persuasion, devoid of the fear of God, with the name 'faith' even though all scripture cries out against it."[22] It is the Holy Spirit who authenticates the living Lord Jesus Christ to men and thereby authenticates true faith; the persuasiveness or perspicuity of a notion as such, however correct, does not. While the Holy Spirit bestows Christ upon life (and therefore upon the understanding as well) the Holy Spirit does not deal primarily with abstractions. Needless to say, faith is not ideology which has "worked up" and added to itself a sentiment of "fear of God": "they are speaking foolishly when they say that faith is 'formed' when pious inclination is added to assent."[23] Faith is ever a relationship (*societas*) with Jesus Christ. Indeed, those who uphold ideology as faith (regardless of the degree of 'formation') necessarily reduce faith to an assent whereby even the "despiser of God" may receive "anything at all" which scripture offers.[24] Calvin's rejoinder is that so long as assent is a purely human development there ever remains divorced from it that witness of adoption which the Holy Spirit effects through faith. Ultimately it is Christian *experience* which indicates the difference—which is to say that the person who remains in the sphere of ideology cannot comprehend the distinction; that knowledge pertaining to faith which Calvin here indicates is a knowledge pertaining to faith only. That assent *is* integral to faith Calvin never denies; nonetheless, he insists that faith cannot be characterized by it or reduced to it. Instead, that assent which is of true faith is "more of the heart than of the brain, and more of the disposition than the understanding."[25] In short, bare

---

[21]Ibid.

[22]Ibid.

[23]Ibid.

[24]*Inst.* 3.2.8: *nihil eorum commento posse fingi absurdius. Fidem assensum esse volunt, qua recipiet quilibet Dei contemptor quod ex scriptura profertur.* Battles' "whatever" for *quilibet* could have the nuance of "that which." I have altered it to "anything at all," as Calvin's meaning is "whatever turns up," "the first that comes along," and so forth.

[25]*Inst.* 3.2.8: *assensionem scilicet ipsam . . . cordis esse magis quam cerebri, et affectus magis quam intelligentiae.*

ideationality is related to the nature of faith as the empty title of faith is to faith itself.[26]

RELIGION

Faith is not religion. Religion certainly flourishes; it is a dimension of the Fall, however: so far from being incipient faith or even the ante-chamber to faith it is a monument to human concupiscence. It is *never* religiosity as such which constitutes faith or proximity to faith; rather, it is proximity to the true God (which is nothing else than the proximity of Jesus Christ to men) which "reduces the whole of the world's religion to nothing."[27]

Calvin realizes that religion is endemic to man. Since it cannot be eradicated it needs to be converted. For this reason he can speak of the truth or genuineness of religion, but always with the proviso that that content which renders "religion" true is the true God;[28] indeed, "if our religion is to be approved by God, it must needs rest on knowledge conceived of his Word."[29] "Religion" and "faith" are not only not co-terminous; of themselves they are categorically distinct. Thus Calvin can speak of those "in whom there gleams some sort of empty piety" as being on their way to ruin.[30] God, he reminds us, is worshipped rightly in no other way than according to his "appointment."[31] His appointment is Jesus Christ exclusively.

Despite religion's being idolatry, is there not a witness to God in the creation? Calvin insists there is; indeed, God has never left himself without witness. However, this witness serves only to render man inexcusable; it does not advance him toward salvation in any way.[32] Religion is not the form whose content is revelation; religion is not incipient faith or faith-in-process. One can be both pious and condemned.

"GOD"

Neither can a vague, imprecise, undefined "God" be that object which renders faith *faith*. God dwells in inaccessible light; the person who does

---

[26]*Comm.* Rom. 10:10.

[27]*Comm.* Acts 17:17.

[28]*Comm.* Acts 14:17.

[29]*Comm.* John 4:22.

[30]*Comm.* Matt. 15:13.

[31]*Comm.* Acts. 14:15.

[32]*Comm.* Rom. 1:19-20; *Comm.* Acts 14:17; *Inst.* I.3-4.

not know Jesus Christ but thinks he knows God is simply deluded:

> "There are two reasons why faith cannot be in God unless Christ intervenes as
> a Mediator. First, the greatness of the divine glory must be taken into
> account, and at the same time the littleness of our capacity. Our awareness is
> very far from being capable of ascending so high as to comprehend God.
> Hence all thinking about God without Christ is a vast abyss which imme-
> diately swallows up all our thoughts. There is clear proof of this not only in
> the Turks and the Jews who worship their own dreams under the name of
> God, but also in the Papists.[33] It is a common axiom of the schools that God
> is the object of faith. Thus they extensively and carefully speculate about his
> hidden majesty, leaving out Christ, but with what success? They entangle
> themselves in astounding delusions so that there is no end to their wander-
> ings. They think that faith is nothing but imaginative speculation. Let us
> therefore remember that Christ is not called the image of the invisible God in
> vain, but this name is given to him for this reason, that God cannot be known
> except in him.[34]

> The second reason is that, as faith ought to unite us to God, we shun and
> dread every access to him, unless a Mediator comes who can deliver us from
> fear; for sin, which reigns in us, renders us hateful to God and him in turn to
> us. . . . It is evident that we cannot believe in God except through Christ.[35]

In brief, then, God in himself is simply incomprehensible; whoever claims
to reach to him without the Mediator is making an ersatz claim. If God
were apprehended apart from the Mediator, his transcendence and his
holiness would overcome the apprehender. The complacency (indeed, the
very survival) of those who claim "God" as the object of their "faith"
indicates how wide of the mark they are—which is to say that their "faith"
is not faith at all.

Then what is the "God" whom such persons claim to apprehend?
Calvin maintains it is but an idol which has nothing to do with him who is
God. God *is* he whose Son is Jesus Christ. Not to have the Son is not to
have God incomplete or even distorted; it is simply not to have God: "we
learn that he is wholly in the Father and the Father wholly in him. In
short, whoever separates Christ from the divinity of the Father does not
yet know him who is the only true God, but rather invents for himself a
strange god."[36]

---

[33]With respect to Jews, see below where Torah pertains to that faith Calvin calls
"preparatory."

[34]Calvin says the same in *Comm.* Acts 20:21: "For unless Christ the Mediator comes to
meet us, all our senses fade away to nothing in the search for God." He repeats it in *Comm.*
I Tim. 6:16.

[35]*Comm.* I Pet. 1:21. Calvin says the same in *Comm.* Acts 20:21: ". . . seeing he is the
judge of the world, without Christ the sight of him cannot but terrify us to death."

[36]*Comm.* John 17:3.

Related to this vague deity is the "common faith" many persons possess instead of a "living faith";[37] the object of this common faith is but a certain common ("uninformed") opinion of God which no more brings God and man together than looking at the sun lifts us up into the sky.[38] It was seen earlier that opinion, "however strong," was not faith; to that it must now be added that the "common" understanding of God has nothing to do with him who is God. When men remain ignorant of the Son, and thus ignorant of the true God, they inevitably put in his place "an idol or an empty image."[39]

Undeniably the common man has his god (or gods); there may be even a phenomenological similarity between god and God. Nonetheless, the phenomenological similarity must not betray us into thinking that the natural man can inform himself of the true God—that is, grant himself faith or put himself on the road to faith; rather, it must ever be remembered that "since true knowledge of God is a special gift of his, and faith, by which he is properly known, proceeds only from the illumination of the spirit, it follows that with nature alone as our guide our minds cannot penetrate to him."[40] The "God" who is but a god is nothing more than the "empty imagination of men."[41]

IMPLICIT FAITH AND ITS INADMISSIBILITY

"Is this what believing means—to understand nothing, provided only that you submit your feeling obediently to the Church?"[42] Calvin maintains that such a notion "wears down the whole force of faith and almost annihilates it"; indeed, the "almost" can be deleted: "this fiction not only buries but utterly destroys faith."[43] It is not surprising that Calvin disqualifies as "faith" an assent to doctrines promulgated by the Church

---

[37] *Inst.* 3.2.12.

[38] *Comm.* James 2:19: *sed de vulgari* ("uninformed") *notitia.*

[39] *Comm.* John 4:22.

[40] *Comm.* Acts 17:27: *Imo quum vera Dei cognitio singulare sit ipsius donum; et fides, qua sola rite cognoscitur, non nisi ex spiritus illuminatione procedat. . . .*

[41] *Comm.* John 17:3. Concerning the foregoing discussion Calvin says, with respect to the "devout" of Acts 17:24, "for they were convinced that there was some divinity; their perverted religion was merely requiring to be corrected." In the light of what he says elsewhere about opinion, religion, etc., his remark here is wholly inexplicable (*Comm.* Acts 17:24).

[42] *Inst.* 3.2.2.

[43] Ibid.

where that assent entails no understanding of that to which assent is given. As has been indicated, there can be no faith without knowledge; now Calvin adds that faith never rests on "pious ignorance." In this vein he writes unambiguously, "we do not obtain salvation either because we are prepared to embrace as true whatever the Church has prescribed or because we turn over to it the task of inquiring and knowing. But we do so when we know that God is our merciful Father, because of reconciliation effected through Christ, and that Christ has been given to us as righteousness, sanctification, and life. By this knowledge, I say, not by submission of our feeling, do we obtain entry into the kingdom of heaven. For when the apostle says 'with the heart a man believes unto righteousness, with the mouth makes confession unto salvation' he indicates that it is not enough for a man implicitly to believe what he does not understand or even investigate. But he requires explicit recognition of the divine goodness upon which our righteousness rests."[44]

Just how far the ignorance of implicit faith is from the knowledge appropriate to genuine faith Calvin indicates in his comment on the Johannine text concerning Christ's bestowal of life upon those men whom he enlightens with the true knowledge of God: "Not any kind of knowledge is meant here, but only that which transforms us to the image of God from faith to faith. Indeed, *it is the same as faith*, by which we are incorporated into the Body of Christ and made partakers of the divine adoption and heirs of heaven."[45]

So essential is knowledge to faith that Calvin can speak of faith *as* knowledge. Needless to say he is not reducing living faith to reflection upon an abstraction; yet since "implicit knowledge" is a contradiction in terms he is reminding us that "implicit faith" is equally an absurdity. The object of faith ever remains Jesus Christ (who as properly "object" must be *known* to be such) and thus faith cannot be an ignorance which excuses itself as reverence for the Church; covering a notion with the umbrella

---

[44]*Inst.* 3.2.3: *nec enim eo salutem consequimur, vel quod parati sumus pro vero amplecti quidquid ecclesia praescripserit, vel quod inquirendi cognoscendique provinciam ad ipsam relgamus; sed quando Deum agnoscimus nobis esse propitium patrem, reconciliatione per Christum facta; Christum vero iniustitiam, sanctificationem et vitam nobis esse datum. Hac, inquam, cognitione, non sensus nostri submissione, ingressum in regnum collorum obtinemus. Nam quum dicit apostolus, corde credi ad iustitiam, ore confessionem fieri ad salutem, non satis esse indicat siquis implicite credat quod non intelligat, nec etiam inquirat; sed explicitam requirit divinae bonitatis agnitionem in qua consistit nostra iustitia.*

[45]*Comm.* John 17:3 (italics mine): *imo eadem est cum fide.*

"Church" does not render that notion an oracle from God.[46]

Moreover, it cannot be assumed that whatever the Church teaches now and is presently not understood will become (part of) the proper object of faith as soon as it is rendered explicit and becomes understood, for it cannot be assumed that whatever the Church teaches does in fact attest Jesus Christ. That knowledge which is of faith ever presupposes truth; "coming to faith" therefore must involve more than coming to understand doctrine: truth itself must be discerned. Such discernment is made as the truth authenticates itself to faith. Church proclamation can be erroneous; in such a case "the very clarity of truth itself will of itself provide a sufficiently ready refutation."[47]

As he does everywhere else, Calvin here insists that Jesus Christ *alone* can authenticate himself; while the Church bears witness to him the Church does not authenticate him. He only can authenticate himself because *in him alone* (that is, not "in the Church"—see fn. 46) are those blessings which God in his mercy wills to pour upon men: "we do not seek any part of our salvation from any other person than from him, and we do not search anywhere else than in Christ alone . . . for there is no part of our salvation which may not be found in Christ. He has made expiation for our sins by the sacrifice of his death; he has borne the punishment to acquit us; he has made us clean by his blood; he has appeased the wrath of the Father by his own obedience; he has procured righteousness for us by his resurrection. Therefore, it is no wonder that we have said that faith must be fixed upon the consideration of Christ."[48] Implicit faith, according to Calvin, never fixes itself upon the consideration of Christ; giving assent to the authority and judgment of the Church in things unknown constitutes a dependence on the authority of men as the only firmness to faith—which is to say, no firmness at all; it is to supplant the Word of God by merely human decrees.[49]

Implicit faith, then, is not merely erroneous, and not merely futile: it is disobedience and ingratitude. The attempt to replace the only valid object

---

[46]It must not be thought that Calvin has a cavalier attitude to the Church. It *is* the Body of Christ and must not be trifled with, belittled, or abandoned. The precise nature of the relation between the Church and faith (especially with respect to the teaching ministry of the Church) is considered in Chapter Seven.

[47]*Inst.* 3.2.3.

[48]*Comm.* Acts 20:21: *mirum ergo non est quod diximus, fidem debere in Christi intuitu prorsus esse defixam.* Calvin says the same in *Comm.* Acts 26:18: "But faith is properly directed to Christ because in him are included all the aspects of our salvation; and the Gospel tells us not to seek them anywhere else but in him."

[49]*Comm.* Eph. 4:13 and *Inst.* 3.2.3.

of faith who comes only to bless by a specious object indicates that implicit faith is idolatry. Jesus Christ alone is the one Word which men are to hear and heed, and in doing that recognize the spurious claims to "faith." Calvin concludes pithily, "In short, the truth is that pure and right knowledge of God which frees us from every error and falsehood."[50]

In the context of the discussion of implicit faith it can yet be asked *how* men come to possess that knowledge of God which frees them from error and falsehood; how does genuine faith arise and thus perceive and receive what is exhibited in Christ? Calvin contrasts the "bare and confused knowledge about God" with the "proper contemplation of Christ." This latter occurs only when the "power and office of Christ are understood."[51] His power and office are understood only by those whom he renews; apart from his renewing men they cannot see him.[52] Calvin is ever eager to maintain that faith is not a natural human propensity; spiritual discernment does not fall within the many capabilities of the natural man. Only those whom Christ draws into his fellowship recognize him in that action; only those whom the New Man makes new perceive him in his power and office rather than "barely" and "confusedly". Thus Calvin iterates tirelessly, "without a doubt no one can duly know him without at the same time apprehending the sanctification of the Spirit; . . . (indeed), Christ cannot be known apart from the sanctification of his Spirit."[53] Regeneration is not connected with implicit faith in any way. Such "faith" is simply not the action of the One who creates that human perceiving and embracing of himself.

In the material which follows concerning preparatory faith and the growth of faith it is important that the foregoing paragraph be kept in mind, for regardless of how weak, doubt-ridden, ignorance-beclouded, obscure, and even seemingly implicit *faith* may appear from a human perspective, the sanctification of the Spirit is determinative. While it is true that Christ cannot be known apart from the sanctification of the Spirit, it is also true that wherever such sanctification occurs Jesus Christ is most certainly known. The sanctification of the Spirit (which, of course, is a reality not publicly verifiable) precludes understanding faith as implicit faith, religion, ideology, opinion, or "God" as the object of faith (and hence as determinative) even though aspects of religion, and so forth, may be present and evidently present. God's having begun a good

---

[50]*Comm.* Titus 1:1.

[51]*Comm.* Eph. 3:12.

[52]*Comm.* 1 Tim. 6:16.

[53]*Inst.* 3.2.8: *Christus nisi cum spiritus sui sanctificatione cognosci nequit.*

work in any man does not entail its having been completed.

PREPARATORY FAITH

To be sure, a dead man can do nothing to attain life. Nonetheless, does not scripture indicate that from a human perspective, there are those unbelievers who welcome Jesus and those who reject him? that there is a not unimportant difference as to the sorts of soil of men's hearts upon which the Word is cast? Is there not the suggestion that some men are more "open" to faith? that some men are more ready to be taught than others? Ultimately, Calvin wants to answer these questions affirmatively. At the same time he does not want to affirm a semi-pelagianism, or suggest that nature anticipates grace, or imply that man is merely sick rather than dead and hence needs medicine (which might be at least self-administered) rather than resurrection.

With the foregoing caution Calvin yet raises or allows to be raised questions which cannot be set aside: in drawing men to himself does Christ grant them *full* knowledge of himself? Is the moment of coming to faith the moment in which the "fullness of the Godhead" is understood fully? If knowledge is essential to true faith, then how much knowledge is necessary for faith to be "true"? Is there a human attitude which is relatively conducive to faith? Can there be a genuine "hungering" for the One who is the bread of life—even a hungering on the part of someone who is dead *coram Deo?*

It must be stated here that Calvin is not perfectly consistent in his treatment of this matter. Undeniably, material can be adduced which appears to contradict, or at least weaken, what he says on the same topic in other places; in addition his treatment in the *Institutes* appears starker, harsher, more rigid than that in the *Commentaries.* Nevertheless, the overall discussion certainly suggests that there is a preparation for faith, that the extent of this preparation varies with human "teachableness," and that this preparation is possible at all only because of the action of Jesus Christ.

"We may also call that faith implicit which is still strictly nothing but the preparation of faith."[54] Here Calvin states overtly that he is not dealing with the development of true faith as he is in the case of the

---

[54]*Inst.* 3.2.5: *Vocare etiam fidem implicitam licet, quae tamen proprie nihil aliud est quam fidei praeparatio.* Calvin would have rendered the discussion less confusing if he had chosen a word other than "implicit," since its meaning here is not what is presumed in his repudiation of implicit faith.

disciples or the women at the tomb, but rather with those who were attracted by Christ's miracles and who affirmed him to be the promised Messiah but who, up to this point, had not "advanced further."[55] They had not reached the sort of knowledge appropriate to true faith; yet neither were they vague or indifferent. They were, at some level, responding positively to the presence of Jesus Christ in their midst. Thus concerning Zacchaeus Calvin insists, "But although faith was not yet formed in Zacchaeus, this was a certain preparation for it. He was *moved by God* to desire so much to see Christ. . . . For no doubt empty curiosity moved some to come to see Christ, even from a distance. But from what happened it is clear that there was a seed of godliness in Zacchaeus' mind. The Lord often, before he reveals himself to them, inspires in men a blind feeling which brings them to him although he is still hidden and unknown."[56]

It should be noted that in the above Calvin is not leaning in the direction of works-righteousness (which would be absurd in the case of Zacchaeus); nor is he suggesting that Zacchaeus was already a believer whose faith Christ merely confirmed. He is insisting that God alone anticipated Zacchaeus' faith; *God* moved the man; the Lord is at work in unbelievers drawing them to himself and creating in them a longing for him even as he remains (as yet) unknown to them: that is, Calvin leaves no suggestion of semi-pelagianism. While the action of the Lord will be recognized only *by* faith, the prior activity of the Lord renders inadmissible the notion that Zacchaeus' reception of Christ is merely human—that is, a purely creaturely activity of no spiritual significance.

Persons like Zacchaeus Calvin describes as not being "imbued with even a trace of the gospel teaching";[57] which is to say that they had no explicit understanding of the gospel and therefore could not be of faith. Nonetheless, Calvin does say that their attitude, wherein they willingly and reverently submitted themselves to Christ, is given the title "faith."[58] Ambiguities are evident at this point: why should the title of faith be given if, at bottom, the reality is absent? Moreover, how can faith *not* be predicated to those who "willingly and reverently submit themselves to Christ"? Is it possible, in Calvin's understanding, to submit oneself to Christ *reverently* without *some* understanding? How much understand-

---

[55]*Inst.* 3.2.5.

[56]*Comm.* Luke 19:1 (italics mine).

[57]*Inst.* 3.2.5: *quamvis ne tenui quidem evangelii doctrina imbuti essent.*

[58]Ibid.: *quae eos subegit ut Christo libenter se subiicerent, ornatur fidei titulo, cuius tamen nonnisi initium fuit.*

ing is necessary? Calvin does contrast utter lack of understanding with "explicit recognition of the divine goodness upon which our righteousness rests."[59] The minimal understanding is that Christ bespeaks God's mercy. Then cannot faith be predicated accurately of Zacchaeus? Calvin is obviously ill at ease at granting *merely* the title "faith" to such persons, for he immediately adds to the passage referred to in fn. 58, "yet it was only the beginning of faith."[60] Why "only"; was it or was it not the beginning of faith? And if it was genuinely the beginning of true faith— that is, faith in its incipience rather than the presupposition of faith, why does Calvin discuss it in a paragraph which begins, "We may also call that faith implicit which is still *strictly nothing but* the preparation of faith"?[61]

To be sure, Calvin does not clarify this matter definitively. Nonetheless, scattered through the *Commentaries* there is the unambiguous statement that some persons are predisposed to faith or enter upon incipient faith through their "teachableness"; for instance, with respect to the classes of men referred to in the parable of the sower Calvin notes that "there is no mention here of the despisers who openly repulse God's word. It is concerned only with those who seem to be *teachable.*"[62] (It should be noted here that the fact that one is teachable does not guarantee that one is taught; there are those who are teachable in principle and yet who do not come to the full flowering of faith; they "do not inwardly conceive the seed because there is no preparation for it within their hearts."[63]) In acknowledging the place of human affirmation in the matter of faith as a human event Calvin admits that a human attitude can encourage or inhibit faith: "For we know how great an obstacle to truth obstinacy is. This, therefore, is the best preparation for teachableness, when we do not take pleasure in error. Paul, therefore, teaches indirectly that we must make way for the revelation of God, if we have not yet attained what we seek."[64]

Although Calvin indicated heretofore that he affirms a distinction between the development of true faith and the conviction that Christ is the promised Messiah, he collapses that distinction in the case of Barti-

---

[59] *Inst.* 3.2.2.

[60] *Inst.* 3.2.5 (see fn. 59).

[61] Ibid. (italics mine).

[62] *Comm.* Luke 8:11 (italics mine): *sed eos tantum notari, in quibus aliqua videtur esse docilitas.*

[63] *Comm.* Matt. 13:19 (same parable of sower in *Harmony of the Gospels*): *quia nulla est in eorum cordibus praeparatio.*

[64] *Comm.* Phil. 3:15.

maeus: the fact that the text predicates faith of the man indicates not merely his trust that he would recover his sight, "but a deeper conviction, in that the blind man acknowledged Jesus to be the divinely promised Messiah. We must not imagine that this was some confused idea, for we have already seen that this confession was taken from the Law and the prophets. For the blind man did not thoughtlessly give Christ the name 'the Son of David,' but embraced him as the one whom the divine oracles had taught him would come."[65] While the blind man has *not* come to the point of confessing that Jesus is Lord, the admission that he is Messiah and Son of David renders appropriate the assessment "faith" without qualification. Bartimaeus is "teachable."

The slight variations in Calvin's willingness to use "faith" of those who have not yet come to a full-orbed Christian confession and his different provisos concerning such are indicated again in his discussion of the Samaritan woman in John 4. The text informs us that the witness of the woman is the occasion of the "believing" of the townspeople. In expounding the text Calvin appears to oscillate between affirmation and reservation; he does not want to equate their belief with faith unqualifiedly, but neither does he want to relegate it to seeming faith or mere credence: "The word *believe* is used loosely here and means that they were moved by the woman's word to acknowledge that Christ was a prophet. It is *in a way the beginning of faith when minds are prepared to receive teaching. Such an entrance to faith* is here dignified as *faith* that we may learn how highly God esteems reverence for his word when he *confers so great an honour upon the teachableness of those who had not yet been instructed.* And *their faith* is shown by their being seized with a desire to advance. . . ."[66] When the text informs us that many more believed because of Christ's word (John 4:41) Calvin adds, "the word *believe* is now used in a different sense, as meaning not only that they were prepared for faith but were actually filled with faith itself."[67]

Admittedly, this latter remark lends some weight to E. A. Dowey's contention (cf. *The Knowledge of God in Calvin's Theology*, pp. 169-70) that Calvin affirms the people of John 4:39 to believe "improperly" (*improprie*), since Christ is not the object of this preparatory "faith" and this teachableness. To

---

[65]*Comm.* Mark 10:52.

[66]*Comm.* John 4:39 (italics mine): *Hoc autem est veluti fidei initium, quum anim ad recipiendam doctrinam parati sunt. Talis ad fidem ingressus hic honorifice vocatur fides, ut sciamus quanti Deus verbi sui reverentiam faciat, quum tanto honore dignatur solam eorum docilitatem qui nondum edocti sunt. In eo autem se demonstrat fides illa quod proficiendi desiderio tenentur. . . .*

[67]*Comm.* John 4:41: *quia non tantum ad fidem praeparatos fuisse significat, sed recta fide imbutos primis.*

be sure, the people were moved to believe that Christ was a *prophet*.

However, Calvin's exposition of the text indicates that "loosely" is to be preferred to "improperly" of their belief; their belief was "in a way the beginning of faith"; indeed, this "entrance to faith" could even be "dignified as faith." Dowey remarks, "No general trust in Christ as a prophet is accepted as a beginning of faith. Such, however great, is entirely superseded by knowledge, however slight, of Christ as God's salvation" (p. 170). Of course there is, in principle, a distinction between a confession of Christ as prophet and as God's salvation. Yet in the gospel passages under examination Calvin certainly implies that under the initiative of God (q.v. *Comm.* Luke 19:1) a confession of Christ as prophet becomes, ultimately, that "entrance to faith" wherein Christ *is* confessed as God's salvation. Dowey has attempted to force an inflexible dichotomy upon Calvin where Calvin, at least in the *Commentaries*, rejects it.

Dowey's understanding is further weakened by Calvin's explicit asseveration that "from these instances it is clear that even those who are not yet imbued with the first elements but are still inclined to hearken are called 'believers'; not in an exact sense, indeed, but in so far as God in his kindness deigns to grace such pious affection with his honour."[68]

Yet the above material does force questions upon us: since Calvin has insisted that faith cannot rest upon pious ignorance (*Inst.* 3.2.2.), is he contradicting himself here, or does he presuppose a significant distinction between pious ignorance (which God disdains) and pious affection (which God honors)? Evidently the latter is the case, as his following remark attests: "but this teachableness, with the desire to learn, is far different from sheer ignorance in which those sluggishly rest who are content with the sort of 'implicit faith' the papists invent."[69] We must then ask whether Calvin is psychologizing here when he speaks of those who "sluggishly rest." The answer is no. Instead, he intends to contrast a sincere "groping" for God (which arises *after* we have learned that our salvation rests with God—*Inst.* 3.2.7) with the cavalier character of inadmissible implicit faith. Since our salvation rests with God, any "groping" after him is but the consequence of his prevenient dealing with us. While "believer" is applied somewhat inexactly to those who are inclined to hearken, utimately it is not applied inappropriately; God's "kindness" in honoring pious affection with the title "faith" is not a fiction born of indulgence; "faith" here properly denotes the beginning of belief.

That passage over which Calvin lingers longest in this matter concerns the healing of the nobleman's son. Calvin says, "Thus the court official

---

[68]*Inst.* 3.2.5: *Ex his patet, eos etiam qui primis elementis nondum sunt imbuti, modo ad obediendum ferantur, vocari fideles, non quidem proprie, sed quatemus Deus pro sua indulgentia pium illum affectum tanto honore dignatur.*

[69]*Inst.* 3.2.5: *sed haec docilitas cum proficiendi desiderio longe distat a crassa ignorantia, in qua torpent qui fide implicita (qualis fingitur a papistis) contenti sunt.*

who believed Christ's promise concerning the healing of his son, having returned to his house, as the Evangelist testifies, believed anew because he first received as an oracle what he had heard from the mouth of Christ, and then submitted to Christ's authority to receive the teaching. Yet we must know that he was so *teachable and ready to learn* that in the first passage his admission of belief signifies a particular faith, while in the second passage he is counted among the disciples who had enlisted with Christ."[70]

Are the man's teachableness and readiness to learn grounded in a merely human capacity? Calvin explicitly rejects this elsewhere as a general human possibility, and there is no reason to presume it operative here. Moreover, while the "particular faith" is certainly not to be equated with that faith "which is accompanied by a full and distinct knowledge of sound doctrine,"[71] yet Calvin does use the word "faith" to denote it. Surely it bears a positive relation to "full" faith; that is, it is not merely a credulity concerning the bizarre which is temporally contiguous to but logically unrelated to a subsequent "full" faith. As was indicated at the beginning of this section, Calvin's rather rigid distinction in the *Institutes* is rendered more flexible in the *Commentaries*. There, in his discussion of this episode he speaks of the nobleman's particular faith as that whereby he "binds Christ's power to his bodily presence, so that he had no other idea of Christ than that he was a prophet sent by God with the authority and power of proving that he was God's minister by performing miracles."[72] Following the nobleman's importuning Jesus to heal the boy Calvin notes, "as he perseveres in asking and at last gets what he wants, you can infer that Christ did not reprove him as if he were going to reject him altogether and refuse his prayer, but that he did it (that is, reproved him) to correct the fault that was obstructing his way into true faith."[73] Jesus Christ does not ignore the "faith" that he is a prophet with the ability to perform miracles, but rather corrects it. Indeed, in the verse following the description of the nobleman's request as reflecting something other than *true* faith, Calvin maintains it to be evident that Christ values even a *weak faith* (*pusilla fides*)[74] which is yet *faith*. This being the

---

[70] *Inst.* 3.2.5 (italics mine): *docilem et paratum ad discendum . . . inter discipulos qui nomen Christo dederant.* N.b. "Particular faith"—". . . because it does not lay hold of Christ in his wholeness but only of his power in effecting miracles" (*Comm.* I Cor. 13:2).

[71] *Comm.* Matt. 15:22.

[72] *Comm.* John 4:47.

[73] *Comm.* John 4:49.

[74] *Comm.* John 4:50.

case, we must ask how rigid can be the distinction between that which is "strictly nothing but the preparation of faith" and that which is "entrance to faith," "beginning of faith," and "weak faith"? The distinction Calvin states in the *Institutes* he obviously does not maintain in his exegesis of those passages which are supposed to illustrate the distinction. Indeed, so fluid is the boundary pertaining to "preparation," "teachableness," and "true faith," that following his description of the nobleman's weak faith Calvin states that the man was "the more ready to believe because he had come with the conviction that Christ was a prophet of God. And so, as soon as he grasped *one word he fixed it in his heart*. Although he did not honour Christ's power as he ought to have done, a little promise suddenly begot a new trust in his mind."[75] In Calvin's own frame of understanding a *promise* (however "little") can only point to mercy; that is, to the Word who is author and object of *faith*.[76] That the man *fixed the one word in his heart* which ultimately begot a *new trust in his mind* confirms this interpretation.

Note 1. In the *Institutes* Calvin contrasts the reception of an oracle with the submission to Christ's authority in order to receive the "teaching." Surely, however, in one's receiving Christ's utterance *as* oracle there is presupposed a recognition of authority; "oracle" implies "authoritative teaching." In dealing with unformed (= non-existent) faith Calvin, admittedly, does speak of unbelievers who, lacking the sanctification of the Spirit, yet "hold the Word of God to be an indisputable oracle; they do not utterly neglect his precepts and are somewhat moved by threats and promises."[77] Such persons obviously are attempting to conform themselves to threats, promises and injunctions without moving at all beyond their moralism. The use of "oracle" notwithstanding, the nobleman is different: his attitude is that of casting himself upon the effectual mercy of Christ at whatever level he understands "Christ"—and he understands at least that Christ possesses and manifests mercy and power.

Note 2. In his comment on John 4:47 Calvin states that the mere fact of the nobleman's seeking help is itself a sign of *faith*. His remark, then, that the use of "believe" in 4:53 with respect to that of 4:50 does *not* "refer

---

[75]Ibid. (italics mine): *quia hac persuasione imbutus venerat, Christum esse Dei prophetam, ideo tam facilis ad credendum fuit, ut vocem unam vox arriperet, arreptam in animum defigeret.*

[76]Cf. Chapter One, where it is demonstrated from Calvin's *Commentaries* that the promises ultimately subserve the promise of mercy: i.e., there can be no promise which is not an expression of God's will to save.

[77]*Inst.* 3.2.9.

to the progress of faith"[78] is enigmatic to say the least. In precisely the context where he insists that the activity of God reduces the world's religions to "nothing" Calvin speaks of that "teachableness" which is "an entrance to faith, and indeed, a kind of beginning of faith . . . ."[79] Is not this exactly what the nobleman manifested? Surely "progress" is an appropriate word to denote the movement from "entrance to faith" or "beginning of faith" to "full faith."

Note 3. Calvin's understanding of the episode of the nobleman must not be construed as a subtle case of grace correcting and perfecting nature. Jesus Christ creates the capacity for one to believe in him at all, however obscure or misinformed that belief might be. It is *Christ* who, at the foot of Zacchaeus' tree, "inspires in men a blind feeling which brings them to him although he is still hidden and unknown." When Calvin says that Christ "corrects the fault that was obscuring the way to true faith" he does not mean to suggest that this "preparatory faith" is an instance of the creation mediating God or that it arises from a merely human capacity. It must not be forgotten that Calvin's doctrine of election, which is never far from his mind in his discussion of these passages (especially those in John) estops any propensity one might have to think that he is suggesting creation mediates God. Simply as creatures it is possible for any man to have "mere factual knowledge" of Jesus Christ;[80] such a person, however, is indubitably an unbeliever. Calvin never suggests that the nobleman, Zacchaeus, and so forth, are unbelievers, however "preparatory" their faith might be, or that their knowledge of Christ is of this order.

Calvin insists that the nobleman, *qua* Jew brought up in the teaching of the law, "had already been given some taste of faith when he came to Christ";[81] that is, his preparatory faith had much to do with his knowledge of God's action gained through the law. Not everyone who comes to faith is a Jew. What does Calvin have to say about the situation of Gentiles?

Calvin insists, at least in the case of Cornelius, that he too was somewhat schooled in the law. Cornelius was "singularly privileged to fall in with some upright worshipper of God who was untouched by false doctrines and who expounded the law to him faithfully and without the addition of any leaven."[82] It is this exposure to the law which grounds Cornelius' being a

---

[78] *Comm.* John 4:53: *ad fidei progressum referri.*

[79] *Comm.* Acts 17:17: *quia autem talis docilitas ingressus erat ad fidem, imo quoddam fidei initium.*

[80] *Comm.* I Cor. 12:3.

[81] *Comm.* John 4:53.

[82] *Comm.* Acts 10:1.

"rare specimen because he was a soldier whose piety to God was so great . . .
he yet worshipped God conscientiously . . . he rejected the superstition in
which he had been born and bred and embraced the pure worship of the
true God."[83] Calvin agrees that Luke is correct in regarding the fear of God
and the habit of prayer as "fruits and proofs of piety and the worship of
God"; indeed, Cornelius' praying in itself attests a proper relationship to
God.[84] Proper relationship necessarily implies faith; then it cannot be
surprising that Calvin speaks of the Gentile as one who, "inspired by such a
frail and rudimentary faith, was such a splendid mirror of uprightness and
sanctity."[85] In Calvin's estimation, then, Cornelius was a man of some faith
prior to Peter's visit, address, and baptism. Indeed, Calvin regards the faith
of Cornelius as a rebuke to us who are more privileged: "if a small spark of
faith had such a great effect on him, what ought the full splendour of
knowledge be bringing about in us?"[86] Faith may be "frail and rudimentary"; it is yet authentic.

Calvin then states that by means of the vision ("a kind of oracle")
Cornelius was led to the "faith of Christ."[87] This appears to contradict what
was said above about the veridicality of Cornelius' faith, worship, and
prayer. However, it must be remembered that for Calvin, Jesus Christ is the
content of both law and gospel (promise); for Cornelius to have become
apprised of the law "without the addition of any leaven" means that he
knew Christ under the economy of the law. The vision bestows the same
Christ upon him, only now under the economy of the gospel. Cornelius is
not being brought from unfaith to faith; he is being brought from genuine
faith of small spark to that of full splendor. Calvin is uncompromising on
this point:

> "No spiritual gifts are offered to us except in Christ. In particular, from
> whence does regeneration itself spring but from the fact that when we are
> implanted into the death of Christ our old man is crucified? And if Cornelius
> was participating in the Spirit of Christ (that is, before the vision) it is not for
> us to think that he was completely devoid of faith in him. For he surely did
> not embrace the worship of the true God, whom the Jews alone used to
> reverence, in such a way that he did not at the same time hear something
> about the promised Mediator; even if this knowledge was hazy and confused,
> yet there was some. . . . Accordingly, Cornelius must be placed in the category

---

[83] Ibid.: *Quod miles tantae in Deum pietatis . . . purum veri Dei cultum esset amplexus.*

[84] *Comm.* Acts 10:2.

[85] Ibid. (italics mine): *quod si tenuibus fidei rudimentis imbutus, tam praeclarum
probitatis et sanctimoniae speculum fuit.*

[86] Ibid.: *si modica fidei scintilla tantum in illo potuit, quia in nobis efficere debere
plenus scientiae fulgor?*

[87] *Comm.* Acts 10:3: *ad Christi fidem.*

of the fathers of old who hoped for salvation by a Redeemer not yet revealed.
. . . Cornelius could not have prayed if he had not been a believer."[88]

In other words, there can be faith in Christ where "Christ" is not rendered fully explicit—but only where the object of that faith is the salvific activity of the living God: Israel's anticipation of Jesus Christ.[89]

It must be noted that Calvin has not turned his back on what he has insisted upon heretofore; he repudiates the "papist" interpretation of this event: "for, taking the fact that God had regard to the prayers and alms of Cornelius so that he endowed him with the faith of the Gospel, they twist it to the preparations made by themselves, as if a man acquires faith by his own diligence and virtue, and anticipates the grace of God by the merit of works. . . ."[90] Indeed, Calvin maintains that any interpretation is incorrect which suggests that Cornelius' works were acceptable to God before he had been enlightened by faith: Cornelius' fear of God and his piety unarguably attest his being born of the Spirit. "It is therefore extremely foolish to imagine here, in the person of Cornelius, a man who aspires or presses towards eternal life *with nature as his guide*."[91] Cornelius was not rewarded for his works and religiosity; rather, "he obtained full*er* knowledge of Christ from his prayers and alms; but his having God well-disposed and favourable to his alms and prayers was already dependent upon his faith."[92] Fuller knowledge of Christ is granted to obedience; but no man by *nature* can grant himself any fuller knowledge of Christ, however "frail and rudimentary."

In brief, then, Calvin is willing to use "faith" of that preparatory faith which as yet lacks the richness and the completeness of mature faith; this preparatory faith is logically related to full faith (that is, is not related only negatively). Calvin consistently maintains, as well, that no man can enter upon such faith merely *qua* creature. It is ever the Lord who, before he reveals himself to men, inspires in them in the first instance even this "pious affection" which brings them to him.

---

[88]*Comm.* Acts 10:4 (italics mine).

[89]In *Comm.* Acts 17:17 Calvin refers to the God-fearers who, like Cornelius, had been instructed in the law and were worshiping the God of Israel even though they were not yet properly imbued with true godliness. "True godliness" here means "fuller knowledge of Christ"; Calvin is not suggesting that their faith was ungodly, and therefore no faith at all.

[90]*Comm.* Acts 10:4.

[91]Ibid. (italics mine).

[92]Ibid. (italics mine).

THE GROWTH OF FAITH

Calvin speaks of a legitimate implicit faith in a second sense: true faith itself ever remains imperfect. For one thing, many things are yet hidden from believers; they see through a glass darkly and therefore remain somewhat ignorant. This much is unarguable: believers' acquaintance even with passages of scripture which are as yet obscure to them point up their ignorance. For another, they are surrounded on every side by error. While such ignorance and error are not those of that inadmissible implicit faith (and hence Calvin is speaking of another order of ignorance and error than when he speaks of "that knowledge which is faith which frees us from every error and falsehood"[93]) they are not yet to be discounted. Indeed, "most things are now implicit for us and will be so until, laying aside the weight of flesh, we come nearer to the presence of God. In these matters we do nothing better than suspend judgment and hearten ourselves to hold unity with the Church."[94] By "suspend judgment and hold unity with the Church" Calvin is certainly not reintroducing what he has repudiated: that the title "faith" can be given to that ignorance which is covered by the cloak of "reverence for the Church," where such reverence is an excuse for knowing nothing of Jesus Christ. Instead, he is enjoining believers not to become schismatic over doctrinal matters which are yet somewhat obscure but which are not such as to be the occasion of rending the Body of Christ, since as "believers" they already understand what is essential to salvation; viz., that Jesus Christ is Mercy, and as Mercy (and therefore gift) can be only *received*, never merited.

Not only is this ignorance and error of a different order from that of inadmissible implicit faith; the attitude pertaining to it is different: there, complacency was present; here, believers aspire after increased understanding. Faith is compatible with error and ignorance (other than ignorance of Christ as Mercy); it is not compatible with complacency about error and ignorance. While it is true that God has assigned each a measure of faith (and therefore a measure of understanding) it must not be concluded that one can no longer be taught. In other words, while the Christ who bestows faith in himself and therefore understanding of himself comes to us in the totality of his reality as the One in whom the fullness of the Godhead dwells bodily, his self-bestowal does not necessitate an instantaneous transformation from sheer ignorance to perfect

---

[93]*Comm.* Titus 1:1.

[94]*Inst.* 3.2.3: quin plurima nobis implicita nunc sint . . . animum autem offirmare ad tenendam cum ecclesia unitatem.

knowledge. For this reason Calvin admits, "I do not deny that in some sense there may be a kind of implicit faith which is not accompanied by a full and distinct knowledge of sound doctrine, provided that we hold this, that *faith always springs from the Word of God* and takes its origins from true principles, and therefore is always connected with some light of knowledge" (*aliquam scientiae lucem*).[95] (Inadmissible implicit faith, of course, does not spring from the Word of God but from the opinions of men, and hence bears no relation to the light of knowledge.) Jesus Christ need not be fully understood before faith is genuine; in fact, he will never be understood fully prior to the *eschaton*. What is crucial is that such understanding as men have arise from *him*.

The manner in which all true faith is implicit Calvin illustrates from the disciples. Before they are fully enlightened they "taste the first rudiments, halting over the slightest matters, and though hanging on their Master's words, make but little progress."[96] They regard the Resurrection as a dream. At the same time, Christ has spoken previously of their faith; then it cannot be the case that prior to the Resurrection they were devoid of it. In other words, *the veridicality of faith is not attested by the appearance of such faith but solely by the attestation of Jesus Christ*. This point must be pondered: Calvin does not attempt to examine and assess religious phenomena in order to ascertain true faith. Regardless of what error and ignorance are present, faith is authentic on the strength of Christ's attestation.

Concerning the women at the tomb Calvin writes, "But although they had faith in the words of him whom they knew to be truthful, the ignorance that as yet occupied their minds so enveloped their faith in darkness that they were almost dumbfounded. Not that they then began to believe, but because the seed of hidden faith—which had been dead, as it were, in their hearts—at that time burst through with renewed vigour. For there was in them a true but implicit faith because they had reverently embraced Christ as their sole teacher. Then, taught by him, they were convinced that he was the author of their salvation. And finally, they believed that he came from heaven that, through the Father's grace, he might gather his disciples thither."[97] Again, it is evident that the beginning of faith is not the *apparent* beginning of faith; that the faith of the women, however properly implicit, was veridical in that its object had ever

---

[95]*Comm.* Matt. 15:22 (italics mine).

[96]*Inst.* 3.2.4: *antequam plenam illuminationem adepti essent. Videmus quam difficulter rudimenta ipsa gustent, ut haesitent in minimis quibusque, ut a magistri ore pendentes, non tamen multum promoveant.*

[97]*Inst.* 3.2.4.

remained Christ as their sole teacher, even though their faith was but a "seed" and hidden as well. It is evident too that while it is the object which delineates ignorance- and error-beclouded faith from outright idolatry, such delineation is *not* available to public inspection; just where the line is crossed from ignorance- and error-beclouded faith to that error and ignorance of inadmissible implicit faith is known to Jesus Christ alone. The fact that the former may be phenomenologically indistinguishable from the latter is an irrelevant consideration.

Faith is always mixed with unbelief, but remains *faith* nonetheless: the seed is only dead "as it were." True faith, it must be added, is always advancing so as to shrink, proportionately, the element of unbelief. This is indicated in Calvin's reflection concerning the appearance of the risen Jesus to Thomas, who, prior to that visitation had been "stupid." Such stupidity notwithstanding, however, his exclamation, "My Lord and my God" "shows that faith was not entirely extinguished in him, though it had been smothered. . . . He suddenly comes to himself after forgetfulness and somnolence. It therefore shows the truth of what I have already said, that the faith which seemed to be destroyed was, so to say, hidden and buried in his heart. This is not an uncommon event among many people. They grow wanton for a time, as if they had cast off all fear of God, *and no faith is apparent in them* . . . when obstructions have been removed, the good seed, which had lain smothered, springs up."[98]

New believers must imbibe milk before they can digest strong meat. While Jesus Christ presses *all* of himself (that is, his entire truth and reality) upon them, yet he accommodates himself to their infancy: "it is the same unvarying truth which Christ teaches his own from first to last; but first he enlightens them with small sparks, as it were, and finally pours out a full light upon them. Thus until they have been fully confirmed, believers are in a sense ignorant of what they know. Yet this knowledge of faith is not so small or obscure that it is not efficacious for salvation."[99] Heretofore Calvin has insisted that that knowledge requisite for faith is knowledge of God's will—that is, mercy. Here he admits that one can certainly apprehend that Christ bespeaks mercy in such a way as to constitute faith, even though one may not be able to articulate the fact that Christ has expiated sin and may not be able to expound the doctrine of justification. Believers whom Christ has as yet enlightened only to the

---

[98]*Comm*. John 20:28 (italics mine). In the same passage Calvin refers to David: "None but would have thought that faith was then completely wiped out of his mind. But by a brief warning from the prophet he is so suddenly recalled to life that it is easy to infer that some spark, though smothered, still remained in his mind and quickly burst into flame."

[99]*Comm*. John 8:32.

degree of "small sparks" are ignorant of what they know. The paradox is significant: they know it in so far as they live in the reality of it and have discerned something of its meaning; they are ignorant of it in so far as they cannot expound it and indeed cannot comprehend it with that clarity appropriate to true faith. The distinction Calvin makes here must be contrasted with that "absolute infancy" where there is no growth at all and likely no understanding at all.[100]

> In considering Acts 10:4 Calvin states, "The question can be asked here whether faith requires the knowledge of Christ, or is it satisfied with a simple conviction of the mercy of God?"[101] Everywhere else he implies that a simple conviction of the mercy of God *is* the knowledge of Christ apart from which there can be no faith. The implied dichotomy in this passage is baffling and must be regarded as a surd remark.

In allowing for a development within faith Calvin is moving between two pitfalls: (i) the notion that "belief" can include no understanding at all; here the object of faith bears no relation at all to faith itself. Such a position he regards as sheer superstition. In addition, it indicates faith to be a purely creaturely activity; (ii) the notion that true faith presupposes no little theological sophistication. This is to confuse a capability for expounding doctrine with an effectual apprehension of the object of faith, the reality of true faith, (however weak, rudimentary, or error-beclouded) with ideological articulability. Calvin wants his readers to realize that someone's inability to explicate precisely the meaning of "atonement" does not mean that he cannot be the beneficiary of God's mercy. The understanding required for faith (that Christ is the mercy of God) need not be that of full-orbed doctrinal formulation.

It must be noted that Calvin does not restrict the title or the fellowship "Christian" to those mature in faith: "we must bear for a time with ignorance in our weak brethren and pardon them if it is not given them immediately to be altogether of one mind with us. Paul was assured as to his doctrine, but he allows those who could not yet receive it *time to make progress*, and he does not cease on that account to regard them as brethren; only he cautions them against flattering themselves in their ignorance."[102] Believers can do no better than Abraham, the prototype of faith, and cannot be faulted for doing as much as he, who throughout the course of his life "showed the increase of his faith."[103]

---

[100]*Comm.* Eph. 4:14.

[101]*Comm.* Acts 10:4: *requiratne fides Christi notitiam, an simplici misericordiae Dei persuasione sit?*

[102]*Comm.* Phil. 3:15 (italics mine).

[103]*Comm.* James 2:21.

DIFFICULTIES IN CALVIN'S EXPOSITION

There remain problems which not even the most favorable reading of Calvin can obviate. One such is Calvin's handling of the case of Simon Magus.

In the *Institutes* Calvin states that Simon Magus merely pretended to a faith he did not have. Conquered by the majesty of the gospel, he showed a "certain sort of faith," recognized Christ to be the author of life and salvation, and enlisted under him.[104] It is not surprising that Calvin judges Magus to be of unbelief: the only word which creates faith is the word of mercy, and Magus has merely been overwhelmed by the sheer power of God.

In the *Commentary* Calvin confirms this by informing us that the man did not surrender himself to Christ in a love (*affectu*) that is sincere and from the heart. Then Calvin immediately adds that he disagrees with those who think that Magus really did not believe and hence made only a pretense of faith, since Luke insists that he did in fact believe. Faced with having to explain how Magus "betrayed himself as a hypocrite a little later" Calvin advances an argument that "there is some middle position between faith and mere pretense."[105] What is this middle position? Calvin describes it as a being *conquered* by the power of the Word (but obviously not being determined by the word of mercy), acknowledging the truth of what is taught, fearing God, recognizing that God is judge, but all the while lacking the Spirit of adoption and therefore not yielding to God with genuine love from the heart.[106] Persons who occupy this middle position differ from "ordinary" unbelievers in that they *think* they believe: they are not making a pretense to non-existent faith *in the eyes of men*. Magus was in such a position; Calvin concludes, however, that his *mind* was involved in pretense.[107] In the *Institutes* Calvin maintains that such persons have some taste of the Word, begin to feel its divine power, and eventually delude others *and themselves* that they are of faith in that their reverent attitude to the Word precludes an open and admitted reproach thereof. Whatever assent they bring to the Word it is not such as

----

[104] *Inst.* 3.2.6: *sed potius arbitramur evangelii maiestate victum qualemcunque fidem adhibuisse, atque ita Christum, vitae et salutis autorem agnoisse, ut libenter illi nomen daret.*

[105] *Comm.* Acts 8:13.

[106] Ibid.

[107] Ibid.

to penetrate to the heart.[108]

Several things must be said about this matter. Calvin is correct in denying the status "faith" to assent which does not penetrate to the heart; that is, to an attitude which evidently reduces the Word to ideology. However, since faith is participation in or fellowship with Christ, one must ask how there can be a middle position between faith and pretense. Indubitably there are degrees of clarity of understanding; there is an "entrance" to faith and a weak faith which require development; but it is still *faith*, the "instrument" by which we become Christ's and he becomes ours. But how can there be partial participation in Christ? What is the status of a man who is mid-way between being dead and alive? Admittedly, one can remain in unbelief and still fear God, dread the judgment, and attempt to conform one's life according to the precepts of the gospel; but to be conquered by the Word is to be subdued by effectual mercy— which is what Calvin means by faith. Then how can one be conquered by the power of the *Word* and remain in unbelief? Calvin confuses the issue when he adds, "Simon's hypocrisy is laid bare now. Not that there had been any pretence about his believing before, for having been convicted he surrendered himself to Christ in earnest. Similarly, many yield to the gospel so as not to carry on a war with God, but at the same time they remain as they were, when, in fact, denial of ourselves ought to follow true faith."[109] Did Magus surrender himself to Christ in earnest? Surely the text denies this. Furthermore, is it possible so to yield to the gospel as to have peace with God and yet not undergo that self-denial integral to faith? Is there a middle position between yielding to the gospel (Christ's becoming ours) and withholding self-denial? For Calvin, it must be remembered, self-denial is not principally something that we do, but rather our Christ-facilitated affirmation of our fellowship with the One who denies himself to the point of death for us (otherwise "self-denial" is but another form of concupiscence).

Calvin involves himself in such convolutions and contradictions here because he has been betrayed by that which beguiled him concerning election: empirical observation, and the conclusions he thinks he has to draw from those observations. Calvin is concerned as to what value to place on the "faith" of people who do not advance, or who appear defective, or who appear to fall away. He has forgotten already that the

---

[108] *Inst.* 3.2.10: *tales non dubitamus quodam verbi gustu affectos ipsum avide arripere, et divinam eius virtutem persentiscere; ut fallaci fidei simulatione non hominum oculis modo imponant, sed suis ipsorum animis.*

[109] *Comm.* Acts 8:18: *non quod prius se credere finxisset; convictus enim serio Christi dederat.*

life of faith is hid with Christ in God, and so wants to go behind what he was seen to insist on earlier: that Thomas was a man of faith when no faith was *apparent* in him; that the admissible implicit faith which sprang from the Word of God could be phenomenologically indistinguishable from that implicit faith which did not; that true faith is attested by Jesus Christ alone and never attested by its appearance; that the beginning of faith cannot be read off the apparent beginning; that true faith may be dead "as it were." The problems arise in this area of Calvin's work because he contradicts himself and attempts to do what he denies men to be able to do, viz., evaluate adequately religious phenomena.

The same problem is evident in his discussion of the "appearance" of faith in the reprobate, and as will be seen, is evident for the same reason. Calvin notes that there are many persons who appear to come to faith and yet who fall away. On his understanding of predestination anyone who falls away is *ipso facto* reprobate. But how can the appearance of seeming faith be accounted for?

> "For though only those predestined to salvation receive the light of faith and truly feel the power of the gospel, yet *experience* shows that the reprobate are sometimes affected by almost the same *feeling* as the elect, so that even in their own judgment they do not in any way differ from the elect. Therefore it is not at all absurd that the apostle should attribute to them a taste of the heavenly gifts—and Christ, faith for a time; not because they firmly grasp the force of spiritual grace and the sure light of faith, but because the Lord, to render them more convicted and inexcusable, steals into their minds to the extent that his goodness may be tasted without the Spirit of adoption."[110]

Again, it must be noted that Calvin is eager to draw eschatological conclusions from his assessment of experience. Moreover, what is the point of saying that the reprobate have *almost* the same feeling as the elect; does he want to distinguish between faith and unfaith, between elect and reprobate, at least in part, in terms of feeling? Does God, can God act apart from his Word of Mercy? (In Chapter One it was seen that all promises subserve the promise, all words the Word, and all acts the act of mercy. The evidence adduced from the *Commentaries* was compelling in the matter.) Since it is the function of the witness to God's power and deity in the creation to render men inexcusable (cf. *Comm.* Rom. 1:19-

---

[110]*Inst.* 3.2.11 (italics mine): *quia etsi in fidem non illuminantur, nec evangelii efficaciam vere sentiunt, nisi qui praeordinati sunt ad salutem; experientia tamen ostendit reprobos interdum simil fere sensu atque electos affici, ut ne suo quidem iudicio quidquam ab electis differant. Quare nihil absurdi est quod collestium donorum gustus ab apostolo, et temporalis fides a Christo illis adscribitur: non quod vim spirituallis gratiae solide percipiant ac certum fidei lumen, sed quia Dominus, ut magis convictos et inexcusabiles reddat, se insinuat in eorum mentes, quatenus sine adoptionis spiritu gustari potest eius bonitas.*

20), then why is "faith for a time" granted to render them *more* inexcusable? (Are there even degrees of inexcusability?) Again, "goodness" (*bonitas*) always pertains, in Book III of the *Institutes*, to *misericordia*. But how can God's goodness be tasted without the Spirit of adoption: is Christ divided? Is there a knowledge of Christ (*bonitas*) which his Spirit does not engender? Can there be any apprehension of goodness which is not a (Spirit-empowered) apprehension of Christ? Calvin, in a manner inconsistent with his major consideration of faith, says that there can be:

> "But I do not see that this is any reason why he should not touch the reprobate with a taste of his grace, or illumine their minds with some glimmerings of his light, or affect them with some sense of his goodness, or to some extent engrave his word in their hearts."[111]

This inconsistency mars the *Institutes* as well: ". . . although there is a great likeness and affinity between God's elect and *those who are given a transitory faith*, yet only in the elect does that confidence flourish which Paul extols, that they loudly proclaim Abba, Father. . . . But this does not hinder that *lower working of the Spirit* from taking its course even in the reprobate . . . the reprobate never receive anything but a *confused awareness of grace*, so that they grasp a shadow rather than the firm body of it. . . . Yet the reprobate are justly said to believe that God is merciful toward them, for *they receive the gift of reconciliation, although confusedly and not distinctly enough.*[112]

Such reprobates are not partakers of the same faith or regeneration as the elect, but they do *seem* to have a beginning of faith (although of course no real beginning). Concerning these persons Calvin adds,

> "And I do not deny that God illumines their minds enough for them to recognize his grace; but he so distinguishes that awareness from the exclusive testimony he gives to his elect that they do not attain the full effect and fruition thereof. He does not show himself merciful to them to the extent of truly snatching them from death[113] and receiving them into his keeping, but only manifests his mercy to them for the time being. . . . Nothing prevents God from illuming some with a momentary awareness of his grace, which afterward vanishes."[114]

How can there be a "lower" working of the Spirit, when the Spirit is the

---

[111]*Comm.* Heb. 6:4: *verbumque suum utcumque eorum animis insculpat.*

[112]*Inst.* 3.2.11 (italics mine): *quamvis magna sit similtudo et affinitas inter Dei electos, et qui fide caduca ad tempus donantur, vigere tamen in solis electis fiduciam illam quam celebrat Paulus. . . . sed hoc minime obstat quin illa inferior spiritus operatio cursum suum habeat etiam in reprobis . . . reprobi nunquam sensum gratiae nisi confusum percipiunt, ut umbram potius apprehendant quam solidum corpus. . . . merito tamen dicuntur reprobi Deum credere sibi propitium, quia donum reconciliationis, licet confuse nec satis distincte, suscipiunt.*

[113]Cf. *Inst.* 3.2.13: "faith . . . by which we cross from death to life"; i.e., the reprobate are not snatched from death in that they are not granted faith.

[114]*Inst.* 3.2.11: *quia nihil obstat quominus praesenti gratiae suae sensu, qui postea evanescit, Deus aliquos illustret.*

power in which Christ acts, and *qua* mercy acts only for blessing? What is a confused awareness of grace? If it is an awareness of *grace* at all, then it is sufficient for salvation, as Calvin indicated when he acknowledged that the knowledge requisite for faith may be (and in fact is) error- and ignorance-beclouded. And if the reprobate receive an awareness of *grace*, no matter how confused, can that *grace* be called a shadow rather than reality? How can one receive the gift of reconciliation and not be of faith, when the One who is our reconciliation is also our sanctification, where sanctification certainly implies faith?[115] What does it mean to receive reconciliation but with insufficient distinctness? It must be remembered that for Calvin intelligibility is a consequence of soteriology; there is no knowledge of God apart from the knowledge of faith. Then why does Calvin say that the reprobate are "illumined" in any sense, especially when illumination arises from the Spirit, whose sole function is to bestow faith? Can God show himself merciful to anyone without *being* merciful? Is he "showing" something other than himself? Is this how the eternal God can manifest his mercy "for the time being"?

Calvin's propensity to draw theological conclusions from empirical observations is evident once more: the reprobate do not "grasp the will as it is immutable, or steadfastly embrace its truth, for they tarry in but a *fleeting awareness.*" Employing his favorite metaphor he notes that God "illumines wicked persons with some rays of his grace, which he later allows to be quenched. Nor does anything prevent him from lightly touching some with knowledge of his Gospel, while deeply imbuing others."[116] Jesus Christ is the sun whose rays are inseparable from him; since the sun's work is not fleeting, how can the rays be such? How can grace be fleeting when grace *is* Jesus Christ in his will to save? Weak, wavering, or hesitant faith is not the consequence of the "lightness of God's touch"; the elect have all of this despite their being "deeply imbued." Calvin contends that the Holy Spirit does not give life to the "seed" in the hearts of the wicked to keep it incorruptible as he does with the elect, and this should not be taken to imply that the Holy Spirit is false. Why should the Holy Spirit not be regarded as false here, when his action is not that of Christ?[117]

Calvin lands himself in these difficulties because of his understanding of election and of the place of human affirmation in faith. Since election guarantees perseverance, any who are presently of genuine faith must

---

[115]Q.v. 1 Cor. 1:30 and *Inst.* 3.2.8.

[116]*Inst.* 3.2.12 (italics mine).

[117]Ibid.

continue to be so; any not of genuine faith must never have been. This notion is a warping of parts of the New Testament witness. To be sure, in one place (the only place of which I am aware) Calvin does admit that apostasy is possible: there can be someone "who has utterly renounced God's grace. The man who falls is the one who forsakes the Word of God, who extinguishes its light, who denies himself the taste of the heavenly gift, and who *gives up participating in the Spirit.*"[118] Elsewhere, of course, Calvin denies that anyone who participates in the Spirit can give it up—and this latter must be regarded as characteristic of his thought. When Calvin sees fall away those who were of faith, he has to engage in the convolutions of saying that it was a fleeting appropriation of mercy, or a seeming effectual call, or a momentary illumination, in order to accommodate the "fall" to his understanding of unfaith.

If Calvin could say that *all* men are elect and that there is a genuine human affirmation integral to faith (without thereby, needless to say, moving into a semi-pelagianism) then the empirical data he cannot overlook need not cause him logical difficulty. The difference between faith's being a gift, and faith's being a gift exercised (which means as well a gift which can be negated) may appear slight. In fact, the difference is huge. His appreciating this distinction would have relieved him of the difficulties which he cannot avoid and which he can consider only awkwardly and inconsistently concerning those who appear, at one time, similar to those who endure to the end, but who in fact fall away.

---

[118]*Comm.* Heb. 6:4 (italics mine): *qui participationem spiritus deserit.*

CHAPTER 6

THE LAW AND FAITH

"To be Christians under the law of grace does not mean to wander unbridled outside the law, but to be engrafted in Christ, by whose grace we are free of the curse of the law, and by whose Spirit we have the law engraved in our hearts." (*Institutes*, 2.8.57)

JESUS CHRIST: THE SUBSTANCE OF THE LAW

Jesus Christ is the author and object of faith. Faith is engendered by Christ; faith "puts on" Christ; faith subsequently looks only to Christ. Faith is but an empty vessel whose content can be only Christ.[1] Accordingly, any discussion of the law and faith must indicate the relationship of law to Jesus Christ. Indeed, if the relationship of the law to Jesus Christ is other than merely negative (that is, Jesus Christ contradicts the law) then ultimately Jesus Christ must be the substance of the law.

In many places Calvin suggests that this is the case. He insists that the law was given for the purpose "of keeping the (ancient) people in the faith of Christ."[2] Since Jesus Christ, the manifestation of the Father's kindness and favor, *is* the initiator, consummator, and content of faith, ultimately the purpose of the law and the purpose of Christ are one. Thus: "for what is the *design of the law*, except that the people should call upon him (the Father) and that he should exercise a care over his people? For wherever God declares that he will be our God, he offers to us his paternal favour and gives us free access to himself, bids us to rely on his grace, and, in short, this promise contains everything needful for our salvation."[3] The law is evidently God's provision whereby his creatures call upon him (that is, come to faith) in response to his paternal favour and from which they learn to trust him for everything necessary to life, and to await from him the final manifestation of their salvation, when he completes in them that good work which he has already begun (Phil. 1:6).

---

[1] See Chapter One.

[2] *Comm.* Gal. 3:19: *ut populum veterem in Christi fide contineret.*

[3] *Comm.* Jer. 31:33 (italics mine).

Now it is incontestable that the Word of God alone engenders faith; the purpose of the law according to the passage just cited is finally to bring to salvation those whom it has constrained to call upon God. Then the law must *be* the Word of God. In other words, there is but one Word of God which both calls men to faith and subsequently informs existence-in-faith.[4] Indeed, Calvin maintains that ultimately the law is the living God himself (or Word of God) "shaping" the believer's life: "none are truly wise but those who take God for their conductor and guide, following the path which he points out to them, and who are diligently seeking after the peace which he offers and presents by his Word."[5] The lives of the faithful are "framed" by God's Word.[6]

Obviously, Calvin is using "law" to mean much more than mere statute or injunction or code. He argues that scripture often speaks of law with this extended meaning: Moses understood "law" to include the gospel; in urging the law upon his people Moses "endeavours to commend God's great kindness to his people, because he had taken them under his discipline and government. This commendation could not have applied merely to the law" (that is, to mere statute).[7]

Calvin confirms this assessment in stating that the substance of the New Covenant is precisely that of the Old Covenant and adds, "by substance I understand the doctrine; for God brings forward in the gospel nothing new but what the law contains. Hence we see that God has so spoken from the beginning that he has changed not a syllable with regard to the substance of the doctrine. For he has included in the law the rule of a perfect life, and has also shown what is the way of salvation, and by types and figures led the people to Christ, so that the remission is there clearly made manifest and whatever is necessary to be known."[8]

Calvin speaks in his New Testament *Commentaries* of Jesus Christ as both grace and claim. And in his commentary on the Psalms he declares that the law reflects both "true religion" and "godliness"[9]—which should be the occasion of no surprise, since David apprehended the Mediator in the law.[10]

---

[4]E. A. Dowey maintains that for Calvin there are many words, and they are not related to the one Word which begets faith. See my criticism of Dowey on this matter in the Appendix to Chapter One.

[5]*Comm.* Psalm 19:8.

[6]*Comm.* Psalm 119:104.

[7]*Comm.* Rom. 10:6.

[8]*Comm.* Jer. 31:31.

[9]*Comm.* Psalm 19:7.

[10]*Inst.* 2.7.12: *praesertim vero ostendit David, se in lege mediatorem apprehendisse.*

Indeed, how could one properly suggest that the substance of the law be altered when the apostolic writings "contain nothing but a simple and natural explanation of the law and the prophets" (and the prophets were but interpreters of the law)?[11] Developing the same point in his major work on election, the work in which he maintains that election is always in Christ, Calvin insists that the *law* calls men to life and that "law" and "light of life" are synonyms.[12] Truly, it is "preposterous" to suggest that under the law the Fathers lacked regeneration.[13]

In Book III of the *Institutes* Calvin emphasizes, as has been indicated, that there can be no "blind" faith; authentic faith in Jesus Christ must discern that in him God is propitious, merciful, paternal, benevolent, and so forth; in short, that in Jesus Christ God is ever *pro nobis*. This understanding, of which men are destitute by nature, is to be derived from the law; for the law contains the free promises of salvation, and by the law in this extended sense Jesus Christ is apprehended.[14]

Again, Calvin insists that there is but one Mediator between God and men. Accordingly, God has ever communicated with men only through the intervention of his "eternal Wisdom or Son. . . . As he is the Meditator of reconciliation, by whom we are accepted by God, the Mediator on intercession, through whom the way is opened for us to call upon the Father, *so he has always been the Mediator of all teaching*, because by him God has always revealed himself to men. He . . . held the primacy in giving the law."[15] This is not to suggest that the Mediator somehow inhered or suffused the law: the life that the Fathers enjoyed and the remission of sin that they knew were theirs only in virtue of Jesus Christ.[16] While he was present to them under the law it was ever possible for men to contemplate the law and not discern the Mediator (something which would be impossible, of course, if he inhered the law). Calvin does wish to impress upon his readers, nonetheless, that prior to the appearing of the

---

[11]*Comms.* II Tim. 3:17, I Cor. 14:21; and *Inst.* 2.7.1.

[12]*De Aet. Dei Praed.* 106, 108.

[13]*Comm.* Jer. 31:33. Admittedly, Calvin does say two verses earlier that while the substance of law and gospel are identical, the new "form" was the Spirit of regeneration which Christ brought with him. If this were the case then the substance of law and gospel would *not* be identical. Calvin is struggling here to preserve both the identity of substance and genuine newness with respect to the gospel. He should not be held to this uncharacteristic remark, which he counters in numerous other passages (e.g., *Comm.* Jer. 31:33).

[14]*Comm.* Psalm 19:7.

[15]*Comm.* Gal. 3:19 (italics mine).

[16]*Comm.* Heb. 9:15.

Incarnate One the men under the law were not necessarily without his benefits.

Indeed, since Jesus Christ was present to men under the law the sacraments of the law were as efficacious as those of the gospel. The former did not merely "figure" grace but conferred it; indubitably the reality of the sacrament was conveyed.[17] While Jesus Christ was not present to these persons in his flesh and blood as he is to those under the gospel, yet under the law they partook of the same spiritual food as those under the gospel. Since the "food" is the fruit of Christ's death and resurrection, and therefore of his flesh and blood, Calvin is forced to declare that in a proleptic way they did receive that flesh and blood— through the secret work of the Spirit.[18] The point that Calvin wishes to make by this strange argument is simply that the law has no other content than Jesus Christ. Ultimately God can confer "benefits" on people only as he confers the one benefit: his Son. Under the law men are visited with the Mediator as they are under the gospel.

When Calvin maintains that Jesus Christ is present under the law he has the ceremonial cult in mind as much as the moral law. It is Christ's presence to the former and his adoption of it which render it an instrument of his bestowal of himself upon men. Viewed in themselves, the ceremonies are at best cabalistic and at worst repulsive. Calvin is not reluctant to admit that to unfaith (that is, to those who do not understand Jesus Christ to be the substance of the cult) the sight and smell of the sacrifices would not suggest the effectual presence of the Mediator: "For what is more vain or absurd than for men to offer a loathesome stench from the fat of cattle in order to reconcile themselves to God? Or to have recourse to the sprinkling of blood and water to cleanse away their filth? In short, the whole cultus of the law, taken literally and not as shadows and figures corresponding to the truth, will be utterly ridiculous."[19]

> It is in the light of the foregoing that one must understand Calvin's contention that the ceremonies are worthless and empty until the time of Christ is revealed.[20] It is not that they are worthless and empty until the chronological advent of Christ (a nonsensical understanding, since with that advent they are rendered obsolete; see below, "Substance and Shadow"), but rather when they are abstracted from Jesus Christ and regarded in themselves. They are worthless until the *logical* "advent" of Christ. Their worth resides in their being a God-ordained proleptic anticipation of Christ.

---

[17]*Comm.* I Cor. 10:3: *rem sacramenti exhibitam.*

[18]*Comm.* I Cor. 10:4.

[19]*Inst.* 2.7.1.

[20]Ibid.

Earlier it was noted that since Christ does not inhere the law, the sacrifices of themselves do not remit sin. Indeed, so weak (*infirma*) are the sacrifices of the law that they have to be repeated yearly.[21] Calvin moves one step further and exclaims that if the law is so weak (*imbecillitas*) that whatever remedies it applies to atone for sin do not accomplish what they represent, then "who can find refuge in it (that is, the law) as a safe harbour?"[22] The point is that one is not supposed to seek refuge in the law in so far as law is abstracted from Jesus Christ. In numerous places Calvin insists both that sin is remitted in Christ alone and that under the law the fathers knew their sins remitted.[23] Obviously sin is remitted under the law only because Christ is the substance of the law. Yet it must never be assumed that mere performance of the law is "putting on" Christ.

Since God condescends to accommodate himself to men and use this apparent primitivism it cannot be denied that grace was offered to the ancient people, for grace is God's condescension and accommodation. If grace is offered, then the ceremonies cannot be devoid of reference to Christ.[24] Again, mere compliance with the cult does not generate spiritual efficacy; yet the cult is the means whereby God is effectually present with his people, and present in no other way than he is at the appearing of Jesus Christ.[25] Accordingly, the cult bears everywhere the mark of Christ; its exercises are that by which worshipers are led by the hand to Christ; and since Christ is given only to be "put on"—that is, remains of no benefit as long as he is contemplated outside of us—the effect of the cult was to excite the people to faith in the coming redeemer.[26] Indeed, the cult should not be reduced to a "holding action" which kept people from wandering into the surrounding paganism; rather it was to "foster hope of salvation in Christ until his coming."[27] Veritably, the *purpose* of the legal practices was to effect faith in the one Mediator.[28] Through such faith Christ forms and informs a people anew after himself.[29] He accomplishes this through the instrumentality of the cult. The cult admits one "in a sacramental way" to the truth and reality which actually (*re*) via this instrumentality reach men. What "actually reaches" men, of course, is

---

[21] *Comm.* Heb. 10:3.

[22] *Comm.* Heb. 9:15.

[23] E.g., *Comm.* Heb. 10:16; cf. *Inst.* 2.7.1.

[24] *Inst.* 2.7.1: *iam ex gratia Iudaeis oblata certo colligitur, legem Christo non fuisse vacuam.*

[25] *Comms.* John 1:1 and I John 1:1.

[26] *Comm.* Gal. 3:24.

[27] *Inst.* 2.7.title.

[28] *Comm.* Heb. 8:5.

[29] *Comm.* Heb. 8:5: *formo*—"form," "fashion," "educate."

nothing else than Jesus Christ; and his efficacy is the "reality" of the signs; that is, Jesus Christ is present to people under the law prior to his appearing.[30]

It must be stressed that since Jesus Christ is the substance of the law, the law becomes effective in people as Christ himself does; that is, only through faith. Throughout his treatment of the law Calvin never suggests that prior to the manifestation of Jesus Christ his benefits were received in any mechanical manner, that the performance of a rite as such guaranteed spiritual efficacy. Whether under law or gospel, Old Covenant or New Covenant, Jesus Christ and his benefits become ours only in faith. To suggest anything else is to declare law and gospel contradictory.

Calvin avers that law and gospel could be contradictory only if "God were unlike himself"—which Calvin dismisses as absurd.[31] To be sure, since Jesus Christ does not inhere the law, the law cannot bring salvation apart from grace;[32] but then the law, properly understood, is not without grace since the law is a manifestation of God's mercy (Christ). Hence Calvin asseverates that "the agreement between the law and the gospel is established, because God, who is always like himself, and whose Word is unchanging, and whose truth is unshakeable, spoke in both together."[33] Despite the diversity of scripture there is set before us one God, in case anyone should think that the law is "at variance with the gospel, or that the author of the latter is different from that of the former."[34] Indeed, since God is revealed to us in no other way than in Christ,[35] then the law of God pertains to faith in the same way that Christ does. In short, God's intention for the law is recognized and affirmed only in faith. Where faith is lacking the law has been regarded as something other than that whose substance is Christ. Conversely, wherever the law is discerned and expounded in accord with its own nature and purpose, it engenders faith.

Thus Calvin, interpreting St. Paul, states that there are people who look to the law for righteousness, but who do not look in accordance with what the law prescribes (that is, faith); in fact such *legal* righteousness (*legalem iustitiam*) is the reason for their falling from the *law* of righteousness (*a lege iustitiae*).[36] The law itself points to faith; a "legalistic" reading

[30]*Comm.* Heb. 9:13: *sacramentali modo . . . quia rei effectus intervallo praecedit signorum veritatem.*

[31]*Comms.* Gal. 3:12 and Matt. 5:18.

[32]*Comm.* Gal. 3:17.

[33]*Comm.* Heb. 1:1.

[34]Ibid.

[35]*Comm.* Heb. 1:3 and *Inst.* 4.8.5.

[36]*Comm.* Rom. 9:31.

of the law obscures this, and dooms the pursuit after righteousness to futility: the law does not yield what perversity attempts to pry out of it. Where the substance of the law is not discerned Jesus Christ is not apprehended, not "contemplated," not put on, and therefore his righteousness never becomes ours. What the law does *not* prescribe is precisely a "legal" righteousness. The law *does* prescribe that which will lend us "another righteousenss," viz., faith.[37] In fact, every aspect of the law points to him who shares his sonship by bestowing faith in him upon us. Again, to suggest anything else would be to render law and gospel contradictory; Calvin confirms the non-contradiction as he reminds us that the faith-bestowing and faith-soliciting One did not begin to be manifested in the gospel.[38]

In accord with the foregoing Calvin notes that because the nobleman was brought up in the teaching of the law he was already of faith when he encountered the historic Jesus.[39] Similarly, the fact that the ceremonial law witnesses everywhere to Christ indicates that all the rites were given for one purpose: the support and increase of that which is the correlate of Jesus Christ: faith.[40] Calvin insists that "Christ alone" ("Mercy alone") *always* implies "faith alone."[41] Since the fathers discerned Christ to be the substance of the law, it follows that they pleased God only by faith.[42] Abel, Noah, Abraham, Moses and David benefited only through their faith; "when Paul says that grace was revealed to us by the appearing of Christ, he does not exclude the fathers from participation in it; for *the same faith* gives them a part with us in this appearing."[43] Enoch did not "please God" by anything he did; that is, any performance which God recognized and rewarded: "the fact that he pleased God is properly attributed to his faith."[44] It must not be thought, of course, that faith lends substance to the law; faith does not bring or add Christ to the law; rather, faith apprehends the Christ who is already there. The men under the law who made a "proper use" of the Word were those endowed with the Spirit of faith.[45]

---

[37] *Comm.* Rom. 10:4.

[38] *Comm.* John 5:39.

[39] *Comm.* John 4:53 (same argument concerning Cornelius—*Comm.* Acts. 10:1).

[40] *Comm.* Acts. 13:39.

[41] *Comm.* Rom. 3:21.

[42] *Comm.* Heb. 11:6.

[43] *Comm.* II Tim. 1:10 (italics mine).

[44] *Comm.* Heb. 11:5.

[45] *Comm.* I Cor. 10:11.

In short, since the law is empty and insubstantial apart from Christ, those who repudiate him—that is, do not hear the law in faith—are simply not disciples of Moses.[46] The law is expounded incorrectly if it binds men to itself or inhibits their apprehending Jesus Christ.[47] And this is to say that the law is falsified where it does not engender and elicit faith. Faith is the human response which God expects and with which alone he is pleased.[48] Those who do not yield that response have never become apprised of the "heart" of the law; not putting on Jesus Christ, they merely pursue the "shadow" of the law.[49]

APPENDIX

(i) E. A. Dowey fails to understand Calvin at this point. He maintains that the law "cannot be the object of saving faith because it throws responsibility back upon man."[50] Dowey concentrates upon the law in terms of Calvin's notion of natural law. He does not indicate that according to Calvin the nature of the law or the chief function of the law is not burdening man with a demand or responsibility which he must fulfill out of his own resources. Calvin does not deny that men do attempt to do this; he does deny that such is God's intention, first of all, for the law. He does not deny that there *is* human responsibility with respect to the law, as will be made plain in the discussion concerning the third use: there must be a *living* of that existence which Christ bestows as he bestows faith. However, Dowey is not correct to declare that Calvin understands law *only* in terms of that demand which is understood as inculcating "works."

Elsewhere Dowey contrasts Luther (love and law compete) with Calvin (love and law "are by definition the same thing in essence"),[51] and then adds, "it is grace or gratuitous mercy in the gospel that is of another order." His interpretation ignores Calvin's fundamental premise that the substance of the law *is* gratuitous mercy. So far from law's not being the object of saving faith, saving faith (which for Calvin is created always and only by mercy) is found only where that mercy is discerned as the "heart" of the law. The Fathers under the law were saved by faith.

---

[46]*Comm.* John 5:38: *inanis nec habet solida*; for the same idea see *Comms.* John 4:46 and Rom. 10:5.

[47]*Comm.* John 1:17.

[48]*Comm.* Heb. 11:6.

[49]*Comm.* I Tim. 1:9.

[50]E. A. Dowey, *The Knowledge of God in Calvin's Theology*, 157.

[51]Dowey, *The Knowledge of God in Calvin's Theology*, 230.

(ii) A. M. Hunter accuses Calvin of exegetical legerdemain in affirming there to be no contradiction between the psalmist's finding the law to be soul-restoring and Paul's finding it to be death-dealing.[52] Hunter scorns Calvin's perception that for the psalmist "law" does not mean bare demand but rather includes God's gift to and action upon men; that is, "law" is God's gift of mercy and his subsequent claim on the recipients of that mercy, regardless of whether that recipient lives in the era of the Old Covenant or the New. Hunter disagrees with Calvin's insistence that it is pernicious to suggest that the evangelical law is superior to that of Moses. He argues that "law" is to be understood only as bare requirement, since many of those requirements are inapplicable if not incomprehensible in eras after the eras in which they were first heard and heeded.

In defense of Calvin's teaching it may be asked if Hunter has taken into account the understanding of the nature and function of law present in such passages as Psalm 1, Psalm 19 and Psalm 119. Because he attempts no consideration of passages such as these, it is not surprising that he is not entirely fair in his assessment of Calvin's presentation of the third use of the law.

THE FIRST USE OF THE LAW

While the law is indubitably a promulgation of God's mercy, it is, of course, a promulgation of his claim as well. God has an intention for human life, and he insists on its being honored: "God's will, as it is revealed in the law, is here appointed as the guide and instructor of what is rightly to be approved."[53] God has made known what shape he wishes for human existence, and he expects to be obeyed. Simply put, "the law was given to men in order to govern this present life."[54]

It must be stressed that the law is *given*; natural man, who is utterly blind, deaf, and even dead spiritually, is wholly incapable of informing himself as to God's intention for his life.[55] Attempts at such self-informing Calvin regards as "dreaming" and "playfulness"; they are means of avoiding that obedience which God everywhere requires.[56] Faith knows that God's will can be sought only where he has revealed it: in his action upon men wherein he claims men for himself.[57]

---

[52]A. M. Hunter, *The Teaching of Calvin,* 78.

[53]*Comm.* Rom. 2:18; for same idea see *Comm.* Rom. 8:7.

[54]*Comm.* Rom. 7:1; for same idea see *Comm.* Rom. 6:15.

[55]I am ignoring for now Calvin's understanding of natural law.

[56]*Inst.* 2.8.5.

[57]*Comm.* Rom. 8:7.

Despite the "rigorous" aspects of obedience, Calvin iterates the law to be a manifestation of God's pity in the face of that human blindness, confusion and morbidity to which men would be abandoned were there not *appointed* a governor of this life. Regardless of how death-dealing the law may become in view of human corruption, it is in itself an expression of the Father's paternal kindness. The "will of God," however exacting its requirements, has no other source than that Mercy which is the substance of the law and through whom alone God reveals himself to man.

> Admittedly, Calvin speaks of the law as the will of God when he is expounding the law, while in Book III of the *Institutes* "will of God" means mercy or benevolence exclusively. Yet it must not be thought that God ultimately has two different wills—one the "rule of righteousness"[58] (the *requirements* of the law) and the other the *free gift* of adoption. For Calvin, two wills are tantamount to two Gods. In *Institutes* 3.2.*passim* the knowledge of God's will which faith possesses is the knowledge that God is propitious, fatherly, in short, *pro nobis*. While it would be forcing Calvin to say that "will of God" with respect to requirements can be equated with mercy, it must be allowed that since his propitiatory action is determinative, the requirement must be understood as an expression of that mercy. This point is most significant for the discussion of the circumstances under which the law becomes death-dealing and the discussion of the third use of the law. Calvin must not be pushed in the direction of Luther: the law is not *essentially* the antithesis of mercy.

Since God is good and the law is an expression of his will, the law too is good. There is nothing in the law that is contrary to "goodness, righteousness, and holiness."[59] Hence no blame can be attached to the law if in apprehending it men are constrained to describe their situation as other than good. And all men are so constrained because of their sin.

Calvin affirms mankind to be sin-saturated and sin-enslaved: "we are so completely driven by the power of sin that our whole mind, our whole heart and all our actions are inclined to sin. . . . We are so addicted to sin that we can do nothing of our own accord but sin."[60] In the wake of the encounter of this pervasive sinfulness with the law the latter is no longer apprehended as the instrument of the gospel (Jesus Christ in his propitiatory efficacy as well as his claim); this particular "advantage" and aim of the law becomes obscure.[61] In his own day Moses could not bring the sin-vitiated and sin-intoxicated people to a knowledge of the Mediator (mercy) through his proclamation of the law, even though the Mediator continued to be the substance of the law; he could but "discharge faith-

---

[58] Ibid.

[59] *Comm.* Rom. 7:12.

[60] *Comm.* Rom. 7:14.

[61] *Comm.* II Cor. 3:13.

fully the duty laid upon him."[62] In other words, he could but continue to declare the claim or requirements of the law even as his people persisted in repudiating grace (the Mediator). While the nature of the law has not changed (and cannot change unless God becomes "unlike himself"), the function of the law has. Its function is now to render sinners aware of their predicament as they become apprised of their deserved condemnation: they have ben exposed by the law as people who do not "agree" with God and whose purposes and practices God finds wanting.[63] The function of the law now is that of revealing transgressors.[64] Since the law delineates the "shape" that God intends for human existence and thereby indicates that righteousness which alone is acceptable to him, it now acts to "warn, inform, convict and lastly condemn every man of his own unrighteousness."[65] As a disobedient sinner man is excluded from the promise of life and falls under the law as *mere* curse.[66] He must be informed of that situation, for in this manner alone can human pride and pretense be collapsed. What room for pride is there left to the man who knows that the judgment against him is definitive and therefore will not accommodate a plea of extenuation?[67]

It is not the case that God has altered the nature of the law; the law ever remains holy, just and good. Nonetheless, the contiguity of sin and the law means that "the inseparable and unvarying circumstance" (*accidens*) of the law is "to show man his sin and cut off his hope of salvation."[68] Condemnation does not pertain to the essence of the law; condemnation arises through the encounter of the law and sin. The power of slaying ever remains "accidental" to the law. Just as certainly, however, that accident is "perpetual and inevitable."[69] The law which was given for obedience never fails to expose disobedience; that which was meant for life now effects death. Not only does the law conclude all men in disobedience; it also points up to sinners the exceeding sinfulness of sin: it is the law which

---

[62]Ibid.

[63]*Comm.* Rom. 8:7.

[64]*Comm.* Gal. 3:19.

[65]*Inst.* 2.7.7.

[66]*Inst.* 2.7.3: *a vitae promissionibus exclusi in solam maledictionem recedimus.* The use of "mere" is significant; the purpose of the law is not to curse—except when the law confronts sin.

[67]*Comm.* Rom. 3:19.

[68]*Comm.* Rom. 3:20. Calvin stresses the accidentality of the law's condemning again and again; e.g., *Comms.* Jer. 31:32, Matt. 5:21, Rom. 5:13, Rom. 7:9, Gal. 3:10.

[69]*Comm.* II Cor. 3:7.

causes sin to "sting." As the force or power (*vim aut potentiam*) of sin the law renders consciences disquieted. By the law sinful man *knows* that he exists under judgment of death.[70]

While Calvin is always careful to indicate that such deadliness is but accidental to the law, at the same time he insists that in view of the inevitable presence of the accident to the substance it is not incorrect to assert the death-dealing property to be part of the *purpose* of the law: "let it therefore be established that the law was given not only for instruction so that men might follow what they had learnt from it to be right, but also to convict them of their iniquity, that they might acknowledge themselves to be lost; as if they saw in a mirror their destruction through the just vengeance of God."[71]

Men are condemned, of course, in that they have failed to discern Jesus Christ as the substance of the law: ignoring that putting on of Christ which is faith, they prefer to relate themselves only to the claim of Jesus Christ, that is, to the requirements of the law. The refusal to put on Christ is sheer unfaith; unfaith remains confident of its ability to achieve its own righteousness through complete compliance with the law's requirements. Undeniably, a "good will," completely conformed to obedience, would attain that righteousness.[72] A good will, however, is precisely what unfaith lacks; the will which is *in se curvatus* can continue to will only its own disobedience. While the law does not fail to show men perfect righteousness, men fail to fulfil that law.[73] This is the occasion of no surprise, for the attempt to heed the claim of Christ while refusing to put on Christ is an essential contradiction; the claim of Christ is that we be as he is.[74] The totality of that claim guarantees men's condemnation.

The effects of repudiating the total claim of Jesus Christ while betaking himself to the requirements of Christ means that man lives under the wrong lord. Instead of hearing and heeding him who is indeed Lord, he has decided to live under the *dominus* or the *imperium* of the law's requirements.[75] When the *dominus* of Christ and the law are opposed— that is, when the law is no longer seen as Christ's *dominus*—then that willful disobedience which is unfaith meets with condemnation. And for as long as the *domini* of Christ and the law are opposed, that of the latter

---

[70]*Comm.* 1 Cor. 15:56.

[71]*Comm.* Deut. 10:12.

[72]*Inst.* 2.7.7.

[73]*Comms.* Luke 10:28 and Rom. 4:14.

[74]*Comm.* Gal. 2:21.

[75]*Comms.* Rom. 4:16 and Gal. 2:19 respectively.

remains in effect.[76]

"Life and death do not issue from the same fountain," Calvin insists, for the *dominus* of Jesus Christ and the *dominus* of the requirements are distinct and have different implications.[77] Nonetheless, Jesus Christ does remain the substance of the law. Accordingly, while "law" in the sense of bare requirement (the understanding proper to unfaith) is deadly, "law" in the sense appropriate to faith is life-producing: "for as soon as the law begins to live in us it inflicts a fatal wound by which we die; at the same time the *law* breathes life into the man who is already dead to sin."[78]

How does the law begin to breathe life into the man whom it has condemned and whom it has informed of that condemnation? Since Jesus Christ, who is the substance of the law, is given only for life, therefore the law, however negative its function in the face of sin, is ultimately given only for life: the aim of the law in exposing the exceeding sinfulness of sin is not merely that man becomes apprised of it or terrified by the judgment it brings down or even reduced to despair, but that through the awareness of his own utter poverty and humility and self-abasement he might be "moved to seek and await help from another quarter."[79] Indeed, in itself despair is not God-honoring; it has value only in so far as it is the incipient movement to a situation beyond despair: it is fitting that man despair *in order that* he embrace the grace of Christ (heretofore in unfaith he has "embraced" only the requirement) and be delivered from his melancholy state of guilt.[80] Since man is *commanded* to *love* God, the ultimate purpose of the law even in the face of human sin cannot be condemnation. While the law acquaints a man with his condemnation, the purpose of that revelation is to shock the subject into seeing the impossibility of attaining righteousness through requirement-keeping and lead him to embrace in faith the One who wishes to include him in his own righteousness. For this reason the death-dealing, negative function of the law, Calvin insists, does not detract at all from understanding the law as the law whose substance is the One who is Life. Indeed, even the condemning function of the law commends God's beneficence, since in revealing man's sin it demonstrates that God is under no obligation to do anything at all on behalf of man who has become sinner and he could abandon him to the fate he deserves. This makes it clear that the law wounds for the sake of

---

[76]*Comm.* Rom. 6:17.

[77]*Comm.* Rom. 3:20.

[78]*Comm.* Gal. 2:19 (italics mine).

[79]*Inst.* 2.8.1 (see also *Inst.* 2.8.3).

[80]*Comm.* Deut. 27:26.

healing; it dissolves self-confidence only in order that one might look to and put on him who is wholeness. Calvin maintains that there is no point in indicating, through the law, that sin abounds unless grace abounds the more and is seen to abound: "Paul teaches us that the extent of grace is more strikingly revealed because it is poured out in so copious a flood while sin abounds as not only to overcome the flood of sin, but even to swallow it up. From this we may learn that *our condemnation is not set before us in the law for the purpose of making us continue in it, but to acquaint us intimately with our misery and lead us to Christ*, who is sent to be a physican to the sick, a deliverer to the captives, a comforter to the afflicted, and a defender to the oppressed."[81] The purpose of the law's exposure of sin is the magnifying of the grace of God, which is to say, the magnifying of the One who wills not to be who he is apart from the people who embrace him in faith. While as the substance of the law Jesus Christ (and therefore the Holy Spirit—the power by which he effects faith as he binds men to himself) was never remote from the sinner, the latter, in his preoccupation with attaining righteousness through requirement-keeping, persisted in "neglecting" the Spirit who ever sought to bind him to Christ.[82] Hence it is expedient that men be slain by the law—that is, slain by that from which in their unfaith they sought life but found only death—in order that that death might ultimately be life-giving—through faith. In brief, condemnation under the *law* (-requirement) always subserves righteousness under the *law* (-substance); condemnation always subserves faith.

Calvin does admit that while condemnation subserves faith, it may not issue in faith; the sinner may be terrified and yet not flee to mercy. His recalcitrance is due to the 'obstinacy of his heart.' Persistent obstinacy increasingly renders it difficult for the sinner to "receive any taste of God's goodness."[83] Obstinacy renders it increasingly difficult for the heart to move towards faith.

Notwithstanding the above possibility, the negative function of the law is but the converse of the positive: condemnation under the law is but the action of Jesus Christ as he moves to overturn sin's wilful repudiation of him; condemnation is the action of the substance of the law upon the abuse of the law to effect the fulfilment of the law: faith. It is in this sense that Calvin speaks of the law-wrought humiliation as a *preparation* for

---

[81]*Comm.* Rom. 5:20 (italics mine). Cf. *Inst.* 2.7.2: "For it would be of no value to know what God demands of us if Christ did not succour those labouring and oppressed under its intolerable yoke and burden."

[82]*Comm.* Deut. 10:12.

[83]*Comm.* Jer. 29:13.

faith.[84] That preaching of the gospel which includes the awakening of men to their predicament *coram Deo* is "what is properly meant by *encouraging*."[85] While faith, strictly speaking, is only the putting on of Christ, so closely related to it is the negative assessment generated by the law that Calvin can speak of the ensuing self-dissatisfaction as the beginning of faith; being moved by an apprehension of God's displeasure is itself incipient faith.[86] Of course, Jesus Christ is the author of faith; that preparation for faith, encouragement of faith, and even incipient faith which arise from the law's condemnation, then, are yet the action of Jesus Christ as he deals with men who in their unfaith repudiate him and who in their brazen self-confidence think they can honor his claim while scorning him.

THE MISUNDERSTANDING OF THE LAW

Despite Calvin's insistence that Jesus Christ is the substance of the law and his insistence that law and gospel cannot contradict each other, he does frequently juxtapose law and gospel so as to suggest a strong antithesis; for example, "in the precepts of the law, God is but the rewarder of perfect righteousness, which all of us lack and, conversely, the severe judge of evil deeds. But in Christ his face shines full of grace and gentleness, even upon us poor and unworthy sinners."[87] Should not God's face shine as much in the law? How can God's face fail to shine there when the goal of the *law* is to effect our calling upon the paternal favor and care of God? When in the law God provides everything necessary for our salvation and in the gospel God brings forward nothing new but what the law contains?[88] If Jesus Christ is the substance of the law then how can the law bespeak the God whose face is set against us while the gospel bespeaks the God whose face is turned towards us? This antithesis is often presented to us by Calvin in his New Testament *Commentaries*. The gospel, which is "enlightenment," "partaking of the Holy Spirit," "the taste of the good word of God" is not "revealed to us in any kind of way, but as that which agreeably pleases us." Quite different, then, is the law from the gospel. The former contains nothing beyond (*nihil praeter*) sternness and

---

[84]*Inst.* 2.7.2.

[85]*Comm.* I Thess. 2:12 (italics mine).

[86]Ibid.

[87]*Inst.* 2.7.8.

[88]*Comm.* Jer. 31:31.

judgment, but the latter is a pleasing evidence of the divine love and fatherly kindness towards us."[89]

However, of paramount importance is the context of these passages where Calvin describes law and gospel as antithetical. The context of the remarks in *Comm.* Heb. 6:4 is that of those *who have forsaken the gospel.* In other words, the law becomes death-dealing only when it is torn from the gospel. In this situation unfaith hears the claim of Christ (or rather thinks it can hear and understand that claim; obviously it does not properly hear even the claim in its failure to discern mercy as the ground of the claim; see below). Faith recognizes that the claim of Christ can be fulfilled only in Christ. In other words, that deadliness which unfaith finds in the law is not God's primary intention for the law. Nonetheless, because God insists on obedience, any attempted "obedience" which is not the obedience of faith can be only sheer disobedience—that is, the repudiation of the One who is righteousness and life.

In the *Institutes* where Calvin expounds Paul's apparently anti-gospel understanding of the law in Galatians, Calvin is careful to qualify Paul's comments, reminding his readers that Paul 'was disputing with perverse teachers who pretended that we merit righteousness by works of the law. Consequently, to refute their error he was sometimes compelled to take *the bare law in a narrow sense*, even though it was otherwise graced with the covenant of free adoption.'[90] In short, Paul wishes to indicate to the Judaizers that their understanding of the law is a misunderstanding, and the consequence of this misunderstanding. The "bare law" is the law torn from its context of grace. The consequence of so misunderstanding the law is condemnation. It is crucial to realize, then, that the bare law is something which God does not intend (even though, of course, in his providence he now makes that misunderstanding and its consequent condemnation serve his purpose: the salvation of men, which he calls the first use of the law). Quoting Augustine, Calvin notes that "if the Spirit of grace is absent, the law is present only to accuse and kill us."[91] But the Spirit of grace is absent only when men arrogate the law to their own ends and refuse to acknowledge the place and function of law in God's economy of grace. Such arrogation has never been God's purpose: Moses was not made a lawgiver to wipe out the blessing promised to the race of

---

[89]*Comm.* Heb. 6:4.

[90]*Inst.* 2.7.2 (italics mine): *ut eorum errorem refutaret, coactus est interdum nudam legem praecise accipere; quae tamen gratuitae adoptionis alioqui vestita est.*

[91]*Inst.* 2.7.7.

Abraham.[92] Indeed, Abraham is the faith-exemplar of the *one* covenant which God has made; that covenant (of which faith is the only adequate human response) God confirmed through Moses;[93] to "embrace the doctrine of Moses" is to "choose life"—that is, affirm Jesus Christ.[94] The law, in God's intention, is not opposed to the promise, and therefore not opposed to faith as the implication of the promise. Accordingly, Calvin insists, "the gospel should not seem to be contrary to the law in conferring free righteousness. As, therefore, Paul has denied that the righteousness of faith needs the assistance of the law, so he now asserts that the righteousness of *faith is confirmed by the testimony of the law*. And if the law bears testimony to free righteousness, it is evident that it was not given to teach men how to obtain righteousness for themselves by works. Those, therefore, who *wrest the law for this purpose, pervert it*."[95] The purpose of the law has never been works-righteousness (nor was its original purpose the revelation to men of the exceeding sinfulness of their sin); its purpose has been the inception of faith and the shaping of existence within faith. Both law and gospel are "from faith to faith"; when faith apprehends the law, faith itself is confirmed.

Regrettably, it is only too easy to preoccupy oneself with the law of God and convince oneself that one is glorifying God as the law enjoins, when one is merely misusing the law for self-glorification, refusing to yield *faith*, which is that glorification of God the law demands. Indeed, faith *is* that God-glorifying, human attitude and act to which the law summons men. And it is here that the greater part of Israel has rendered God unfaith in arrogating the law to itself as its *possession*, all the while extolling itself. These people, Calvin insists, have devoted themselves to keeping the law, but have failed to discern the obedience of faith as the end for which it was given, convinced as they were that the oracles of God belonged to them: "in the same way they gloried in God, but not as the Lord commanded us, . . . that we should humble ourselves and seek our glory in him alone. Without any knowledge of the goodness of God they made him peculiarly their own, although they did not inwardly possess him."[96] Unfaith fails to realize that the oracles of God properly "belong" to God alone; the human attitude which insists that the law is "now ours"

---

[92] *Inst.* 2.7.1: *Neque enim datus est Moses legislator qui benedictionem generi Abrahae promissam aboleret.*

[93] *Comm.* Jer. 31:31.

[94] *Comm.* Deut. 30:20.

[95] *Comm.* Rom. 3:21 (italics mine).

[96] *Comm.* Rom. 2:17: *sine ulla bonitatis Dei cognitione, illum quo intus vacui erant, apud homines, vanae ostentationis causa, peculiariter suum faciebant.*

is an attitude which has not discerned grace (Jesus Christ) as the substance of the law and hence never responds in faith. The appropriate human attitude is to come, through the law, to a knowledge of God's "goodness"; such faith-knowledge is acquired only as God is "possessed inwardly"—that is, as Christ, who *is* the pledge of the Father's goodness, is "put on" in the power of the Holy Spirit. To know God's goodness is, everywhere in Calvin, to know his mercy (for example, *Comm.* Rom. 9:32); and everywhere in Calvin mercy is the origin and object of faith. Israel, however, did not recognize the law as the coming among men of the gracious God himself, but rather "wrested" the law into something it could possess and to which it could relate itself in an attitude other than that of grateful receptivity. While the law was given as that means through which the gracious God comes to possess men as they yield themselves to him in grateful faith, Israel regarded the law as that by which it could control God and extract from him his verdict of approval on their self-accomplishment. In this their unfaith found the law a savor of death instead of a savor of life. The problem occurs, Calvin reminds us, when the gospel and law are torn asunder, for the law, properly understood, always includes the gospel.[97] Unfaith fails to realize that even when the law is wrapped abundantly in figures (*figuris implicita*), it is *ever* transparent to God's "goodness."[98] Faith finds transparent what unfaith finds opaque.

In so far as the law is meant to be transparent to God's "goodness" or his mercy, it is meant to be transparent to faith; in that the law mirrors Jesus Christ *it must* mirror faith. When this discernment is not made, however, the law becomes an exitless labyrinth;[99] those persons who do not apprehend Christ-in-his-power-to-effect-faith have failed to refer the law to its own end (*ad suum finam*) and wander about forever in the maze without penetrating to the "true meaning" of the law.[100] That warping of the law which ensues invariably "closes the gate of faith."[101]

Yet it may be asked: Does the law always point to the promise and therefore to faith? Does not circumcision, which was so very significant to the Judaizers, point away from the promise of free mercy? Calvin maintains that circumcision does not point to an act in the mere performance of which man's status before God is altered or enhanced. No one has any

---

[97]*Comm.* Psalm 19:8.

[98]*Comm.* II Cor. 3:13.

[99]*Comm.* II Cor. 3:16.

[100]Ibid.

[101]*Comms.* II Cor. 3:16 and Acts 13:39.

ground to claim anything on account of the sign *alone*. Rather, the true character of circumcision was "a spiritual promise *which required faith*. The Jews neglected both the promise and faith, and for this reason their confidence was vain."[102] Indeed, in Calvin's estimation the nature and purpose of circumcision presuppose grace, the free promise, and therefore faith.[103] The meaning of every item in the law is, ultimately, promise and faith. Indeed, the law pertains essentially not to a meritorious performance of any sort, but to the "spiritual worship of God" and "piety."[104] ("Piety" for Calvin is not a pejorative term but rather refers to those who have the gospel sealed on their "heart" as well as their mind, who know that "the knowledge of faith consists in assurance rather than in comprehension" (*Inst.* 3.2.14) and so forth. In short, "piety" for Calvin always refers to faith.) Promise and law (and therefore faith and law) are contradictory only where the law is misrepresented. It was given to quicken and maintain faith; it fails to agree with faith only when Jesus Christ is torn from it;[105] this in turn is an entirely false view of the law.[106]

Since Jesus Christ is not naturally intelligible (that is, his reality cannot be apprehended naturally) neither is the law: the law does not disclose its meaning (Jesus Christ and faith) to any who have not been enlightened by the Holy Spirit.[107] Where the Spirit of Christ does not so vivify the law as to render its meaning understandable, the law is mistakenly thought to be intelligible in itself.[108] The "meaning" which unfaith "sees" in this false intelligibility is a formula or code by which men can give themselves standing before God. Such men think that their law-perusing yields that knowledge which pertains to the law, viz., works-righteousness. However, their knowledge is never that which is essential to faith: the knowledge of sheer mercy and the concomitant knowledge of human inability. Their ignorance of the intent of the law indicates that many who have the greatest zeal for the law show themselves to be its greatest despisers.[109]

Nonetheless, the failure of unfaith to find the knowledge of mercy in the law does not impugn God's intention for the law; indeed, unfaith's

---

[102]*Comm.* Rom. 2:25 (italics mine).

[103]Ibid.

[104]*Comm.* Rom. 2:27.

[105]*Comm.* Rom. 10:5.

[106]*Comm.* Rom. 3:31.

[107]*Comm.* Gal. 3:2.

[108]*Comm.* Gal. 3:19.

[109]*Comm.* I Tim. 1:9.

very failure serves "to show, on the other hand, that *right* knowledge must be sought from the law."[110] God's chief intention for the law is that it attest promise and faith. Only a misunderstanding of the law suggests anything else.

THE LAW VERSUS THE LETTER

That mutual relation between unfaith and the misrepresentation of the law Calvin describes as unfaith's rendering the law a "letter." Faith is formed and informed by law; unfaith looks only to the letter. Since Jesus Christ is the *proprium* ("characteristic", "essence") of the law, unfaith ever separates Christ from the law (*a Christo separata*).[111] Upon this procedure Calvin comments pithily, "now what is the law without Christ but a dead letter?"[112] Indeed, it is the "theology of the letter" which prevents the law-abusers from seeing the One who is the light and life of the law.[113]

This distinction between law and letter Calvin returns to again and again throughout his *Commentaries*, approaching the issue from several different angles, yet always insisting that the distinction consists in Christ's having been abstracted from the law. For instance, in answer to the question, "How can the psalmist speak of delighting in the law?", Calvin affirms that while the letter is indeed deadly and utterly without power to remedy mankind's fallen condition, the law can in fact restore him to purity in that God uses it as an instrument of his *Word*.[114] Similarly, he maintains that the law becomes letter when the Spirit of Christ or the grace of Christ does not quicken it.[115] Again, the letter lacks the grace of regeneration or the Spirit of regeneration and hence cannot penetrate to the heart.[116] Indeed, the letter is the law minus the grace of adoption.[117] Grace, Calvin insists, is the "spiritual fulfilment of those things of which the bare letter was contained in the law."[118] In other

---

[110]*Comm.* Rom. 2:20 (italics mine).

[111]*Comms.* II Cor. 3:6 and James 1:25.

[112]*Comm.* Phil. 3:6; for same idea see *Comm.* John 5:39.

[113]*Comm.* Rom. 7:9.

[114]*Comm.* Psalm 19:7.

[115]*Comms.* Matt. 5:17 and Psalm 19:8.

[116]*Comm.* Jer. 31:33.

[117]*Comm.* James 1:25.

[118]*Comm.* John 1:16.

words, the law, unlike the letter, is replete with "spiritual blessings," the letter being but an "empty shape."[119]

Calvin's most protracted metaphor for the law/letter distinction is that of soul and body: the letter is soulless while the soul of the law is Jesus Christ.[120] He argues, "Add the soul to the body and you have a living man endowed with understanding and perception and fitted for all the activities of life; but remove the soul from the body and there will remain a useless corpse devoid of all perception . . . for Christ is the life of the law."[121] As soulless the letter is "unsubstantial" and "lacks life."[122] Where there is no connexion with the Spirit of Christ (*non cohebitur*) there is only "literal teaching" (as opposed to "spiritual").[123] While there pertains to the law that knowledge requisite for faith, the letter merely points to an inability to understand.[124]

Not surprisingly, Calvin associates the law with that action of the Holy Spirit wherein God forms faith's will according to his will: the concupiscent will is replaced by the will of the ever obedient One as he is "put on"; the letter leaves the will willing only itself.[125] This is in fact the predicament of the Rich Young Ruler whose thinking himself to be righteous points to the law's being a "dead letter" for him—as he moves *away* from Jesus Christ.[126]

While the law bespeaks life, the letter, which is a mutilation of the law in that Christ is separated from it, can bespeak only the mutilation of life: death.[127] While the law penetrates to the heart, the letter merely sounds in the ear and can produce only condemnation.[128] Otherwise put, unless the letter becomes the law, the depravity of men's hearts is not corrected.[129] Indeed, in their depravity men find that the letter (their repudiation of

---

[119]Ibid.

[120]*Comms.* Rom. 10:4 and John 1:16.

[121]*Comm.* II Cor. 3:17. Cf. Niesel's appropriate comment: "Whoever does not pay heed to the soul of the law, whoever disregards the fulfiller of the law, must in any event perish by the law. He does not see it as an invitation from the Father of grace, and strives in vain to fulfill its requirements in will and deed" (*The Theology of Calvin*, 95).

[122]*Comms.* John 1:66 and 5:39 respectively.

[123]*Comm.* Rom. 7:5.

[124]*Comm.* II Cor. 3:12.

[125]*Comm.* Rom. 7:6.

[126]*Comm.* Matt. 19:20.

[127]*Comm.* Rom. 10:4.

[128]*Comms.* II Cor. 3:6 and Deut. 10:12 respectively.

[129]*Comm.* Deut. 30:12.

Christ) kindles in their hearts a hatred of God and his law (a hatred of Christ).[130] Thus, where there is the bare letter (*litera nuda*) of the law, there is the lordship of sin.[131]

In short, since Jesus Christ is the substance and meaning of the law, and since Christ never comes to us without the power to make us his (that is, to effect faith) the distinction between the law and the letter is precisely the distinction between faith and unfaith.[132]

Appendix. E. A. Dowey draws attention to the fact that the formula "Christ and faith" is found throughout the *Commentaries*, sometimes with the explicit intention of excluding the law as the source and origin of faith.[133] In support of his contention he quotes *Comm.* Gal. 3:6: "Faith looks at nothing but the mercy of God and a dead and risen Christ." Herein he attempts to indicate that the law is the antithesis of mercy and can pertain to faith only negatively. Dowey fails to realize that the law regarded as a means to salvation is a misuse of the law, the use God makes of it in this context (that is, to apprise men of their condemnation) being but accidental.

Elsewhere Dowey writes, "Next to the revealed orderly will of God in scripture, which makes equal demands on all men and promises rewards, is the special gratuitous mercy of God."[134] Admittedly, God does make demands on all men—for he claims the obedience of faith for all men. When that obedience is not forthcoming, men pervert God's gift into a curse. Dowey does not realize, as his use of "next to" indicates, that it is precisely the gratuitous mercy of God which makes the demand. Moreover, what is the force of "next to" for Dowey? In what manner are the orderly will of God and mercy proximate to each other? Dowey is close to suggesting that God has two wills; for Calvin this would be tantamount to affirming two deities.

A few lines later Dowey speaks of the law as "having its ground in God's gratuitous mercy."[135] However, in the light of what both precedes and follows this remark, one must wonder if Dowey is fully cognizant of the implications of the remark; for instance, preoccupied as he is with the

---

[130] *Comm.* Psalm 19:8.

[131] *Comm.* II Cor. 3:17.

[132] The *locus classicus* of the law/letter distinction is II Cor. 3:6. Regrettably, Calvin is preoccupied here with a sharp criticism of Origen's school of scripture allegorization. What he stresses elsewhere concerning the law and the letter he fails to mention here at all.

[133] E. A. Dowey, *The Knowledge of God in Calvin's Theology*, 158.

[134] Dowey, *The Knowledge of God in Calvin's Theology*, 233.

[135] Ibid.

relation of Jesus Christ to God's orderly will, Dowey states that the God of gratuitous mercy works within the frame of his eternal orderly willing.[136] Does God work in a frame? Is not his action both frame and content? Despite the weaknesses in Calvin's doctrine of election, at bottom he does affirm, as I have indicated elsewhere, that the *whole* God is found in Jesus Christ—which is to say, found in gratuitous mercy.[137] In Christ God appears to us "essentially."[138] Jesus Christ *is* the eternal God.[139] Can there then be a frame apart from gratuitous mercy? Calvin cannot be pressed to say that gratuitous mercy is but an aspect of God's "orderliness."

THE SECOND USE OF THE LAW

The second use of the law is the inculcation of the fear of punishment in order to protect society from persons whose socially acceptable behavior can be constrained only through terror.[140] Of course this second use does not pertain *immediately* to faith: those whose appetitive natures must be restrained in this manner have not been renewed at all; while the consequences of their depravity have been restricted, the depravity itself has not been undone. Indeed, such men continue to hate both the law and the lawgiver; "they do not have hearts disposed to fear and obedience toward God."[141] These men do not obey the law "voluntarily"; they comply with it outwardly while inwardly opposing it.[142] God's action upon these men is yet an expression of his loving-kindness: in addition to protecting society from them, he protects them from falling away completely from the pursuit of righteousness.[143] For "where the Spirit of God does not yet rule, lusts sometimes so boil that there is danger lest they plunge the soul bound over to them into forgetfulness and contempt of God. And such would happen if God did not oppose it with this remedy."[144]

---

[136]Ibid., 237.

[137]See chapter on Election, and *Comm.* II Pet. 1:3.

[138]*De Aet. Dei Praed.* 88.

[139]*Comms.* John 1:1 and I John 1:1.

[140]*Inst.* 2.7.10.

[141]Ibid. The fear of punishment which restrains evil-doers Calvin refers to passim as "servile"; he contrasts it with godly fear, i.e., "that chaste and pure fear which ought to be in God's sons" (*Inst.* 2.7.11).

[142]Ibid.

[143]It is only the regenerate who "voluntarily" obey the law. See below on third use of the law.

[144]*Inst.* 2.7.11.

Thus, even here, there are two aspects of this second use of the law which Calvin maintains are a propaedeutic to faith. The first is that the law here serves as a "holding action" whereby God preserves from utter ruin those whom he has decided to favor by bringing, one day, to faith. To be sure, this holding action presupposes an attitude of unfaith: sheer terror. Although this attitude contradicts the understanding of God as propitious and fatherly and thus belongs wholly to unfaith, yet in the providence of God this negative attitude orients the recalcitrants towards godliness "according to their capacity."[145] The holding action preserves for faith those whose capacity is presently but the capacity for unfaith. In this respect the law is a bridle by which God restrains those whom he will one day visit with his Spirit; it is a schoolmaster which "starts its pupils off and then hands them over to the *theology of faith* for their completion."[146]

In the second place, the fear-engendered obedience which the unregenerate yield the law accustoms them to that obedience integral to faith which they will yield when they have been called effectually; "as a consequence, when they are called they are not utterly untutored and uninitiated in discipline."[147] While their obedience is certainly not the obedience of faith, nevertheless a human attitude and propensity is being fostered in them which will eventually be baptized into the service of faith.[148]

THE THIRD USE OF THE LAW

The third use of the law is for Calvin the chief purpose of the law, which purpose is "the fulfillment of righteousness to form human life to the archetype of divine purity. For God has so depicted himself in the law that if any man carries out in deeds what is enjoined there, he will express the image of God, as it were, in his own life."[149] Here Calvin has in mind those whom God has brought to faith and who henceforth live for the

---

[145]Ibid.

[146]*Comm.* Gal. 3:24 (italics mine).

[147]*Inst.* 2.7.10.

[148]For a statement of the different attitudes in which faith and unfaith obey the law see *Comm.* Rom. 7:16.

[149]*Inst.* 2.8.5: *quorsum vero spectet lex universa, non erit nunc difficile iudicum, nempe in iustitae complementum: ut hominis vitam ad divinae putitatis exemplar formet.* While the third use is merely adumbrated in the following paragraph, it will be considered throughout the balance of this chapter.

praise of his glory. Their existence in faith is to the glory of God as they render obedience to him even as he impresses upon them the "shape" of their obedience or new life. Now since Jesus Christ is the image of God *par excellence*, and since obedience to the law reflects that image, the third use of the law is that by which God conforms persons of faith to Jesus Christ. Those who have put on Christ *become*, through the law, what they *are* eschatologically. This is the force of Cavlin's declaration that "the third and principal use, which pertains more closely to the proper purpose of the law, finds its place among believers in whose hearts the Spirit of God already lives and reigns."[150] The third use is the closest to the proper use of the law; indeed, the first use of the law, as Calvin everywhere insists, is but "accidental"; while the law condemns and convicts unfaith, that condemnation is not the proper purpose of the law.

FAITH'S MOTIVE IN OBEYING THE LAW

What is the motive for the Christian's obeying the law? Undeniably Calvin speaks of an obligation binding all men (and therefore believers) in that as Creator God has the right to be heard and heeded and insists on that right:

> "God designed that the whole human race should be accustomed from the beginning to reverence his deity . . . that man might know he had a Director and Lord of his life, on whose will he ought to depend and in whose commands he ought to acquiesce. And truly this is the only rule of living well and rationally, that men should exercise themselves in obeying God . . . from the beginning God imposed a law upon man for the purpose of maintaining the right due to himself."[151]

> ". . . the law should be reverently obeyed because the Creator of heaven and earth justly claims supreme dominion. . . ."[152]

> "And surely it was necessary that first of all the right of the legislator should be established, lest what he chose to command should be despised or contemptuously received. In these words, then, God seeks to procure reverence to himself before he prescribes the rule (*vivendi regulam*) of a holy and righteous life. . . . He . . . declares himself to be Jehovah, the only God to whom men are bound by the right of creation. . . ."[153]

> "For since we, with all that is ours, are deep in debt to his majesty, whatever he requires of us he claims with perfect right as a debt."[154]

---

[150]*Inst.* 2.7.12: *tertius usus, qui et praecipuus est, in proprium legis finem proprius spectat, erga fideles locum habet, quorum in cordibus iam viget ac regnat Dei spiritus.*

[151]*Comm.* Gen. 2:16.

[152]*Comm.* Exod. 19:36.

[153]*Comm.* Exod. 20:1.

[154]*Inst.* 2.8.4; for same idea see *Inst.* 2.8.13.

As Creator of all men God has established his lordship. The fact that men owe their existence to him grounds his claim upon them: "we must obey out of natural obligation."[155]

Nonetheless, Calvin, in presenting his understanding of scripture, maintains that the ground of obedience peculiar to *faith* is the mercy which God has poured upon men and in which faith recognizes its origin. Faith, knowing itself *constituted* by that mercy, cannot question God's claim upon it. In this respect Calvin is careful to indicate that the promise of God (mercy) always precedes the claim of God.[156] It is because the Lord has made us his own by his mercy that we are to keep his commands.[157] The fact that mercy always precedes the claim of God is crucial, for it alters the spirit or attitude in which the claim of God is acknowledged. Faith receives the claim not as an imperious demand but as an invitation, a "permission": "the promise stands first because God chooses rather to *invite* his people by kindness than to *compel* them to obedience from terror."[158] It is mercy which both grounds the claim of God and gives the claim its peculiar nature or spirit.[159] Calvin reminds us that the recounting of deliverance from Egypt (which deliverance was sheer mercy; what can a slave *do*?) has the force of a preface to the entire law.[160] This "preface" which determines the attitude in which faith hears and heeds the law Calvin recollects again and again:

> ". . . Moses adds that God is the peculiar God of the Israelites; for it was expedient not only that the people should be alarmed by the majesty of God, but also that they should be gently attracted, so that the law might be more precious than gold or silver, and at the same time sweeter than honey; for it would not be enough for men to be compelled by servile fear to bear its yoke, unless they were also attracted by its sweetness, and willingly (*libenter*) endured it. He afterwards recounts that special blessing wherewith he had honoured the people and by which he had testified that they were not elected in vain; for their redemption was the sure pledge of their adoption. But, in order to bind them the better to himself, he reminds them also of their former condition; for Egypt was like a house of bondage from which the Israelites

---

[155]*Inst.* 2.8.2.

[156]Here I must disagree with G. Racke, "Das Gesetz . . . kommt in heilsgeschichtlichen Ablauf von dem Evangelium zu stehen" ("Gesetz und Evangelium bei Calvin", *Theologische Literaturzeitung*, 1955, no. 3, 179.

[157]*Inst.* 2.8.14.

[158]*Comm.* Deut. 7:9 (italics mine).

[159]Calvin states that the expression, "God . . . who keeps covenant and mercy," has the force of "keeping the covenant of mercy" or "the covenant founded on mercy" or "the mercy which God covenanted" (*Comm.* Deut. 7:9). The point is that mercy alone grounds and gives structure to the claim.

[160]*Inst.*2.8.13: *vice prooemii cuiusdam esse in totam legem.*

were delivered. Wherefore, they were no more their own masters, since God
had purchased them unto himself. This does not literally apply to us, but he
has bound us to himself with a holier tie, by the hand of his only-begotten
Son. . . ."[161]

Libenter has the force of "with pleasure, with goodwill": Calvin uses the word
frequently to indicate the form of the law as invitation rather than unrelieved
burden; for example, "Moses sets before them the blessing of redemption
that they may submit themselves *libenter* to his law, from whom they have
obtained their safety."[162]

Similarly Calvin argues, "for there was nothing which should have stimulated them more effectually to obedience than that more than paternal love
and the gratuitous kindness with which he had gone before them."[163]

Apprehension of God's "majesty" can, and likely will, render one afraid;
servile fear, however, is not the attitude by which faith is constrained to
obey the law. Accordingly, the God whose nature *is* mercy forms the
"atmosphere" of invitation or permission as he dispels that fear through
coming to those of faith "intimately" (*familiariter*) and commends to
them his free mercy.[164]

In short, those who know themselves to be the beneficiaries of mercy
know themselves to have been given the status of righteousness freely;
those who have received so great a gift cannot object to the claim
wherewith God thereafter claims them. Indeed, *not* to derive the ground
for the observance of the law from the righteousness of *faith* would be
illogical.[165] Faith knows that that which rendered it faith claims it henceforth; it knows as well that the mercy which rendered it faith determines
the form of the claim: invitation is the corollary of God's mercy.

Since faith acknowledges sheer mercy as the ground of the law and
receives the claim as invitation, then gratitude is the only appropriate
attitude in which faith is to render its obedience. Faith knows that it has
(and therefore is) only what it has been given. Awareness of the gift can
imply only gratitude. Calvin leaves no doubt on this matter:

"The people should attest their gratitude by obeying the law. . . . It would
have been too base and absurd for them to refuse God as their lawgiver when
they knew that by him they had been purchased for himself."[166]

---

[161] *Comm.* Exod. 20:1.

[162] *Comm.* Exod. 19:36.

[163] *Comm.* Deut. 27:9.

[164] *Comm.* Matt. 22:37.

[165] *Comm.* Rom. 10:6.

[166] *Comm.* Deut. 6:20.

"In his promises God takes the initiative and anticipates us by his pure grace; but having thus freely granted us his grace, he immediately requires gratitude of us in return."[167]

The most moving exposition of gratitude as the motive of faith's obedience Calvin reserves for his sermon: "Ought we not to think, morning and evening, day and night, about the grace which is made ours in our Lord Jesus Christ, who is the sun given to illumine us? Would we not necessarily be dull and stupid if we did not know that he makes his spiritual brightness to shine upon us in order to bring us to salvation? And how does that occur except by the mercy of God? Afterwards, when we contemplate the grace that God gives us in order to maintain us in this present life, are we worthy of being nourished at his expense? No, we are not. But the whole of it comes through our Lord Jesus Christ. Then it is necessary that in our sleeping and our waking, in our drinking and our eating, in our rest and our work, in everything and through everything, we acknowledge the mercy wherein God has dealt with us, the remembering of which is a never-ending exercise. Also, when we pray to God it is necessary that his grace be kept before us. For what access should we have in speaking privately to him and in depositing all our cares and worries in his lap and even in calling him our father, except that we are carried along by his free goodness in our Lord Jesus Christ and that he has pardoned our transgressions? If we do not think of all this then we are entirely too dull and stupid."[168]

If in everything we are to acknowledge the mercy wherein God has dealt with us, and if the remembering of that mercy is a constant exercise, then the absence of a complementary gratitude in everything attests but dullness and stupidity. Indeed, faith's realization that mercy alone has turned death into life should draw faith irresistibly (*rapi*) to embrace the lawgiver.[169] For Calvin there is nothing more despicable than ingratitude. Conversely, it is the gratitude of faith which is efficacious in rendering faith obedient.[170] Calvin judges a succinct instance of this to be the account of the healed blind man's joining the company of Christ; this is the sign of the man's proper gratitude.[171] To the invitation of the merciful God faith can speak only a grateful "yes."

FAITH'S NEED OF THE LAW

Since the man of faith is precisely he who has been renewed by the Holy Spirit as he puts on Jesus Christ, the Son with whom the Father is ever pleased, is not the third use of the law superfluous? Does the new

---

[167]*Comm.* II Cor. 7:1.

[168]*Sermon* Eph. 4:31 ff. (translation mine).

[169]*Inst.* 2.8.15.

[170]Ibid. The root meaning of *validius* is "efficacious" rather than "powerful"(Battles).

[171]*Comm.* Matt. 20:34.

man need to be "shaped" in addition to the shape he has received in putting on Christ? The question here refers to the eschatological dimension of Calvin's thought. He insists that believers *are* sons with whom the Father is pleased—eschatologically; while they are not sin-ruled in their present life (Christ is king) they are sin-riddled. While they do possess, for instance, that understanding essential to faith and while they do have a renewed heart and mind eschatologically, they are yet persons of perverse heart and obtuse understanding. They will ever need encouragement in docility and obedience of heart; and they will ever need an understanding wisely regulated by the law of God.[172] Accordingly, believers never move beyond needing the law; they "must learn more thoroughly each day the nature of the Lord's will to which they aspire and be confirmed in their understanding of it. It is as if some servant, already prepared with all earnestness of heart to commend himself to his master, must search out and observe his master's ways more carefully in order to conform and accommodate himself to them."[173] Faith, although real, ever remains weak and prone to indolence. Consequently, faith needs not merely instruction but also exhortation in order to counteract the propensity towards transgression and in order to make "fresh progress" in its obedience to the divine will.[174] Regardless of how intensely faith aspires to realize in the present its sanctification, it is never so successful that the impediment of the flesh is no longer with it in this life. Throughout our life, then, we must contend against it. For this reason the law "is to the flesh like a whip to an idle and balky ass, to arouse it to work."[175]

Calvin preserves the careful balance between "realized" and "unrealized" eschatology in his insistence that believers, whom Christ has already redeemed from all iniquity, Christ must yet purify. Calvin is persistent and penetrating on this point. The law is not merely a rule of life, but, reflecting greater severity, a bridle which keeps faith in the fear of the Lord and a spur to correct the slackness of the flesh, "so far as it is profitable for teaching, correcting, and reproving" (*docendum, corrigendum, redarguendum*).[176] The lattermost word has the force of "confute," "refute," "contradict." In other words, even as Jesus Christ is *for* believ-

---

[172]*Comm.* Psalm 119:5: *mentem expetere atque nonnisi ex lege Dei sapiat.*

[173]*Inst.* 2.7.12: *est enim illis optimum organum, quo melius in dies ac certius discant qualis sit Domini voluntas, ad quam aspirant, atque in eius intelligentia confirmentur.*

[174]Ibid.: *quia non sola doctrina, sed exhortatione quoque indigemus, hanc quoque utilitatem ex lege capiet servus Dei, ut frequenti eius meditatione excitetur ad obsequium.*

. . .

[175]Ibid.: for same idea see *Comms.* Psalm 119:105 and Gal. 3:25.

[176]*Comm.* Gal. 3:25.

ers, and that definitively (that is, his being for them establishes and guarantees irrevocably their identity as believers) it is yet necessary for God (whose law it is) to be against them. To be sure, his being against them can never overturn his being for them; it can never expose them to his wrath definitively. Yet neither is it the case that his being for them eschatologically (and therefore finally) obviates his being against them. As long as believers continue to sin the law continues to be necessary.[177]

Since it cannot be denied that the law reflects God's intention for the shape of existence-in-faith, only "perfectionist faith" suggests that it is not inadmissible to depart from the law. It mistakenly thinks that the pattern of righteousness which the law reflects has been attained by faith here and now.[178] That men of faith are simultaneously sinners it denies. That error-beclouded faith, however, as well as any other misunderstanding which thinks it can depart from the law, will find itself in the ever-proximate labyrinth.[179] Faith needs the law of *God*: for *he* decrees the shape of existence-in-faith in *his* law. Faith does not pursue a "sort of fantastical holiness"; faith does not inform itself as to what it regards as a suitable or requisite "living out" of its life. Rather, the course of the life of faith (*regenda vitae*) is that direction which the Lord imparts.[180] Moreover, Calvin insists that God imparts a specific shape; he does not utter a plethora of principles which men snatch at and attempt to press into the service of their pursuit of holy living, only to find that other men have adapted other principles, so as to render the Christian life formless and vague. Rather, there is "but *one* everlasting and unchangeable rule."[181]

It is clear that Calvin contended that the believer ever needs to be "shaped" by means of the law. Earlier it was seen that the believer is "invited" rather than "compelled" to obey the law. How are these two aspects related? Calvin carefully maintains a dialectical balance on this matter: while the law must contradict (*redarguo*) the believer, at the same time the law is not alien to the life of faith, just as Jesus Christ, the substance of the law, is not alien to faith. While the law ever remains *law* and is not suggestion or advice or information, at the same time it is "not now acting towards us as a rigorous enforcement officer who is not

---

[177]For same idea see *Inst.* 2.7.14.

[178]*Inst.* 2.7.15.

[179]*Comms.* Psalm 19:8, Psalm 119:5, I Cor. 9:26, Col. 1:10.

[180]*Comms.* Psalm 119:1 and Psalm 1:2.

[181]*Inst.* 2.7.13 (italics mine): *siquidem non plures, sed una est perpetua et inflexibilis vivendi regula.*

satisfied unless the requirements are kept."[182] Jesus Christ's "contradicting" believers is always included within his being for them definitively.
The law of God ever contradicting ever remains necessary, but it is not
foreign to that which constitutes *faith*: Jesus Christ, who is God for us.

The foregoing dialectic Calvin describes in a variety of ways: while the
law continues to exercise power over faith, it does not have the power to
condemn; while believers are not spared the law, neither are they "under"
the law (since they are "under" grace). While faith is not relieved of the
law, it is relieved of the yoke and curse of the law.[183] Although the law
mirrors that sluggishness and imperfection which cling to faith, the law
has nonetheless lost its "sting."[184] Even as Jesus Christ cancelled that
judgment which the law brought down upon us, he informs believers of
the nature, object and scope of the law.[185] Since faith grounds its righteousness in the remission of sins, it is released from the "rigour" of the
law but not from the spur and the bridle.[186] In short, while it is the
proximity of Jesus Christ which bestows life, it is his very proximity
which insists as well that faith make concrete what it already is eschatologically. While servile fear is incompatible with faith, so is indulgence.

Similarly, Calvin's insistence that faith is "invited" to keep the law is
kept in dialectical tension with his insistence that obedience is *enjoined*;
that faith must obey the law Calvin judges to be "beyond all doubt."[187]
Although the law has lost its capacity to condemn believers, it has not lost
its authority over them—for Jesus Christ, the substance of the law *is* their
authority. As long as faith is constituted by *him*, it must ever receive the
law "with the same veneration and obedience."[188] Indeed, the *purpose* of
God's having accepted men in Christ and having raised them to newness
of life is to "manifest in the life of believers a harmony and agreement
between (his) righteousness and their obedience."[189] The refashioning of
men which occurs as the New Man is put on is precisely an "adjustment to
obedience to God alone."[190] While mercy is always the *prius* of faith,

---

[182]*Inst.* 2.7.13.

[183]*Comms.* Rom. 7:4 and Rom. 6:15.

[184]*Inst.* 2.7.14 and *Comm.* 1 Cor. 15:56.

[185]*Comm.* Matt. 5:21.

[186]*Inst.* 2.7.14.

[187]*Comm.* Gal. 3:12.

[188]*Inst.* 2.7.15.

[189]*Inst.* 3.6.1.

[190]*Comm.* Col. 1:10.

obedience is a necessary and inviolable implication; the law ever remains "only complement" of the gospel.[191]

Conversely, where obedience is lacking, grace is lacking; and where grace is lacking, faith is lacking. Hence Calvin does not hesitate to say that "Christ does not reconcile believers to the Father that they may act wantonly with impunity, but that by governing them with his Spirit he may keep them under the hand and rule of the Father. Whence it follows that *Christ's love is rejected except by those who prove by true obedience that they are his disciples.*"[192] Where there is no obedience there is no faith.

Elsewhere Calvin argues that obedience imparts assurance to faith. Now assurance, he reminds us, does not occur as faith looks in upon itself; assurance arises as faith looks away from itself to Christ, for Christ is Christ *pro nobis*: to contemplate Christ is to contemplate oneself in him. Assurance grows as believers, in obedience, live that life in Christ which their faith is given to envisage. Such obedience confirms their adoption as sons.[193] In other words, to live in accord with the contemplation of Christ and oneself in Christ is to *be* obedient. Again, lack of obedience attests lack of faith.

In a somewhat similar vein Calvin speaks of the law and of obedience as bridles to keep the flesh in check. Evidently the law checks the believer's propensity to sin only as it is obeyed. Hence Calvin can speak of obedience as both an encouraging of faith and as a subduing of the flesh.[194]

In sum, the consequence of God's awakening believers from a deadly sleep is that they are formed to obedience.[195]

Another instance of Calvin's careful dialectical balance occurs in his description of the attitude or spirit in which the law is to be obeyed. Just as there is a fear which is appropriate to faith and a fear which is the denial of faith,[196] in the same manner there is an obedience to the law which arises from unfaith's yielding to external (*alieno*) restraint and an obedience which is faith's willing (*voluntaria*) affirmation of the claim of God.[197] On the one hand, the unbeliever is obligated relentlessly to

---

[191]*Comm.* Matt. 5:17.

[192]*Comm.* John 15:10 (italics mine).

[193]*Inst.* 3.6.1.

[194]*Comm.* Heb. 6:4.

[195]*Comm.* II Tim. 2:25.

[196]*Comm.* Psalm 1:2.

[197]*Comms.* I Tim. 1:9 and Ezek. 11:19.

exercise obedience and thus finds himself under the discipline and "yoke" of the law; on the other hand, in faith he is delivered from that very "yoke."[198] The difference in the two types of obedience arises as faith "puts off" unfaith's attempted works-righteousness and, confronted with the proffered mercy and righteousness of Jesus Christ, finds itself rendered humble and meek. Indeed, the yoke becomes "easy" only through participation in the humility and meekness of Christ himself.[199]

Of course, to participate in Jesus Christ is to know the paternal love of the Father. Calvin maintains that it is precisely faith's awareness of the Father's constant love which effects faith's obedience to the law.[200] From the standpoint of the transformation which that love effects in believers, in turn, the source and cause of obedience is the love wherewith faith embraces God as Father.[201] In that believers know themselves embraced by God they "embrace" (a term which, in Calvin, refers *only* to the putting on of Christ) in turn what he ordains for them: they do not obey reluctantly or grudgingly; they do not approach the law with the attitude of complying with the "bare" requirements; they do not regard it as a lifeless precept to be performed mechanically. Instead, they reflect the dominical utterance, "Blessed are they who hear the Word of God and keep it," by embracing that Word "with whole-hearted affection."[202] Indeed, that obedience alone is of faith which embraces the law with "sincere affection";[203] the *end* of the law is the exciting of faith to yield obedience to God with a "more prompt and cheerful affection."[204]

This affectionate embracing of the law is possible only for faith, because faith, unlike unfaith, does not contemplate merely the precepts contained in the law but also the accompanying promise of grace, Jesus Christ; and his presence "*alone* sweetens what is bitter."[205] Truly, an obedience not marked by affection and cheerfulness is an obedience not elicited by God's love, which is to say, not elicited by God himself; an understanding of the law's demand which troubles and distresses souls points to a God who is less than loving and to a demand which is less than

---

[198] *Comms.* Matt. 11:29 and Gal. 2:20 respectively.

[199] *Comm.* Matt. 11:29.

[200] *Comm.* John 15:10.

[201] *Comm.* Deut. 7:9.

[202] *Comm.* James 1:25.

[203] *Comm.* Deut. 11:18.

[204] *Comm.* Psalm 19:7.

[205] *Inst.* 2.7.12 (italics mine).

serviceable in love.[206] Calvin repudiates both. Godly living commences only as the law of God attracts us to him by its sweetness; proficiency in the law occurs only as faith cheerfully sets its mind upon the law.[207] In the same spirit Calvin insists that the law is the "delight" of faith, compliance with which is "sweetness"; it is unfaith which finds the law bitter and burdensome.[208]

Reflecting the foregoing is Calvin's protracted treatment of the law's not being grievous. He notes that John restricts this assertion to God's children, lest anyone think that it applies to unfaith as well. Nonetheless, Calvin asks whether John's notion is an oversimplification: does not faith, although ruled by the Spirit of God, yet have to contend against the flesh, and that with only fragmentary success? Calvin replies that "the law is called easy (*facilem*) so far as we are endowed with heavenly power and overcome the lusts of the flesh. For however much the flesh may wanton, believers feel that there is no delight save in following God."[209] Calvin's interpretation is not facile, then. He does not pretend that faith's obedience ever becomes easy in the sense of cavalier; there is always a need for a resolve to obedience and a need for struggle. Faith ever has to "wrestle" and "fight" if it is to obey the Lord and serve him.[210] Faith's struggle with the flesh is perpetual. While the believer's heart is "whole" (in so far as it "seriously aspires to God") the believer's heart yet remains unwhole for as long as sin is present.[211] Calvin does not wish to suggest that the need for the believer to "become who he is" can be reduced to the simple (and "fantastical") assertion that he is in fact "who he is." The full force of the imperative the man of faith dare not forget.

At the same time, however, neither is the believer's uncharacteristic, counter-propensity to disobey crushing. He knows that to capitulate in the struggle is to render himself miserable, while aspiration to the Lordship of Christ, while not without its own turbulence, is alone satisfying. While godliness is no cavalier undertaking, God has ordained that in that undertaking alone the man of faith finds his fullfilment in true happiness.[212]

---

[206]Ibid.: *quid enim lege minus amabile, si flagitando tantum et minando metu sollicitet animas, et terrore angat?*

[207]*Comm.* Psalm 119:15.

[208]*Comms.* Malachi 1:6 and Psalm 119:47.

[209]*Comm.* I John 5:3.

[210]*Comms.* Ezek. 11:29 and I John 5:3.

[211]*Comm.* Ezek. 11:19.

[212]*Comm.* I Tim. 4:8 (cf. *Comm.* Gal. 5:18).

In short, since the man of faith does not contemplate the bare law (*lex nuda*) but sees in the law the fatherly kindness of God as well, he knows that succor is promised to him in the struggle and forgiveness in his failure. The knowledge of the Father's kindness renders the believer's obedience to the law "delightful," "sweet," and "easy." In a word, that obedience proper to faith can spring only from faith's *love*.[213]

Nonetheless, since the eschatological fulfilment of faith is never granted to earthly existence (that is, sin continues to riddle faith), may not the man of faith, rendered conscious of his own imperfection and weakness by means of the mirror of the law, find himself plunged into anxiety? Since it is essential that there be progress in obedience, and since the law is the measure of that progress, could not the believer's attempted discernment of that progress render faith anxious?[214] While faith is not subject to the judgment of men, it most certainly is to the judgment of God; while a believer may live unworried that his law-fulfilment is hid "in the opinion of the world," can he live unworried knowing that its veridicality is hid "even to our own senses"?[215]

Calvin replies that the believer's life is hid with Christ in God and therefore its existence is out of danger, even though its reality (including the reality of its obedience) is not disclosed to neutral observers, including the believer himself in so far as he is making a natural assessment. Notwithstanding, *God's* faithfulness dispels anxiety, for he will not "deny what has been committed to him, nor disappoint us in the guardianship which he has undertaken. . . . Hence there is no reason why we should be alarmed if, wherever we look, we nowhere see life. For we are saved by hope."[216] While the renewal which faith puts on is so "secret" as to be hid even from the believer's "senses," it *is* apprehended by faith.[217] By faith the believer discerns the eschatological reality and is hence spared anxiety as the law continues to indicate that the believer's authenticity has not yet been manifested. Assurance of his own authenticity is ever borne in upon the faith of the believer even as there is no inter-subjective evidence of it. While the believer's authenticity is *entirely* hid with Christ in God, faith *knows* this indubitably to be the case: "the life, therefore, which we obtain

---

213*Comm.* Psalm 119:159.

214*Comms.* Psalm 1:2 and Psalm 119:15.

215*Comm.* Col. 3:3.

216Ibid.

217*Comm.* Rom. 7:23.

by faith is not visible to the eye, but is inwardly perceived in the conscience by the Holy Spirit."[218]

Indeed, as has been indicated elsewhere, the man of faith does not properly obey the law if, in his sin and weakness, he is fearful. God can be served only with tranquil mind; to "toss with anxiety" is not to serve him at all.[219] Calvin adds that in the face of the austerity of the command of Christ the disciples became anxious; and Christ freed them from "all anxiety."[220]

Thus, Calvin insists, because Christ dispels the disciples' anxiety the law must be obeyed joyfully or it is not really obeyed. Where joy in obedience is lacking it must be questioned whether Jesus Christ has been put on, for obedience in his Spirit is man's greatest joy.[221]

OBEDIENCE IN FAITH
IS NOT SUBMISSION TO IDEOLOGY

The law requires, in Calvin's vocabulary, that believers "walk in God's ways" and yield obedience to the law's "dictates."[222] The language suggests that prescriptions are made according to which faith is to order its life: believers adjust themselves to a code. Does the law in fact require for faith behavioral conformity to a standard? Does the doing of God's will mean compliance with a statute? A not unusual caricature of the Christian life is that while the believer may be oriented in a direction different from that of unfaith, the orientation itself is not qualitatively different: a religious or secular ideology has given way to a Christian one. Does Calvin, then, assert that faith's obedience is the implementation of an ideology (even though faith, the putting on of Christ, can never be ideology)? Indeed he does not. Calvin insists that faith's doing the Father's will does not mean "to adopt one's life and behaviour to the pattern of virtues in the philosophic sense. . . ."[223] Since God comes to us in the character of a true and faithful husband, that obedience which faith renders can be only love and faithfulness to *him*, and not conformity to a code.[224] While God is indeed lawgiver, the nature of the obedience which

---

[218] *Comm.* Gal. 2:20.

[219] *Comm.* Luke 1:74.

[220] *Comm.* Matt. 19:25.

[221] *Comms.* Psalm 1:2, Psalm 19:7, Psalm 40:8, Psalm 119:115.

[222] *Comms.* Rom. 7:6 and Psalm 119:1.

[223] *Comm.* Matt. 7:21.

[224] *Inst.* 2.8.18.

faith renders is controlled by the nature of the law; *its* nature, in turn, is to be appraised by the "character" of the lawgiver.[225] God's *ingenium* ("character," "disposition") is not that of a bare statute or abstraction, but is rather sheer, self-giving love. Accordingly, any human response to the command which is not generated by and does not revere that self-giving love is simply not *obedience*. The God who is this self-giving love acts from the *heart*; the response he requires of men is from the heart.[226] Mere behavioral adjustment or ideological conformity Calvin speaks of as a pseudo law-keeping which involves feet, hands and eyes, but not the heart; as such it is but a pretence to obedience.[227] Indeed, where hands, feet and eyes only are enlisted there has occurred a fulfillment of the letter without any orientation to the truth.[228]

All of the above indicates that faith's obedience is always rendered to a Person; to obey the commandments is to submit oneself to him; to find his commandments other than burdensome is to discern who has given them. While the law certainly is for Calvin a standard or measure, it is that impersonally only where it is abstracted from Christ. "*God himself*," not precepts or a code, is to be faith's guide.[229] Altering the vocabulary slightly Calvin first reminds his readers that the Word of God (Jesus Christ) and faith are correlates, and then adds that obedience to the law is subsumed under that relationship.[230] Our lives are *directed* by Jesus Christ himself.[231] Elsewhere Calvin stresses at length that God accommodates himself to our capacity in his bestowal of the law.[232] *The* culmination of this accommodation is Incarnation. Herein God does not accommodate himself to us by reducing or weakening the law-requirements, but by living our human existence. The manifestation of life according to the law, then, so far from being adherence to a code, is the shape imparted to human existence by God himself living ("living out") our existence.

The lawgiver wants to possess *us*, and not merely coerce from us an act abstracted from us; to this end he requires of us integrity of soul, spirit,

---

[225]*Inst.* 2.8.6: *id fit quia in legislatorem non respiciunt a cuius ingenio natura quoque legis aestimanda est.*

[226]*Comm.* Matt. 5:21.

[227]*Comm.* Psalm 40:8.

[228]*Comm.* Psalm 119:1.

[229]*Comm.* Psalm 119:59 (italics mine).

[230]*Comm.* James 1:22.

[231]*Comm.* I Cor. 6:20.

[232]*Sermon* Job 9:25-33.

and body.[233] The purpose of the law is that man cleave (*cohaerere*) to *God*
as God joins him to himself.[234]

OBEDIENCE: THE FORMATION OF JESUS CHRIST
IN THE BELIEVER

Once it is acknowledged that the obedience required of faith is faith's
continuing orientation to Jesus Christ, there remains to be specified what
that orientation effects in believers. Does it effect "moral improvement"?
Is the end of putting on Christ moral reformation? Admittedly, on
occasion Calvin can be found suggesting that this is the case; for example,
his speaking of God's shaping (*formo*) his people according to an explicit
plan.[235] However, such assertions must be understood in the context of
Calvin's less ambiguous utterances. He does insist that since Jesus Christ
is the life of believers, and since Jesus Christ is that true humanity which
will finally transform humanity at the *eschaton*, and since God's grace
relieves the believer of the shipwreck of life and restores him to "another
life,"[236] then law-obedience is that by which the One who *is* the life of
believers eschatologically becomes that life now. He is the shape which
existence-in-faith assumes in obedience to him. Jesus Christ is not only
that to which obedience is oriented, but also the reality which is effected in
believers through their obedience. Existence-in-faith is formed as Jesus
Christ "forms himself" in it.

Undeniably, Calvin does not always render this as explicit as he
might; nevertheless, the allusions to it are sufficiently frequent and unambiguous that his intention is not an open question. For instance, he states
that the *law* of God "contains in itself that newness by which his image can
be restored in us."[237] The image of God is Jesus Christ himself; as true
humanity he *is* that newness. Obedience to the law, then, is that by which
the image is formed *anew* in believers, restoring them to their true,

---

[233] *Inst.* 2.8.44: *legislator . . . nempe is, qui quum nos totos possidere debeat, iure suo, animae, spiritus et corporis integritatem requirit.*

[234] *Inst.* 2.8.51. E. A. Dowey appears to regard the law as code, as when he speaks, for example, of the Spirit's work "bringing the believer again into harmony with the law" (*The Knowledge of God in Calvin's Theology*, 237). Nowhere in Dowey's work is there an explicit statement that suggests that obedience to the law is something other than conformity to a code.

[235] *Inst.* 3.7.1; cf. *Comm.* Jer. 31:33, where Calvin speaks of the sovereignty of the *law* in human life.

[236] *Comm.* Gal. 2:20.

[237] *Inst.* 3.6.1: *etsi autem novitatem illam qua imago Dei in nobis instauratur, lex ipsius in se continet.*

essential humanity. Elsewhere Calvin speaks of believers as those who are being "formed" by the hand of God.[238] But after what does God "form" his people except the Man with whose obedience he is always pleased?

It is evident that, with respect to the gospel, *eschatological* newness of life is the characteristic of faith (that is, the characteristic of putting on Christ); with respect to the law the characteristic of faith is the putting on the *present activity* of Christ as he restores believers to that image which he is. The shape of existence-in-faith, so far from being wrought by the inculcation of "philosophic virtues" or "moral reformation," is Jesus Christ himself living and reigning in the believer.[239] Jesus Christ alone is to be the glory of the believer.[240]

The foregoing should be the occasion of no surprise. When Jesus Christ is known to be the substance of the law and the one to whom faith's obedience is oriented, the effect of such obedience can be only the formation of Jesus Christ in believers. That "enlarging of the heart" of which the natural man is wholly incapable and which is found only in faith's obedience can be only the "expansion" of Jesus Christ within the believer. What he commands, God first gives.[241]

Appendix I. In dealing with this aspect of Calvin's theology R. S. Wallace remarks, "to live a life according to the image of God is to live according to the law."[242] The converse emphasis is truer to Calvin: to live according to the law is to live a life according to the image of God; that is, the latter defines the former. Wallace's formulation suggests that the law is or could be code. Wallace appears subsequently to make this very suggestion: ". . . knowing our weakness and seeking to supply our need, (God) accommodates himself to our capacity and gives us in the law an image of his incomprehensible and hidden justice. . . . Calvin sees in the law, especially as we have it in the Ten Commandments, a pattern and image which truly reflects the perfect and yet hidden justice of God."[243] Wallace does not safeguard his readers against the forensic interpretation of "justice" (that is, that believers are arraigned before a court); and nowhere does he suggest that faith's obedience of the law is the formation of Jesus Christ in believers as he "enlarges" their hearts. Wallace does subsequently refer to God's delineating his character in the law, but he

---

[238] *Comm.* Eph. 2:10.

[239] *Inst.* 3.7.1.

[240] *Comm.* Phil. 3:8.

[241] *De Aet. Dei Praed.* 107 and *Comm.* Psalm 119:32.

[242] R. S. Wallace, *Calvin's Doctrine of the Christian Life,* 112.

[243] Ibid.

does not comment upon the precise force of "character" in Calvin. Admittedly, Calvin's language can suggest obedience to a code and moral reformation as the effect of that obedience; for example, the law shows believers what "cannot be adjusted or diminished."[244] However, such an interpretation fails to discern both the coherence and subtlety of Calvin's thought.

Wendel is alive to the theological strengths of Calvin's theology. He notes that a legalistic interpretation of the law disappears for faith since it understands the gospel to "assimilate the law to itself."[245] While Wendel is correct, his vocabulary might lead one to think that Calvin implies an impersonal absorption of one thing by another. A better formulation is that believers are spared condemnation even as they are conformed to Jesus Christ.

Wendel also comments that "what we find (in Calvin's work), in fact, is a spiritualization of the law in its relation to those who have received the gift of the law and have been received into Christ."[246] By "spiritualization" Wendel wishes to indicate, among other things, the fact that for faith the law is not the letter. However, some caution should be exercised in the employment of the word "spiritualization" if it tends to suggest lack of concreteness; according to Calvin human existence is shaped *concretely* as Jesus Christ is put on and the law is obeyed.

THE REWARDS OF THE LAW

Mercy is the gospel-promise. Faith puts on mercy. By definition, then, faith receives the gospel-promise (even where the Mediator has not yet "appeared"). The situation is different, however, with respect to the law-promises, for here the rewards or fruits which the law-promises hold forth God guarantees only to him who performs or fulfils the law: "there is recompense ready for you if you do what they enjoin."[247] The promises of the law pertain to the service or employment (*ministerium*) of the law which faith renders; here the condition attached to the law-promise pertains as much to faith as to unfaith: unless the law is fulfilled, recompense is not forthcoming.

Moreover, it is this very condition which establishes the significance of faith's works: apart from the conditional promises there would be no

[244]*Sermon* Eph. 4:23-26.

[245]P. Wendel, *Calvin*, 205.

[246]Ibid.

[247]*Inst.* 3.17.6.

value to works before God.[248] Admittedly, the value of the works does not inhere the works themselves; value arises solely from the situation of promise/fulfillment which God has ordained. And he *has* ordained it.

Calvin does suggest from time to time that the renewed heart and mind (that is, faith) are indeed able to fulfil the law. Such confidence he exudes as he informs us that "once God has enlarged our hearts there will be no lack of power because, along with proper affection, he will furnish ability."[249] In spite of such remarks, Calvin does fundamentally preserve the determinative eschatological dimension of his theology: believers continue to sin, and *qua* sinners, never meet the requirements of the law so as to enjoy the rewards promised in the law. In truth, so very sin-riddled is the believer's obedience that Calvin speaks of the fulfilment of the law as "nowhere visible."[250] Recompense is promised to perfect law-keepers; not one is to be found.

At the same time, since Calvin is certain that God does not mock believers through the law-promises, then in some manner the rewards pertaining to those promises must be made to accrue to believers. The accrual occurs in so far as God contemplates believers in Jesus Christ; that is, since he is not who he is apart from the people he includes in his own life, the Father's finding him the perfect law-fulfiller implies the Father's regarding those in him as such too.[251] In that Jesus Christ is the fulfilment of the conditions attached to the law there accrue to those in fellowship with him the recompenses that he alone deserves: "for the Lord then freely bestows all things upon us so as to add to the full measure of his kindness this gift also: that not rejecting our imperfect obedience, but rather supplying what is lacking to complete it, he causes us to receive the benefit of the promises of the law *as if* we had fulfilled their condition."[252] Needless to say, it is only by his fatherly kindness and generosity, in sum his mercy, that God "raises works to this place of honour so that he attributes some value to them."[253] In light of this mercy Calvin states that "walking in the commandments of God" is not the precise equivalent of performing whatever the law demands; rather, the expression points to "the indulgence with which God regards his children and pardons their

---

[248]*Comm.* Rom. 3:20.

[249]*Comm.* Psalm 119:32.

[250]*Inst.* 3.17.3.

[251]For a discussion of Christ's perfect obedience see *Inst.* 2.12.3 and 2.16.5-7.

[252]*Inst.* 2.7.4 (italics mine): *perinde atque a nobis impleta conditione, legalium promissionum fructum percipere nos facit.*

[253]*Inst.* 3.17.3.

faults. The promise, therefore, is not without fruit as respects believers, while they endeavour to consecrate themselves to God, although they are still far from perfection. . . . Their obedience is not acceptable to him because it is deserving, but because he visits it with his paternal favour."[254]

God concludes believers in his Son, with whom he is ever pleased. This fact alone effects that accrual of law-reward to believers. However, God concludes in his Son only those who put on mercy, the gospel-promise. Thus the matter of believers' works being regarded as a fulfillment of the law devolves upon the relation of the law-promises to the gospel-promise. Calvin maintains that the promise-element in the law is an instance of God's "goodness" and as such is identical with the gospel-promise; *the* promise, in turn, is sheer mercy. Accordingly, the "goodness" indicated in the law should incite people to lay hold of the gospel-promise, and in doing this, find their situation *coram Deo* altered.[255] That alteration occurs, of course, as persons are engrafted into Christ and their works are "covered" by his. Since this engrafting is effected only through faith, Calvin concludes that the law-promises are changed from fruitless to fruitful "only by the *intervention of faith*."[256] Calvin's contention must not be weakened here: faith alone is the demarcation between life blessed by God in accordance with his promises and life which foregoes blessedness. Similarly, Calvin insists that such blessedness the Lord imparts only to those who respond to his call.[257] God is pleased with faith alone as faith is that by which grace is received; and grace alone procures worthiness and value for works.[258]

With this aspect of faith as well Calvin is concerned to maintain a proper balance: while it would be "fanatical" to claim perfect obedience, at the same time that "intervention of faith" which is of determinative significance eschatologically is not without significance for faith's self-understanding and activity in the present. Even as believers are sin-riddled in their striving to seek God "with all their heart" (and hence never do in fact), there remains a difference in the "heart-condition" of faith and unfaith. Indeed, Calvin contrasts faith's "whole" heart with unfaith's "double" heart. The "perfection" predicated of faith, then, is not that faultlessness which can never be found in men, but "integrity or sincer-

---

[254]*Comm.* Levit. 26:3.

[255]*Comm.* Rom. 10:5.

[256]*Inst.* 3.17.3 (italics mine).

[257]*Inst.* 3.17.6.

[258]*Comm.* Heb. 11:2.

ity."[259] While the flesh ever impedes the spirit's fulfilling of the law, the spirit is sovereign; appropriately, therefore, the believer "judges and estimates himself by that part particularly."[260] In the light of the free imputation of Christ's righteousness believers are to regard themselves as law-keepers in as much as they *apply* themselves to it, regardless of how defective their law-keeping may be in fact.[261] God is pleased with that will and willingness to obey which is a strenuous pressing on to the goal, the imperfection of which God will receive with fatherly indulgence.[262] What matters is that believers aspire (*adspirant*) with serious and sincere affection to keep the law unto death.

Nonetheless, those who know themselves admitted to the blessings of the promises by the sheer mercy of God know as well that they must always rest ultimately in his goodness—or faith will perish.[263] The identification of both believers and their works as righteous will always rest in the *imputation* of righteousness and the non-imputation of sin.[264]

APPENDIX I:
THE GREATER "CLARITY" OF THE GOSPEL

Since Jesus Christ is the substance of both law and gospel, is not the gospel superfluous? If the distinction between law and letter was known under the law, then what does the gospel add to the law? Calvin speaks of the gospel as "the clear manifestaton of Christ" and argues that "gospel," in the broad sense, "includes those testimonies of his mercy and fatherly favour which God gave to the patriarchs of old."[265] Repeatedly he iterates that the gospel imports no new content; gospel and law are qualitatively identical. Nonetheless, there is a quantitative difference: while God certainly manifested *himself* under the law and the gospel, he did so rela-

---

[259]*Comm.* Jer. 29:13; cf. Wallace's remark, "Perfection, for Calvin, consists not in attaining to this and that virtue in the highest possible degree, but in whole-heartedness, integrity, and sincerity" (*Calvin's Doctrine of the Christian Life*, 122).

[260]*Comm.* Rom. 7:22.

[261]*Comm.* John 16:10.

[262]*Comms.* Deut. 30:12, I Cor. 9:24, Matt. 5:48.

[263]*Comm.* Rom. 4:14.

[264]*Comms.* Deut. 12:28 and Psalm 119:1; cf. *Inst.* 3.17.1: "For our assurance, our glory, and the sole anchor of our salvation are that Christ the son of God is ours, and we in turn are in him sons of God and heirs of the kingdom of heaven, called to the hope of eternal blessedness by God's grace, not by our worth."

[265]*Inst.* 2.9.2.

tively "obscurely" in the former and with "fuller light" in the latter.[266] While God himself was indubitably known under the law, and known in "the same image" as now, he was known without "full splendour," without "full light."[267] While faith always apprehends the Mediator, it does so more distinctly through the gospel than through the law. While the fathers did not await salvation (this they already possessed) they did await the clear manifestation (*conspicua manifestione*) of it.[268] Indeed, since the righteousness of faith was not hidden (*latuisse*) prior to the coming of Christ, there is evidently a double manifestation, the second one being the fullfilment of the promises of the first, together with a fuller clarity (*plenior claritas*).[269] Calvin avers explictly that the difference between the fathers and contemporary believers "is only one of degree. . . . What they had in small measure we have more fully (*plenius*)."[270] Since the clarity of faith was not so openly manifested under the law, the new covenant is called the time of faith, "but relatively, not absolutely."[271]

In explicating the reason for the need of a double manifestation Calvin refers repeatedly to God's mercifully accommodating himself to men in their elementary capacity. What was known under the law were the first elements; what is known under the gospel is an advance on them.[272] Children whose weakness cannot bear the full knowledge of heavenly things God spares from knowing him "intimately."[273] Calvin indicates as much in the title to *Institutes* 2.9; "Christ, although he was known to the Jews under the law, was at length clearly (*demum*) revealed only in the gospel." *Demum* means both "at length, now at last," and "precisely." Both meanings are required: there is revelation in history, and God accommodates himself to its recipients; the culmination (fulfil-

---

[266] *Comm.* Jer. 31:34.

[267] *Inst.* 2.9.1.

[268] *Comm.* I Pet. 1:10. This statement is typical of Calvin's thought. Atypical is his remark that the fathers did not yet possess salvation (*Inst.* 2.9.1: *sed quia thesauro potit non sunt*).

[269] *Comm.* Rom. 3:21.

[270] *Comm.* I Cor. 10:3.

[271] *Comm.* Gal. 3:23. Calvin's point may be allowed to stand despite the inadequacy of his exegesis. The verse ("Now before faith came. . . .") does not refer to "relatively" rather than "absolutely." Calvin attempts to redress the inadequacy of his exegeis saying, "The Jews were besieged on every hand by the curse; but against this siege there were built the prison walls which protected them from the curse. So that Paul shows the prison of the law to have been in fact beneficent in spirit." This statement, however, remains inadequate.

[272] *Comm.* Jer. 31:34.

[273] *Inst.* 2.7.2: *nam qui nondum familiariter innotuerat Christus, similes fuerunt pueris.*

lment) of that revelation is also its moment of greatest clarity. Elsewhere Calvin maintains that under the law there was "tasted" the fullness of grace that was shown forth in Christ.[274] His use of "taste" reflects a deliberate multivocality: while not as much is consumed in a mere "taste" as in a full eating, at the same time the flavor is so experienced as to preclude any suggestion that what is consumed in one case contradicts what is consumed in the other.

Admittedly, Calvin's treatment of the precise distinction between the two manifestations is somewhat inelegant. He realizes that he is having difficulty articulating the distinction as he has recourse to "as it were" (in the gospel "God comes near to us, as it were"[275]), "in a manner," "it is said," and so forth.[276] At the end Calvin can say only that while the same light shines in law and gospel, it shines more brightly in the latter.

Appendix II. While that aspect of the law which gives shape to existence-in-faith remains, that aspect which is the cultus of Israel has been abrogated; what the law foreshadowed under types, the gospel now points out with the finger.[277] Through the "shadow" of the cultus (for example, the scapegoat sacrifice) "believers might learn that they were in no wise competent to bear God's judgment, nor could be delivered from it otherwise than by the transfer of their guilt and crime";[278] the "finger" of the gospel points to the One who did in fact bear that judgment, the need for which the shadow but attested. While the sacrifices are "shadows" of the substance, they are never the substance itself.[279]

At the same time, "shadow" does not have the force of "nothing." Admittedly, in his unguarded moments Calvin suggests that it has; for example, "the whole legal worship was nothing more than a picture which adumbrated (*adumbraverit*) the spiritual in Christ," and the sacrifices "had nothing in them but the blood of beasts which does not reach to the soul, whereas the power (*virtus*) of Christ is something quite different."[280] Nonetheless, the undeniable tenor of Calvin's teaching is that the sacrifices were not without effect, and that since the passion of Jesus Christ their

---

[274]*Inst.* 2.7.1: *plenitudinem gratiae, cuius gustum sub lege perceperant Iudaei, in Christo exhibitam esse docens.* For same idea see *Inst.* 2.9.1.

[275]*Comm.* Jer. 31:34.

[276]E.g., *Inst.* 2.9.4.

[277]*Inst.* 2.9.3.

[278]*Comm.* Lev. 16:20.

[279]*Comm.* Daniel 9:27.

[280]*Comms.* Heb. 8:5 and Heb. 10:4.

use has been abrogated but not their effect.[281] To be sure, Jesus Christ *is* their effect; they have none apart from him. But neither were the sacrifices "apart from him." While the sacrifices were operative, with respect to atonement, only in virtue of Christ's death and resurrection, his presence in the shadows obviates their being *mere* shadows.[282] Cessation of use does not imply voiding of significance:

> "It was only the practice of the ceremonies that was abrogated; their significance was actually given more confirmation. So Christ's coming did not take anything away, even from the ceremonies, but rather the truth behind the shadows was revealed, and served to strengthen them. Seeing the concrete fact, we recognize that they were not vain or useless."[283]

> "But the gospel did not so supplant the entire law as to bring forward a different way of salvation. Rather, it confirmed and satisfied whatever the law had promised, and gave substance to the shadows."[284]

> "As God gave rules for ceremonies on the basis that their outward use should last for a period but their significance be everlasting, one does not do away with ceremonies when their reality is kept and their shadow is omitted."[285]

> "In themselves they are vain and shadowy images, and will be found to possess reality only in reference to a better end. Their highest confirmation, therefore, lies in the fact that they have attained their truth in Christ."[286]

The ceremonial law, then, is not a religious accretion of no Christological significance; it is not a species of magic or manipulation unrelated to faith. Its significance lies solely in its being the proleptic, effectual anticipation of that death and resurrection which has occurred "once for all." And since the benefits of that death and resurrection are not received apart from faith, the "power" of the ceremonies could have been apprehended only in faith. Calvin insists that God did not command the sacrifices because of any supposed intrinsic worth, but rather because he "intended to lead the ancient people by such exercises to repentance and faith."[287] Indeed, the *sole* purpose of the ceremonies was the assisting of faith.[288] This point must be stressed. Ceremonies benefit only because Jesus Christ is their substance; but to say this is to say that they benefit

---

[281]*Inst.* 2.7.16 and *Comm.* Matt. 5:17.

[282]*Inst.* 2.7.16.

[283]*Comm.* Matt. 5:17.

[284]*Inst.* 2.9.4.: *sed non ita successit evangelium toti legi, ut diversam rationem salutis offerret; quin potius ut sanciret ratumque esse probaret quidquid illa promiserat et corpus umbris adiungeret.* For same idea see *Comm.* Jer. 31:34.

[285]*Comm.* Matt. 5:19.

[286]*Comm.* Rom. 3:31.

[287]*Comm.* Micah 6:6.

[288]*Comm.* Acts 15:9.

only because they pertain to faith; they do not benefit simply because they are performed. The ceremonies never were a quasi-magical manipulation of "blessings" in contrast to that blessing of the New Covenant for which faith is so essential that Calvin can write, "it is no ordinary praise of faith to call it the *cause* of our salvation."[289] Concerning ceremonial law and gospel Calvin maintains there to be no difference in either Word or faith.[290] The fathers did not obtain righteousness by the ceremonies, but by "cleanness of heart."[291]

Not surprisingly, Calvin avers again that God's instituting the ceremonies was yet another instance of his accommodating himself to men. The sacrifices were "adventitious" in that God "had respect solely for men";[292] they reflect his condescension in his giving himself to "elemental" human understanding pending the appearance of the Mediator. However, they do not, of themselves, pertain to the essence of the Mediator: the substance does not inhere the shadow. When the need for accommodation (of this sort) has passed, the shadow's passing does not impugn the substance.

Calvin insists that the very coming of Jesus Christ (who is the substance and truth of the ceremonies) terminates their use; his passion, which seals their effect, also abrogates them.[293] The fullfilment of the ceremonies also renders them obsolete. Since God, in the gospel, speaks "as it were face to face and not under a veil," it is entirely inappropriate to attempt to contemplate him other than where he speaks "unveiled."[294] Since faith now contemplates God as present in Jesus Christ rather than having him "represented in figures as absent," there is no excuse for preferring the figures.[295] The manifestation of Jesus Christ means that the ceremonial law, in so far as its outward aspect differs from that of the gospel, has ended; indeed, once he has been manifested all "types" *must* cease; to continue the ceremonies is to fail to recognize the uniqueness and sufficiency of Christ's sacrifice.[296] Moreover, since the fathers, in the

---

[289] *Comm.* Luke 8:11 (italics mine).

[290] *Comm.* Heb. 10:16.

[291] *Comm.* Acts 15:9.

[292] *Comms.* Col. 2:14 and Psalm 40:8.

[293] *Comm.* Psalm 40:8 and *Inst.* 2.7.16.

[294] *Comm.* Jer. 31:31. "Veil" here refers to the relative obscurity of the law. Concerning the ceremonies "veil" can have the meaning it has in II Cor. 3:6. See "remembrance" below.

[295] *Comm.* Luke 16:16.

[296] *Comms.* Gal. 3:25, Heb. 1:3, Heb. 9:12, Heb. 10:16.

era of the ceremonies, were united to Jesus Christ only by faith and not in virtue of the cult as such, the continuation of the ceremonies when he whom they foreshadow is present is sheer unfaith.[297] Indeed, it is the appearance of the substance to faith which exposes the shadows as shadows. In other words, while the shadows were not without value for faith, they never were the object of faith: "those ceremonial practices indeed properly belonged to the doctrine of piety, inasmuch as they kept the church of the Jews in service and reverence to God, and yet could be distinguished from piety itself."[298] Jesus Christ, without the ceremonies, is sufficient for piety itself.

Calvin maintains as well that just as letter could be mistaken for law, so shadow may be mistaken for substance—and with the same result. To mistake shadow for substance is, in effect, to deprive Jesus Christ of his power.[299] The unfaith which makes this mistake does not find in the law the One who is the substance of the law, and therefore does not find in the law the exercise of "spiritual worship" or "the simple Word of God"; instead it is dragged along by its own inventions and pursues the flesh rather than the Spirit.[300] In a word, unfaith bows its neck to the wrong yoke.[301]

Since unfaith contemplates only the shadow, it forfeits mercy. Now Calvin argues that the cultus was an organ of worship whereby Israel confessed itself guilty and worthy of death.[302] It looked to Jesus Christ as the remedy for that guilt and death. In so far as unfaith contemplates the shadow, however, it fails to contemplate the Propitiator, and instead repeatedly confirms itself in its guilt. Of itself the shadow can attest guilt but cannot eradicate it.[303] The law minus the "power" of Jesus Christ is the power of Christlessness: the power of sin and condemnation. Indeed,

---

[297]*Comm.* Heb. 11:2.

[298]*Inst.* 4.20.5. However, Calvin does point out that once the substance has appeared, thus exposing the shadow as shadow, faith can yet benefit from the reading of the ceremonial law: "Although the rite of sacrificing is abolished, it yet greatly assists our faith to compare the reality of the types, so that we may seek in the one what the other contains" (*Comm.* I Pet 1:19). Because faith knows that Jesus Christ is the substance of the shadow and thus will not mistake shadow for substance, it can be informed by perusing the shadow.

[299]*Comm.* Col. 2:17.

[300]*Comm.* Acts 7:44.

[301]*Comm.* Col. 2:17.

[302]*Inst.* 2.7.17.

[303]*Comm.* Col. 2:14: *nihil prae se ferebat aliud quam obligationem.*

the ceremonies seal the condemnation.[304] Hence Calvin concludes that "there was not one of all the ceremonies of the law which did not fetter a man in the guilt of sin. . . ."[305] While Christ is the blotting out of the written bond against men, the ceremonies abstracted from Christ are but the rewriting of it.[306]

In the light of the foregoing Calvin insists that there is a "remembrance" of sin in the ceremonies, in so far as in the ceremonies *themselves* God had not dealt definitively with sin.[307] In Jesus Christ, however, he has "effaced the remembrance."[308] He argues that believers, being yet sin-riddled, must remember their depravity, and remember it in such a way as to confess before God their guilt and the necessity of a sacrifice as remedy.[309] Faith "remembers" its sin (and dares to "remember" it) just because God no longer "remembers" it. Unfaith, however, fails to discern that in Jesus Christ, God no longer "remembers" sin, and is therefore determined by sin. Unfaith looks to that which "remembers" sin (the shadow); faith looks to God who does not. To contemplate the substance-less shadow is to go behind what God has "forgotten" and reacquaint him with it.

---

[304]Ibid.

[305]*Comm.* Acts 13:39; for same idea see *Inst.* 2.7.17.

[306]*Comm.* Col. 2:14.

[307]*Comm.* Heb. 10:16.

[308]*Comm.* Col. 2:14.

[309]*Comm.* Heb. 10:3.

CHAPTER 7

THE CHURCH AND FAITH

Calvin introduces his discussion of the Church with the reminder that Jesus Christ becomes ours and we become partakers of his benefits only by faith. Of itself, however, such faith ever remains weak, ignorant, lazy and fickle. It must be both nourished and guided if belivers are to arrive at the goal of faith, the completion of the good work which God has begun in them.[1] Without nourishment and guidance faith does not endure. Accordingly, God is Father (that is, the propitious One who adopts people and brings them to faith) only to those for whom the Church is mother.[2] Since Father and mother are never rent asunder, outside the Church there is no faith. Calvin maintains that Christians are called (which calling, of course, is the *sine qua non* of faith) into union with Christ only inasmuch as they are united with all the elect under Christ the head; Christ is Lord of the believer in so far as he is head of the *body*. Apart from union with that body one receives none of Christ's benefits— now or in the future.[3] Indeed, believers are precisely those who have been gathered into the society of Christ (*societas*) and who, as a community (*communitas*) form one flock.[4]

As was seen earlier the gospel alone creates and maintains faith. The Church can nourish and guide faith, then, only in so far as God has "deposited" the gospel in the Church.[5] Since God has indeed made this deposit Calvin is thoroughly consistent in maintaining that "there is no other way to enter into life unless this mother conceive us in her womb, give us birth, nourish us at her breast, and lastly, unless she keeps us under her care and guidance until, putting off mortal flesh, we become like the angels. Our weakness does not allow us to be dismissed from her school until we have been pupils all our lives. Furthermore, away from her

---

[1] *Inst.* 4.1.1.

[2] Ibid.

[3] *Inst.* 4.1.2.

[4] *Inst.* 4.1.3.

[5] *Inst.* 4.1.1: *thesaurum hunc apud ecclesiam deposuit.*

bosom one cannot hope for any forgiveness of sins or any salvation. . . ."[6] Spiritual food is extended only through the hand of the Church; those who spurn her starve.[7] Believers who ever remain "babes in Christ" despite their steady advance to that which they *are* eschatologically repudiate the Church at their peril.

While the Church thus remains necessary to faith, it yet never becomes (part of) the object of faith: while Father and mother together "parent" believers, and while believers must affirm the Church to be God-ordained (failure to make this affirmation is an attestation of unbelief) and in this sense must "believe the Church," to believe *in* the Church would be idolatrous.[8] While the Church is what it is and can assist faith only because the gospel has been "deposited" in it, it is not metamorphosed into that "treasure"; the body's ever being conjoined to the head does not mean that the body becomes the head. Throughout this discussion of the Church, then, Calvin guards against confusing the society of Christ with its Lord, and also against sundering that society from its Lord.

As God-ordained the Church is indestructible. Calvin adduces several considerations pertaining to this matter, all of which are, at bottom, identical: the Church will endure because of her peculiar relation to the gospel, to the decree of election, and to Christ's death.[9] In "depositing" the gospel in the Church God has bound the Church to Jesus Christ; then the Church can no more be destroyed than Christ's death can be made barren.[10] In other words, the Church exists and will ever exist in that God, having intended a people for himself, intends their continuance and consummation as his "chosen." In periods of persecution and spiritual dissolution the Church may appear to have disappeared; yet the fruitfulness of Christ's death guarantees her survival.[11]

Believers do not attain certainty—that the Church is indestructible or that the Church, as the treasure house of the gospel, offers "sure and firm supports" for their salvation—because they have been "argued into" such an assent. In truth, to be "persuaded" that the Church offers the sure and firm support of salvation is to court the risk of being "persuaded" to the

---

[6]*Inst.* 4.1.4.

[7]*Inst.* 4.1.5: *unde sequitur dignos esse qui fame et inedia pereant, quicunque spiritualem animae cibum divinitus sibi per manus ecclesiae porrectum respuunt.*

[8]*Inst.* 4.1.2.

[9]Ibid.

[10]Ibid.

[11]Ibid.

contrary subsequently. Argument, as elsewhere in Calvin's thought, is an inappropriate means of acquiring assurance concerning God's plan and purpose.[12] Rather, believers acquire assurance concerning the indestructibility of the Church (and its support of their salvation) *only* on the grounds of their being "fully convinced that (they) are members of it":[13] believers "believe the Church" inasmuch as God authenticates to them its nature, reality, and necessity, even as he authenticates to them the One in whose life the Church continues to nourish and guide them. For Calvin, then, ecclesiology is a predicate of Christology: Jesus Christ as the steadfast One guarantees the steadfastness of the Church. The notion of the collapse of the Church is as absurd as the notion of the dismemberment of Jesus Christ himself. In the same way, Jesus Christ as the truth guarantees that the truth will ever be "deposited" in the Church. To forsake the Church is invariably to forsake the truth. On the other hand, participation in the Church is so efficacious that it keeps us in the society of God—and authenticates the same to us.[14]

It must not be thought that Calvin regards affiliation with the Church-congregation as mechanical or quasi-magical. The Church guarantees salvation only as it guarantees faith. And since the Church-congregation is a *corpus mixtum*, faith with unfaith, wheat with chaff, mere adherence to the ecclesiastical institution does not render one a member of Christ's body. Faith alone is fellowship with Christ; the Church guarantees salvation in that God has ordained the Church to be the means whereby he sustains faith. The *corpus mixtum* consists of those who are indeed "children of God by grace and adoption and are true members of Christ by sanctification of the Holy Spirit," as well as those who "have nothing of Christ but the name and outward appearance."[15]

Since God is the searcher of men's hearts, believers do not have to locate the "hypocrites"; that, is, identify the invisible Church within the visible: they are to regard as belonging to the real Church all who claim to

---

[12]Cf. Calvin's discussion of the manner in which believers discern and acknowledge the authority of scripture (*Inst.* 1.7).

[13]*Inst.* 4.1.3.

[14]Ibid. In his discussion of the Church as a *societas* of Christ or of God Calvin maintains that "the communion of saints" "very well expresses what the Church is" (4.1.3). This expression suggests that Calvin will speak of the Church primarily as the people of God. Calvin objects to the understanding of the Church as hierarchy, with the implication that the people of God are somewhat superadded or tangentially related. However, it is arguable that in his discussion of the *notae* of the Church (and their relation to the functions of ordained ministers) he has not developed adequately the notion of the people of God.

[15]*Inst.* 4.1.7.

belong to it and who by their confession, their life-example, and their partaking of the sacraments indicate that they profess the one Christ as authentic believers.[16] At the same time as he insists on not identifying the visible Church with the elect, Calvin wishes to discourage a hypercritical fault-finding which he adjudges to be born of pride and a false understanding of holiness rather than of true holiness and of true zeal for it.[17] Perfection is *not* the mark of the Church. The rigor with which the Anabaptists cast out the weaker brother Calvin finds distressing. Believers are to examine themselves, not each other; and should they observe glaring faults in fellow Church-members, they yet have no pretext for renouncing communion with the Church.[18] They must ever remember that *all* believers continue to sin; that the sinfulness of another's conduct is not to be equated with the unacceptability of the person; that the weakest brother may yet aspire sincerely to the Lordship of Christ; and finally, that "in estimating the true Church, divine judgment is of more weight than human."[19] The Church is holy only in that daily she aspires to the Lordship of Him who alone is holy; Christians who are "cocksure about their perfection" have been deceived by the devil.[20]

All of the foregoing, of course, is known only in faith. It is only as faith puts on Jesus Christ that the Father authenticates to believers the "mother" in whom their salvation is guaranteed. Faith alone is apprised of the nature, reality and necessity of the Church.

THE MINISTRY

Once it is acknowledged that immature faith ever needs nourishment and guidance and that God has ordained the Church to be the sole means by which faith is advanced towards maturity,[21] it must yet be specified precisely *how* the Church provides nourishment and guidance. Calvin's unambiguous answer is, "the ministry." While Jesus Christ is *the* truth in which the Church schools believers, the disappearance of the *ministry* entails the disappearance of the truth.[22] Evidently "Jesus Christ" implies

---

[16]*Comm.* I Pet. 1:1 and *Inst.* 4.1.8.

[17]*Inst.* 4.1.16.

[18]*Inst.* 4.1.15.

[19]*Inst.* 4.1.16.

[20]*Inst.* 4.1.17 and 4.1.20.

[21]*Inst.* 4.1.5.

[22]*Comm.* I Tim. 3:15.

"ministry." Calvin everywhere upholds this notion: God rules his Church by means of the ministry (when Christ alone is King!);[23] the ministry is the chief sinew by which believers are held together in one body.[24] The ministry is not an arrangement devised by men, even Christian men, who regard it their responsibility to make provision for what they understand the well-being of the Church to require. Rather, the ministry is, by Christ's appointment, Christ's *gift* to the Church.[25] Disdainfully to ignore the gift is not mere ingratitude; it is unfaith. Faith ever recognizes that the ministry is essential to that Church which God has ordained to support and confirm faith. Using his favorite analogy Calvin maintains that "neither the light and heat of the sun, nor food and drink, are so necessary to nourish and sustain the present life as the apostolic and pastoral office is necessary to preserve the Church on earth."[26] Just as it is ridiculous to think that the earliest Church could have existed apart from the apostles (they are, in fact, "instruments of the Holy Spirit by which the Church stands or falls"[27]), the contemporary Church cannot *be* the Church apart from the ministry, since ministers have precisely *the same charge* as apostles.[28] In a word, the ministry is the manner in which Christ is present to his Church.[29] In this vein Calvin notes that Paul not only considers himself a co-worker of God, but also "assigns himself the function of imparting salvation."[30] Without the ministry, then, the "deposit" disappears, and there is consequently no Church.

The foregoing should not suggest that the minister is supra-human or any less sinful than any other believer; in fact, he excels the others in nothing.[31] Of himself he is but an earthen vessel. Nonetheless, his undeniable appearance as earthen vessel does not preclude God's giving an inestimable treasure through him, and giving it in order to elicit recognition of the treasure from believers.[32] Through the earthliness of the

---

[23]*Comm.* Luke 10:16.

[24]*Inst.* 4.3.2. Calvin never indicates that there are, in his understanding, no sinews other than the "chief."

[25]*Comm.* Eph. 4:11.

[26]*Inst.* 4.3.4.

[27]*Inst.* 4.1.14.

[28]*Inst.* 4.3.5. Calvin states in one place (4.8.9) that the apostles, unlike ministers, were "amanuenses" of the Holy Spirit.

[29]*Inst.* 4.6.9.

[30]*Inst.* 4.1.6: *denique pluribus locis non modo se cooperarium Dei facit, se partes sibi assignat conferendae salutis.*

[31]*Inst.* 4.1.6.

[32]*Comm.* II Cor. 4:7.

God-appointed ministry, then, "God himself appears in our midst, and, as Author of this order, would have men recognize him as present in his institution."[33] God insists on being recognized in that ministry which he has appointed, therein rendering illegitimate any pretense that the earthen vessel has wholly obscured the treasure. In truth, the greater earthliness of the vessel glorifies and renders more visible the power of God.[34]

While, by God's ordination, the earthen vessel will not fail to contain the treasure, what belongs to the Holy Spirit should not be transferred to the ministry: the creaturely does not penetrate and correct mind and heart; Paul does not credit ministers with any intrinsic power, despite his great esteem of the ministry. The minister who claims as much for himself is simply committing sacrilege.[35] The test of a minister's faithfulness in remaining but an earthen vessel is that he "does nothing of himself."[36] While acknowledging the ministry as essential to the Church he does not claim for himself what will detract from the "treasure."

Calvin reminds us that while God's power is not bound to the means he chooses for nourishing and guiding faith, the fact that he has chosen those means does bind believers to them. Only "fanatical" persons (that is, Enthusiasts) delude themselves that they can safely ignore what God has appointed. The refusal to submit to the yoke of the ministry, Calvin insists in the strongest of language, is tantamount to blotting out God's "face"; which is to say, tantamount to forfeiting mercy and therefore faith, for faith exists only beneath God's propitious, benevolent visage.[37]

Believers who chafe at having to betake themselves to that ministry which consists of fellow-creatures and sinners should remember that to be addressed by God *nudus*, apart from the ministry, would be overwhelming.[38] The ministry is the provision of the ever-merciful God for that faith which ever remains weak. At the same time, the fact that the minister is fellow-creature and sinner means that the singularity of the "treasure" is all the more manifest: Jesus Christ asserts his sole sovereignty.[39]

---

[33] *Inst.* 4.1.5: *ergo ut sciamus ex vasis testaceis nobis proferri inaestimabilem thesaurum, Deus ipse in medium prodit, et quatenus huius ordinis autor est, vult se praesentem in sua institutione agnosci.*

[34] *Comm.* II Cor. 4:7.

[35] *Inst.* 4.1.6.

[36] *Comm.* John 20:23.

[37] *Inst.* 4.1.5: *quod perinde est ac Dei facem, quae nobis in doctrina affulget, delere.* Cf. *Comm.* II Cor. 4:7 where "face" is Jesus Christ (i.e., mercy).

[38] *Comm.* I Thess. 5:12, 13 and *Inst.* 4.1.5.

[39] *Comm.* Luke 10:16.

Since the minister excels other Christians in nothing, power and authority pertain exclusively to his *function*. And the function of the ministry is to preach the gospel and administer the sacraments.[40] Since, as will become evident in the discussion of sacraments, the Word (preached) is entirely the power of the sacraments, the function of the ministry is the declaration or proclamation of the Word. The apostles (whose charge is identical with that of the ministers) were called *in order to* preach.[41] The priests (whose successors the ministers are) had as their office only the responsibility of "answering the people from the mouth of God."[42] Not surprisingly, then, Calvin insists that God chooses ministers "in order that he might disseminate his heavenly wisdom to men through them. For that reason they must confine themselves *strictly to that task*."[43] Indeed in view of the fact that the function constitutes the ministry, a non-preaching minister is a contradiction in terms; the minister who does not preach is simply not to be regarded as a minister.[44] The priesthood which ministers exercise is the slaying (that is, "sacrificing") of men "by the spiritual sword of the Word."[45] In reiterating this point Calvin wishes to impress upon his readers two points: first, that the power and authority do not inhere the person of the minister, and second, that the function of the ministry is exclusively the declaration of the Word. Accordingly, throughout his *Opera* Calvin uses "preaching," "teaching," and "ministry" interchangeably. The face of God which shines upon men through the ministry shines upon them in *teaching*; it was the teaching of the prophets which was a living image of God (*viva Dei imago*); God reflects himself in the mirror of teaching; the yoke which believers must wear is the yoke of teaching.[46] The Church is the keeper (*custodem*) of God's

---

[40] *Inst.* 4.1.1. L. Schummer is making an overfine comparison when he says, concerning the pastor's being a minister of the Spirit, of salvation, and of eternal life, "Ces trois compléments de nom correspondent bien au triple office de prédication, d'administration, et de puissance de clefs" (*Le Ministère Pastoral dans l'Institution Chrétienne de Calvin à la Lumière du Troisième Sacrement*, 42).

[41] *Comm.* Luke 6:13. Frequently Calvin discusses the function of the ordained ministry without any reference to the sacraments. In other words, "preaching" has the force of "declaration of the Word," which is preaching plus sacrament. Cf. *Comm.* II Tim. 3:15 and *Inst.* 4.1.5 and 4.1.22. Throughout the remainder of this discussion of preaching, "preaching" can be understood as "preaching plus sacrament." See *Comm.* I Cor. 4:1 where Calvin speaks of the sacrament as an appendage (*appendix*) to the Word.

[42] *Inst.* 4.8.6.

[43] *Comm.* I Cor. 4:1 (italics mine). For same idea see *Inst.* 4.3.3.

[44] *Comm.* II Cor. 5:20, and *Inst.* 4.3.5, 4.5.5, 4.5.11.

[45] *Comm.* Matt. 28:19.

[46] *Inst.* 4.1.5 and 4.1.6.

truth; through the preaching of its ministers the truth is maintained, by their labor the Word is kept pure, and in their teaching God continues to show himself Father to a family as he nourishes it.[47] Jesus Christ, who is the image of that paternal favor, has instituted the ministry precisely for the purpose of preaching.[48]

THE MARKS OF THE CHURCH

The Church exists wherever the ministry exists. As expected, then, the marks (*notae*) of the Church *coincide exactly with the functions of the ministry*: "wherever we see the Word of God purely preached and heard, and the sacraments administered according to Christ's institution, there, it is not to be doubted, a Church of God exists."[49] These two activities are a "perpetual token" by which the Church is distinguished.[50] Calvin then adds immediately, "that is, wherever the *ministry* remains whole and uncorrupted."[51] As soon as Calvin identifies the two marks of the Church he cites Matthew 18:20: "For where two or three are gathered in my name, there am I in the midst of them." In other words, gathering in Christ's name *is* the preaching and hearing of the Word, together with the administraton of the sacraments; the presence of Jesus Christ is a function or variable of the activities of the ministry.[52] The disappearance of the proclamation of the Word, which for Calvin is identical with the disappearance of the Christ-instituted ministry, entails the collapse of the Church.[53] On the other hand, the "pure ministry of the Word" and the "pure mode of celebrating the sacraments" guarantee that any society in

---

[47]*Inst.* 4.1.10.

[48]*Inst.* 4.1.7.

[49]*Inst.* 4.1.9. In *Comm.* Acts 2:42 Calvin speaks of fellowship and prayer as additional *notae* of the Church. His assertion here does not overturn what he insists on throughout Book III: the Word (preaching and sacrament) delineates the Church. See fn. 14 for discussion of compatability of *notae* with "communion of saints."

[50]*Inst.* 4.2.1: *perpetua tessera.*

[51]Ibid. (italics mine).

[52]Calvin does not mention this in *Comm.* Matt. 18:20.

[53]*Inst.* 4.1.11. Similarly the effacing or destruction of these marks is the removal of the true and genuine distinction of the Church (*veram germanamque ecclesiae distinctionem*, 4.1.11). Calvin does maintain that the "diversity of graces" within the Church impels the members of the Church to share their God-bestowed gifts with one another (4.1.13). However, his protracted consideration of the responsibilities of the ministry virtually eliminates any significant discussion of the "variety of gifts."

which these are found is indubitably the Church.[54] Where these two
marks are found there can be no excuse for separating from that Church,
regardless of what moral turpitude might be present as well. As long as
the ministry remains unrepudiated the Church abides; to forsake it is to
be traitor and apostate and denier of Jesus Christ.[55]

THE RELATION OF JESUS CHRIST, THE GOSPEL,
AND THE PREACHING OF THE GOSPEL

To this point it has been noted that the gospel has been deposited in
the Church, that the ministry *is* the proclamation of the gospel, that the
Church exists to nourish and guide faith; and it has been reiterated
throughout this study that Jesus Christ alone, in the power of his own
Spirit, engenders faith. What, then, are the relations among Jesus Christ,
gospel, preaching, and faith? Is preaching merely an outward sign pointing to the Christ who ever stands behind it? Is it merely a witness to Jesus
Christ, instead of being as well (indeed, essentially) the very coming
among men in power of the Lord Jesus Christ himself, whose power is
attested by the bestowal of faith upon men? The answer to the question of
the relation between Christ and preaching, of course, is suggested by that
between Christ and the gospel: is the gospel merely the apostolic recollec-
tion of Jesus Christ, or is it that by which hearers of the gospel were
brought to faith? In other words, in what sense and under what circumstances is the preaching (and hearing) of the gospel the *self*-declaration of
Jesus Christ (and in what sense and under what circumstances is it not)?

Calvin alludes to the content of his answer in several places where he
suggests that the *purpose* of preaching is identical with the purpose of the
coming among men of Jesus Christ: the object of preaching is that men
take refuge in Christ;[56] "publishing the gospel" facilitates that obedience
which he alone can give;[57] the chief end in preaching is the reconciliation
of men with God;[58] teachers are sent to bring life-giving (*vivificam*) light
to the blind and to transform men's hearts into the righteousness of

---

[54]*Inst.* 4.1.12. Calvin does suggest a criterion for the "purity" of preaching and
sacrament: doctrine which affirms that "God is one; Christ is God and the Son of God; our
salvation rests in God's mercy; and the like" (4.1.12).

[55]*Inst.* 4.1.14, 4.1.18, 4.1.19, 4.1.10.

[56]*Comm.* Matt. 23:37.

[57]*Comm.* Matt. 28:19.

[58]*Comm.* John 20:23.

God.[59] Calvin notes that Peter associates "peace" with "preaching" because preaching is "precisely the *one* means by which the fruit of the reconciliation procured by Christ comes right home to us. In the same way, after Paul has taught that Christ is our peace, he quickly adds that he (Christ) has come to preach peace."[60] Apparently preaching does what only Christ can do.

Before the question of the relation of preaching to gospel is pursued further it must be noted that the question does not pertain to preaching as a *merely* human activity; if preaching is the self-declaration of Jesus Christ (who is the effectual presence of God) then preaching is more than an ordinary human event. Calvin insists that God alone, ultimately, can equip the preacher. While the preacher has natural gifts and talents which are essential to preaching and which God can "adopt" for the purpose of the proclamation of the Word, natural talents do not enable any man to accomplish what has been indicated in the foregoing paragraph. The prophets (whose service is preaching, according to Calvin) relate only what they have received from God.[61] Jesus Christ himself equips the apostles (whose charge ministers share), and it is only his equipping them which grounds his putting them forth "even as angels come down from heaven."[62] While all Christians are constituted such by the Holy Spirit (that is, Jesus Christ in his effectual power), preachers, as watchmen entrusted with special responsibility, require a "special gift"; in them the Holy Spirit "must prevail more than in ordinary men."[63] While Calvin's expression here is inelegant and even theologically questionable, the point he wishes to make is clear: no man can become a preacher of the *gospel* simply on the strength of natural aptitude; no man can create faith in his hearers. God alone renders a man fit for preaching the gospel.[64] And God renders a man fit in so far as he "deposits" the Word of God with the prophet or preacher.[65] Calvin's assertion here bears consideration, for it indicates that the qualification to be a preacher comes entirely from without. In addition, the fact that the Word is "deposited" with the

---

[59]*Comm.* Acts 26:18.

[60]*Comm.* Acts 10:36 (italics mine): *pacem nominatim praedicationi coniungit, quia haec una demum ratio est, qua reconciliationis a Christo partae fructus ad nos usque pervenit.*

[61]*Comms.* Joel 1:1 and Ez. 3:17.

[62]*Comm.* John 7:16.

[63]*Comm.* Ez. 3:17.

[64]*Comm.* Luke 24:49.

[65]*Comm.* Joel 1:1.

preacher reminds us that preaching is constitutive of the Church, for Calvin evidently does not intend any distinction between the gospel's being deposited in the Church and with the preacher. Where the gospel is preached, there is the Church. And God alone can facilitate its being preached.

"For as man's salvation was completed in Christ's death, so God makes us share in it through the gospel."[66] Calvin insists that Jesus Christ is not who he is apart from his making us his and him ours; the gospel (the prophetic-apostolic witness to God's unique activity in Jesus of Nazareth) is unarguably part of the Christ-event in so far as it is the act of his bestowal of himself and his benefits upon men, together with their certainty of this. In other words, while Jesus Christ cannot be collapsed into or reduced to the apostles, neither is he who he is apart from the apostles. "Jesus Christ" *includes* "gospel." For this reason Calvin can speak of the gospel as "the ambassadorship of the mutual reconciliation between God and men."[67] An ambassador bears the authority and effectiveness of him whose ambassador he is; the gospel, accordingly, is in effect Jesus Christ himself declaring and bestowing the reconciliation between God and men which he has brought. Jesus Christ himself is both the One in whom God is propitious, and also, the witness to that propitiation; he is himself the gospel, the announcement that God actually "brings down to us his fatherly love."[68] As the apostle witnesses to God's action and self-declaration in Jesus Christ, Christ himself bestows (through the Spirit) the benefits of that act upon men. Apart from the gospel Jesus Christ remains wholly "outside" men. But since Christ *cannot* remain wholly outside men, Christ-without-his-gospel is not Christ at all; and Calvin does not hesitate to state that without the gospel Jesus Christ is fancied, seeming, or imaginary.[69]

Calvin extends the above argument to preaching, and maintains that as this "sure doctrine" (gospel) is preached, Jesus Christ discloses himself: *revelation* occurs through the preaching of the gospel.[70] Indeed, the *manifestation* of Jesus Christ is not simply the appearance of the historic Jesus, but the proclamation of the gospel as well. In the historic Jesus God has fulfilled what he promised to the fathers; in the "teaching of the

---

[66]*Comm.* II Tim. 1:9.

[67]*Comm.* Matt. 16:19.

[68]*Comm.* Eph. 2:17.

[69]*Comm.* Col. 2:9.

[70]Ibid.

gospel" he makes that fulfillment known to us;[71] that is, "revelation"
comprehends Jesus Christ *plus* gospel *plus* preaching. The fact that Jesus
Christ has appeared in history does not mean that all men are now the
beneficiaries of revelation; he can be said to be "manifested" only to those
whom he illumines by his gospel.[72] Apart from the preaching of the gospel
there is no manifestation of him who has come. In a word, the hidden God
"reveals" himself through the preaching of ministers.[73] The preaching of
the gospel, then, is the self-declaration of Jesus Christ. "Christ has been
made known" and "the gospel has been preached" are synonymous.[74]

Calvin notes that while "name," in scripture, is often a synonym for
"power," it can refer as well to the preaching of the gospel; to believe in
Christ's name, then, is to believe in him when he is *preached*.[75] In the
same paragraph Calvin insists that Christ offers himself through the
gospel. For Calvin "Christ," "gospel" and "preaching" imply each other.
The three terms form a unit whose force, at bottom, is, "the historical
Jesus, as attested by prophet and apostle, acts upon men today as and
only as he is declared." Within his exegesis of one and the same verse
Calvin states both that Jesus Christ is the only true food of the soul and
that it is *teaching* which feeds men.[76]

Since Jesus Christ does not act upon men apart from preaching,
Calvin can condense "Christ-in-his-gospel-through-preaching" to
"preaching" and state succinctly that it is *preaching* which brings life;[77]
the preaching (of Christ's death) affects hearers as much as "the actual
sight of Christ's death" would have;[78] preaching brings the Holy Spirit. A
few lines later Calvin states that the Holy Spirit is the fruit of the gospel.
Again "gospel" and "preaching" imply each other.[79] Preaching is that by
which God begets sons and raises them to maturity[80]—which is to say that
preaching is Christ drawing men to himself as *he* becomes their justifica-

---

[71]*Comm.* I Pet. 1:20.

[72]Ibid. Since the Holy Spirit is the illuminator, for Calvin there is the closest relationship between the gospel and the Holy Spirit. See below for a discussion of this
relationship.

[73]*Comm.* I Cor. 13:12.

[74]*Comm.* Eph. 1:8.

[75]*Comm.* John 1:12.

[76]*Comm.* John 21:15.

[77]*Comm.* I Tim. 2:4.

[78]*Comm.* Gal. 3:1.

[79]Ibid.

[80]*Comms.* Gal. 3:2 and Gal. 3:5.

tion and sanctification; preaching is the "formal cause" by which the goodness of God (that is, mercy of Jesus Christ) flows out to us;[81] preaching facilitates trust in Jesus Christ;[82] since preaching comes to us with the authority of God, our salvation is grounded in it.[83] But to say that preaching effects justification, sanctification, and trust, is to say that preaching effects faith. And Calvin states simply that faith is produced (*nasci*) by preaching, and that without preaching there can be no faith.[84]

In an earlier section of this chapter where it was indicated that the purpose of preaching is one with the purpose of Jesus Christ, it was noted that both of these were most closely related to, even identical with, the purpose of the Church; while the Church is ordained of God to nourish and guide faith and is able to do this in that the gospel has been "deposited" in it, the gospel has been "deposited" with the preacher for the same purpose. Not unexpectedly, then, Calvin speaks of *preaching* as the "mother" who conceives and brings forth faith; faith is the daughter who ought to remember her proper mother.[85] The Church is "mother" in so far as preaching is "mother."

GOD IS UNIQUE TEACHER

The fact that the Church and preaching nourish and guide faith must not be interpreted to mean that Jesus Christ has ceased to do so. Indeed, to transfer to the Church or preaching what belongs essentially to Christ is idolatry. By the appointment of God Jesus Christ is the unique teacher of the Church and is alone to be heard and heeded.[86] Calvin would regard as absurd any suggestion that God "gives up" his unique wisdom, power and authority and entrusts the nurture of faith to men alone. In calling and equipping preachers God certainly employs the work of men for the salvation of men;[87] nonetheless, his using their human activity does not detract at all from the praise of his glory. While scripture does esteem the

---

[81]*Comm.* Eph. 1:8. No particular weight should be assigned to "formal" here. In his exegesis of the preceding verse Calvin speaks of Jesus Christ as the efficient, material, and formal causes. Calvin's point here is that the preaching of the gospel is Jesus Christ himself bestowing his benefits upon men.

[82]*Comm.* Eph. 1:13.

[83]*Sermon* Gal. 1:1f: *nostre salut doist estre fondé là-dessus.*

[84]*Comms.* Rom. 10:17 and I Tim. 3:15. For same idea see *Inst.* 3.23.13 and 3.24.1.

[85]*Comm.* II Cor. 13:5.

[86]*Comms.* Gal. 1:1 and Matt. 17:5.

[87]*Comm.* Eph. 4:12.

ministry, it indicates that the effectiveness of that ministry arises solely from God's power and authority.[88] When Christ informed the disciples that whoever heard them heard him, he was not suggesting that his word inhered theirs or could be equated *simpliciter* with theirs; he was not "resigning to men the right given him by his father" or "transferring to men the honour due to himself."[89] Those whom God graciously employs as his ministers in *his* creating faith he allows to share in his honor, but never in such a way as to diminish that honor.[90]

Admittedly, Calvin can contradict, seemingly, what he has said above: preaching *is* such a transfer.[91] The contradiction is seen to be only apparent as Calvin is allowed to state his precise meaning at greater length:

> "But it is a common thing for God to transfer to his ministers the honour due to himself alone, not in order to take anything away from himself, but to commend the efficacy of his Spirit, which he puts forth (*exserit*) in them. For he does not send them to work so that they may be dead instruments (*mortua organa*), or as if they were play actors, but so that he may work powerfully with their assistance."[92]

> "God sometimes connects himself with his servants, and sometimes separates himself from them: when he connects himself with them he transfers to them *what never ceases to dwell in him*; for he never resigns to them his own office, but makes them partakers of it only."[93]

Calvin wishes to preserve a careful dialectical balance here: God never resigns his own honor, power and authority to the preacher; yet his sending the latter out in his own power and authority would be futile. Accordingly, he condescends to include them in his authority (here is the force of "transfer") without renouncing his sole rule. The "transfer" does not impugn the Lordship of Jesus Christ.[94]

---

[88] *Comm*. Acts 26:18.

[89] *Comm*. Luke 10:16.

[90] *Comms*. I Tim. 1:2 and John 20:23.

[91] *Comm*. Acts 13:47 and *De Aet. Dei Praed.* 107.

[92] *Comm*. Acts 26:18.

[93] *Comm*. Mal. 4:6 (italics mine): *Aliquando coniungit se Deus cum servis suis: aliquando, autem ab illis se separat. Dum se coniungit, transfert ad eos quod apud ipsum tamen residere nondesinit. Neque enim suos partes illis resignat, sed communicat duntaxat.*

[94] *Sermon* II Tim. 2:14f.

THE PREACHER AS MOUTHPIECE OF GOD

"God deigns to consecrate to himself the mouths and tongues of men in order that his voice may resound in them."[95] The preacher's speaking is "just as if" God himself were speaking. However, the "just as if" means neither that God has "changed place" (lost his transcendence) nor that he has "confined us to earthly means" (because by this misinterpretation he is now thought to be limited to the creaturely). It does mean that preaching is the means by which God bears us up to him.[96] While an unqualified equating of the preached word with God's Word would be that commingling of divine and creaturely which Calvin abhors, nevertheless, by God's condescension and accommodation the voice of the preacher can become the voice of God.[97] To listen (in faith) is to hear God himself speaking by the voice of men.[98] While Jesus Christ is no longer in the flesh preachers are; God therefore appoints preachers to Christ's "place" in order to "speak as if out of his (Christ's) mouth."[99] In truth, *even as* Jesus Christ is the sole author of faith, God has ordained that faith be born of the voice of man; those who are sure they can come to faith and be sustained in it while ignoring the voice of man (the Enthusiasts) "act just as if the farmers, giving up the plough, neglecting sowing and leaving all cultivation, were to open their mouths and expect food to fall into them from heaven."[100] On the other hand, once faith acknowledges that the human voice is, by God's ordination, the mouthpiece of God himself, the only response for faith is the submission of itself to what it hears, for through the preached word God confronts men "no less than if he himself had come down from heaven."[101]

God himself assures believers that he has ordained preachers to be his mouthpiece in so far as believers have been assured of their salvation through the "mouthpiece."[102] Intrinsic to each other, then, are the assur-

---

[95]*Inst.* 4.1.5.

[96]Ibid. Note the similarity between the fact that preaching "bears us up" to God and the identical role of the Holy Spirit in the Lord's Supper. For a discussion of this matter see below.

[97]*Comm.* Eph. 4:4.

[98]*Comms.* Luke 10:16 and John 4:43.

[99]*Comm.* Acts 13:47.

[100]*Comm.* I Cor. 3:6.

[101]*Comms.* Luke 10:16 and I John 4:1.

[102]*Comms.* II Cor. 5:20 and Eph. 2:17. *Sed inde tota autoritas* (i.e., of the gospel), *quod homines agnoscimus esse Dei organa, et Christum per os eorum nobis loquentum audimus* (*Comm.* Eph. 2:17).

ance of salvation and the assurance that through the human voice God himself has spoken an effectual word of grace "for me." The assurance which is intrinsic to faith (assurance that Jesus Christ includes believers in his own life) validates the means by which this assurance is born: when "God acts effectually by the voice of man so as to create faith in us by his ministry"[103] believers cannot doubt that the voice of man has become the voice of God.

Again Calvin is careful to preserve a dialectical tension: not everything the preacher says is *eo ipso* "Voice of God," since it is possible and even inevitable that the preacher mixes "his own additions" with the gospel.[104] Nonetheless, in so far as the preacher puts forth "sincerely and in good faith" what he has learned from the Word, he must not be regarded with contempt: God's voice resounds in the voice of the preacher.[105]

Appendix: Preaching as a Human Activity. In view of the foregoing it can be asked whether Calvin comes close simply to identifying God with human speech. Undeniably his vocabulary points in this direction. However, the extent to which Calvin balances this seeming identification with an insistence on preaching as a creaturely (and even sinful) event is not widely recognized. Calvin is at pains to remind his readers that the preacher is not a quasi-mechanical channel for the voice of God; the preacher's mind and will have not been replaced by those of God; preaching is not a species of docetism where the voice of God is connected with a merely *seeming* human event. Indeed Calvin eschews the "fanatical" notion that the Spirit uses the preacher in such a way as to suspend the latter's critical, human faculties. Despite Calvin's suggestion that the apostles were able to expound Jesus Christ as the fulfillment of the Old Testament prophecies "with Christ's Spirit as precursor in a certain measure dictating the words,"[106] the tenor of his discussion on preaching as human activity contradicts any notion that the preacher has had the content of his preaching "funnelled" into him, his sole responsibility (if this lattermost word is even applicable) being to open his mouth and let escape what has been inserted.

Calvin does not deny that God's using human (which is to say, both finite and sinful) activity is "risky"; nor does he deny that in fact some

---

[103]*Comm.* Rom. 10:17.

[104]*Comm.* Matt. 17:5.

[105]*Comm.* 1 John 4:1.

[106]*Inst.* 4.8.8. It should be noted (i) that *dicto* means "declare" or "say" rather than "dictate" in the modern sense, (ii) that *quodammodo*, which Calvin uses frequently in his discussion of the creatureliness of preaching, means precisely "not literally."

preaching is deplorable, so deplorable as to have no apparent usefulness before God: "there are so many stupid, ignorant men who blurt out their worthless brainwaves from the pulpit."[107] Calvin admits as well that defective preaching may arise not only from indolence, unfaithfulness and ignorance, but also from lack of ability: a man whose Christian life, wisdom and faith are uncriticisable may yet lack aptitude for teaching and thus be unable to utter that by which other men are edified.[108] Calvin can make these assessments only on the presupposition that that authentic human activity which is essential to preaching makes possible the negative exercise of that activity. As long as preaching is a human activity there must be scope for "worthless brainwaves."

Again, preaching as human event is attested by Calvin's insistence that preaching is not a mindless hurling of texts of scripture at congregations; while the preacher has the same charge as the apostle, he does not regurgitate or parrot the word of the apostle. The situation in the world of both preacher and hearer differs from that of the apostles; while the preacher does not adjust the message to fit the hearer in terms of a theological correlation between Word of God and word of man so as to compromise the Word of God and disembowel the gospel, neither is preaching a human activity which does not attempt to relate itself to the circumstances of the hearer as participant in both Church and world: "The good and faithful pastor must take prudent note of what the present circumstances of the Church require, in order to suit his advice to the occasion."[109]

While on the one hand scripture is the source and norm of sound preaching, on the other hand "preaching" which is simply a mindless mimicking of the apostolic witness is no preaching at all; it will not be honored by God, and in fact will deleteriously affect the prosecution of Christ's mission in the world, since it renders insipid that Word which alone is life-giving: "there is nothing of greater danger than the pedantry which makes every doctrine become stale."[110]

Preaching ever remains a *personal* engagement of speaker and hearer. As personal engagement and activity are its concern, passion and vigor are

---

[107]*Comm.* I Thess. 5:21.

[108]*Sermon* I Tim. 3:1-4.

[109]*Comm.* Jude 4. Cf. *Comm.* Luke 6:26 and *Sermon* II Tim. 2:14ff.—"We cannot be preachers in order to forge and build what will seem good to us, and in order to visit our fantasies upon the people; but the word of truth lies behind us, both speaker and hearer. For God wishes to rule us: Jesus Christ alone desires to have complete Lordship" (translation mine).

[110]*Comm.* I Thess. 5:21.

unrelenting: "if it is at all possible, we have to drag men out of hell itself."[111]

PREACHING AND HEARING

Calvin insists that in the matter of the bringing of men to faith preaching cannot be set aside in favor of a private reading of scripture without exposition and application.[112] Herein Calvin differs from some of the sectarians not simply because he understands that the circumstances of sixteenth-century Europe differ from those of first-century Palestine or Asia Minor (some sectarians apparently were unwilling to acknowledge this), or even because he understands that a private reading of scripture apart from the knowledge and aptitude peculiar to the ordained minister would inevitably yield "fanaticism," but ultimately on the grounds that scripture itself enjoins preaching.[113] By the same token scripture enjoins hearing. For this reason Calvin stated a mark of the Church to be the preaching *and* hearing of the Word.[114] Preaching as a human activity implies hearing as a complementary activity: "preaching" is utterance plus hearing. There is "teaching" only in so far as it is received.[115] And just as preaching was seen to be not an unthinking repetition of scripture, so hearing is not an unthinking absorption of information. Passivity on the part of the "hearer" indicates unfaith: faith "listens."

Moreover, faith listens discerningly and critically. Such a listening is the antithesis of "the external sound of the voice (which) strikes our ears in vain."[116] Indeed, where spiritual perception and criticism are lacking one can "hear" adequate preaching and, failing to discern Jesus Christ

---

[111] *Comm.* Acts 8:22.

[112] *Letter to Duke of Somerset* (*Calvini Opera*, 13,70).

[113] *Comm.* Heb. 13:22.

[114] J. McNeill is one of the few writers of journal articles on this subject to draw attention to *hearing* ("The Church in Sixteenth Century Reformed Theology," *Journal of Religion*, Vol. 22, 1942). Admittedly, Calvin does speak infrequently of preaching without referring to hearing (e.g., *Comm.* I Tim. 3:15). However, this omission does not reflect his considered theological opinion.

[115] *Inst.* 4.3.1.

[116] *De Aet. Dei Praed.* 94. Cf. L. Schummer's perceptive remark: "Quand le Seigneur commande aux fidèles d'écouter ses ministres, comme si lui-même parlait, il n'entend pas couvrir de son autorité les extravagances et fantaisies de cogitations indépendantes de Lui mais la fidèle administration de sa Parole" (*Le Ministère Pastoral dans l'Institution Chrétienne de Calvin à la Lumière du Troisième Sacrement*, 56).

(with his benefits) to be the content of that preaching, occupy oneself "with frivolous questions."[117] The hearer's responsibility is to be occupied with appropriate considerations as the preaching unfolds. The exercise of such responsibility is all the more important if one is confronted with a "stupid" preacher who afflicts congregations with "worthless brain-waves." Hearers must adjudge whether they are receiving wheat or chaff, the Word of God or *mere* creaturely reflection. Calvin insists that faith can and must distinguish whether what is heard is "from heaven (or) from earth."[118] No preacher can claim to be exempt from criticism on the grounds that he speaks with the voice of God and *that* voice no creature may criticise; his voice can never be equated uncritically with the voice of God. In addition, while what the preacher says may in fact reflect God's intention for the hearers, it must not be assumed that what the preacher says reflects the totality of that intention. No preacher articulates the fullness of revelation: "God has distributed his Spirit to each person to a limited extent only, so that even where his outpouring is at its greatest there is something lacking."[119] No preacher has any grounds for taking offense at his being assessed.

As scripture is the norm of preaching so it is the norm for the hearing of preaching. But since the inner meaning of scripture is not naturally intelligible, scripture cannot be used as a "checklist" against which "items" in preaching can be noted present or absent. The meaning of scripture is apprehended only by means of the Spirit—apart from whom scripture is without profit.[120] Calvin remarks pithily that while gold is tested by fire or touchstone, the testing procedure can be applied only by those who understand the art. This discerning criticism does not mean that men have elevated themselves above the Word of God; it does mean that God himself enables his people to recognize what is of him. God does so only as his people betake themselves to the Word written and yield that obedience which the Spirit enjoins: without the Spirit scripture is reduced to a "checklist"; without scripture the "Spirit" leads to the vagaries of the Enthusiasts. By means of Word and Spirit, then, the hearer can become "experienced in judging" so as to recognize where sound teaching has been corrupted by "worthless nonsense."[121] It is ever

---

[117]*Comm.* Acts 20:21.

[118]*Inst.* 4.8.5: ... *Deo intus dictante, sciebant e coelo esse, non ex terra, quod audiebant.* Again the force of "dictates" here does not overturn the argument of this page.

[119]*Comm.* I Cor. 14:32.

[120]*Comm.* I John 4:1.

[121]*Comm.* I Cor. 14:29.

the task of the preacher not to presume upon a hearing simply because he is the preacher, but rather to demand a hearing only inasmuch as he "proves" that what he says is of God.[122] It is ever the task of the hearer, in obedient faith, to "judge by the Spirit of God whether it is his Word which is declared."[123]

THE AUTHORITY OF PREACHING

"Thus faith is built on no other foundation than God himself; and yet the preaching of men is not wanting in its claim of authority and reverence."[124] In view of what has been said to this point concerning the relation of Jesus Christ to gospel and preaching, as well as the relation between voice of God and voice of man, at once we expect Calvin to argue that the authority of Jesus Christ lends authority to preaching (and to the preacher); that while preaching has no inherent authority, it gains authority through the service it renders to him. Calvin argues precisely in this manner, and does so in his customary vocabulary: "the character (*persona*) of the teaching is applied to those who are entrusted with its administration."[125] Calvin's saying that the preacher has applied to him the *persona* of the teaching is tantamount to his saying that the preacher has applied to him the *persona* of Jesus Christ. Unfaith fails to recognize this and thinks itself to have to do with men *only* when it is confronted with preaching, and thus insults the Father through its disobedience.[126] Faith, on the other hand, acknowledges that the authority by which preachers confirm faith consists *entirely* in their service to the Word; indeed, preachers are divinely ordained sureties (*sponsores*) of salvation; through the preacher God "represents his person."[127] Were the preacher not authoritative he would be but a minister of the letter; his ministry would be without significance for faith. He is a "minister of the Spirit" in so far as *he* "writes the Word of the Lord" in men's hearts[128]—for *Christ's* power appears "openly" (*palam*) in the preaching of the gospel.[129]

---

[122]*Comm.* Joel 1:1.

[123]*Comm.* I Cor. 14:29; cf. *Comm.* II Cor. 13:5.

[124]*Comm.* Gen. 50:24.

[125]*Comm.* Matt. 5:13: *Quod proprium est doctrinae, ad persona transfertur, quibus comissa est eius administratio.*

[126]*Comms.* Matt. 16:19, Luke 10:16, II Thess. 3:14.

[127]*Comm.* John 20:23: *personam sustineat*; cf. *Comm.* I Pet. 4:4.

[128]*Comm.* I Cor. 3:7.

[129]*Comm.* II Cor. 13:5. For same idea see *Comm.* Gal. 2:8.

While Calvin does say that God "substitutes the pastors in his place," the addition of "as it were" is crucial:[130] God does not give himself away to men; while they reflect his light they never shine with any inherent brightness; they are not authoritative because a transmutation has occurred, but because he condescends to use the service they render. While preachers can demand to be heard in view of God's having sent them to teach,[131] they remain authoritative only as long as they claim no authority for themselves. Prophet and apostle are authoritative precisely in that they ever point to him who is the Authority.[132] Jesus Christ does not delegate or relegate his authority to any other person. Preachers are authoritative only inasmuch as they endeavor to keep unobscured Christ's authority for himself, which they do only as they attest that he alone leads and rules the Church. The preacher who claims authority for himself usurps Christ's authority and renders himself tyrannical. In other words, authority is never given to preacher, prophet, or apostle personally, but to the ministry to which they have been appointed.[133] And there is no proper exercise of that ministry (that is, a pointing to Jesus Christ) which is not the preacher's pointing away from himself. The Church is built up only as men aspire to preserve Christ's authority for himself.[134] We are to hear him alone.

Without exception, then, the authority of apostle and preacher is not intrinsic; nor is it derived. A derived authority suggests a partial and shared authority. But the apostles do not share Christ's authority; theirs consists precisely in their service of his. "The power of the Church" (which is to say, the power of the ministry) "is therefore not infinite but subject to the Lord's Word and, as it were, enclosed within it."[135] The authority of the preacher is the authority of the Word. In this way Calvin can say both that "God substitutes pastors for himself" and that "they are nothing but his instrument."[136] Faith discerns that preaching is authoritative as and only as it is that activity through which God secures human recognition of *his* authority.

---

[130] *Comm.* John 21:15: *quasi in locum suum subroget.*

[131] *Comm.* John 7:16.

[132] *Comm.* Joel 1:1 and *Inst.* 4.8 passim.

[133] *Inst.* 4.8.2: *id totum non proprie hominibus ipsis, sed ministerio cui praefecti sunt dari.*

[134] *Inst.* 4.8.1.

[135] *Inst.* 4.8.4.

[136] *Comm.* I Pet. 4:4.

PREACHING BUILDS THE CHURCH

Jesus Christ alone builds up the Church. But in view of everything that has been discussed in this chapter Calvin maintains that the Church is "built up solely by outward preaching."[137] Preaching alone edifies faith. The "essential thing", with respect to the Church, is that God's truth be maintained "by the pure preaching of the gospel."[138] Preaching is the "master builder" whereby God sustains and adds to his Church.[139] In truth, while the saints have been born of imperishable seed, even they will wither unless the germinated seed is watered throughout life; "continual preaching" is that watering.[140]

Jesus Christ alone is the foundation of the Church. Yet the relation between him and the gospel is such that it is equivalent to say that the Church is built on the foundation of prophet and apostle; moreover, to say with Calvin, that Jesus Christ alone builds the Church is equivalent to saying that God has appointed those who hold the teaching office to build the Church.[141]Thus Calvin can say without contradiction that Christ alone is the foundation of the Church, and that in Christ the Church is founded by preaching.[142]

ELECTION AND PREACHING

Calvin is aware that much preaching appears to fall on deaf ears and hard hearts.[143] Then are preachers plunged into anxiety concerning the results of their activity? Worse still, are they to cope with anxiety by attempting (futilely) to generate "success" (that is, faith)? Calvin's answer to this question he regards as a reflection of the answer Jesus gave as he endeavoured to "put right the harm which had been done to their (the disciples') weak minds by the lack of success of the preaching."[144] The "answer" is that election guarantees the efficacy of preaching and thus spares preachers anxiety at its little "success": by virtue of God's eternal

---

[137]*Inst.* 4.1.S.

[138]*Comm.* I Tim. 3:15: *praecipuum.*

[139]*Comm.* I Cor. 3:10.

[140]*Comms.* I Cor. 3:10 and Eph. 4:12.

[141]*Comm.* Eph. 2:20.

[142]Ibid.

[143]*Inst.* 3.21.1.

[144]*Comm.* Matt. 15:13.

decree preaching cannot fail to engender faith in the elect, since preaching is the God-ordained means by which election becomes effectual calling. Believers will remember that at one time their situation was exactly that of the unbeliever who at present lacks even a capacity for the gospel:

> ". . . there is no reason why those who have some hope of salvation should despair of others. Whatever they may be, they have been like all others. If, by the mercy of God alone, they have emerged from unbelief, they ought to leave room for that mercy to operate among others also."[145]

The decree of election guarantees that some men will invariably be brought to faith through the preaching of the gospel.

At the same time, believers should not be "partially disheartened" in view of the preaching of the gospel's bringing life to but part of mankind. It is not the case that the gospel is but partly effective. Rather, the same preached gospel brings life to some and justly condemns unbelievers in such a way as to subserve the praise of God's glory. In other words, election guarantees the effectiveness of preaching, inasmuch as that preaching brings life and/or glory to God.

> "The good name of the gospel is in no way brought into disrepute by the fact that it does not profit all. For God is glorified when it brings about the ruin of the reprobate, as must happen. And if anything is a sweet savour to God, it ought to be this to us as well; that is, we should not be offended if the preaching of the gospel does not result in the salvation of all who hear it but should think it quite enough if it promotes God's glory by bringing to the reprobate a just condemnation."[146]

Since the spiritual corpse has no capacity for response, preaching can elicit that response appropriate to the declaration of the gospel (viz., faith) only as God creates it in men. The decree of election is God's promise that he will use preaching to do just this. Christ has been given for life; that life will arise from the proclamation of him faith cannot doubt.[147] The *double* decree guarantees that even where men are not brought to faith, preaching is still not futile: something *happens*.

---

145 *Comm.* Rom. 11:32.

146 *Comm.* II Cor. 2:15.

147 *Comm.* II Cor. 1:20. There runs throughout Calvin's discussion of election and preaching his insistence that God calls all men *promiscue* by the outward preaching (and hence "invites even the reprobate"), yet calls effectually only the elect (*De Aet. Dei Praed.* 70, 102, 106, 109; *Comms.* Matt. 23:37, Acts 13:48; *Inst.* 3.22.10, 3.24.8). Calvin maintains that life is the only intent (*illius proprium*) of the gospel; its becoming death-dealing is but "accidental" (*Comm.* II Cor. 2:15). However, he contradicts this latter assertion in *De Aet. Dei Praed.* 153. See chapter on election for a discussion of the difficulties in this matter.

"THE KEYS" AND PREACHING

As was seen earlier, perfection cannot be the ground of membership in the Church, since Christians continue to sin. Accordingly, mercy, which is to say forgiveness, is. Mercy both initiates and maintains faith; forgiveness is both the believer's adoption and his preservation since he continues to carry the "arrears" of sin throughout his life.[148] Fellowship in the Church (the *societas* of Christ) is maintained only by continual pardon.

Calvin insists as well that mercy (pardon) God has promised to the Church and indeed placed *solely* in the Church; outside the Church the "benefit" of forgiveness is not enjoyed.[149] The keys which open the door to the "treasure" have been given to the Church alone. Again, as was seen earlier, the fact that the gospel has been "deposited" in the Church does not mean that the gospel has been collapsed into the Church or inheres the Church; similarly, the keys have not been "given over" to the Church. Then how do the keys operate? It must be remembered that entry to the kingdom (remission of sins) is gained only through faith. But faith is created by and embraces the living Word alone. Accordingly, the power of the keys is simply the power of the Word; that is, the power of the living Christ, fellowship with whom and knowledge of whom are granted through the prophetic-apostolic witness to him. Since the remission of sins is granted through their witness and not through their person, the promise is made to all of the apostles in that Peter is but their spokesman; the other apostles have the same power to bind and loose *since they preach the same gospel.*[150] In other words, the power of the keys operates wherever but only wherever there is true apostolic witness to the living Word.

Calvin maintains that believers receive the benefit of pardon through the ministry of the *Church* itself when those "to whom this office has been committed strengthen godly consciences by the gospel promises in the hope of pardon."[151] The force of Calvin's contention should be noted carefully; sins are forgiven by the ministry of the Church, yet in doing so

---

[148]*Inst.* 4.1.21. Battles' "traces" for *reliquias* is much too weak, suggesting only a taint. Calvin's point is that sin is so pervasive that apart from Christ's *continual* forgiveness even the Christian would be expelled from the Church. While Calvin does speak in several places of baptism as that which initiates into the Church, this expression is a telescoping of his statement that "we are initiated into the Church by the sign of baptism, which teaches us that entrance into God's family is not open to us unless we are *first* cleansed of our filth by his goodness" (4.1.19, italics mine).

[149]*Inst.* 4.1.20, 4.1.22.

[150]*Inst.* 4.6.3.

[151]*Inst.* 4.1.22.

the Church does not usurp the place of him who alone can pardon. In truth, the Church remits sin in so far as she does not claim, *of herself*, to remit them. Again, while the power of the keys is conferred on the society of believers as a whole (Peter is a symbol of the whole Church),[152] it is "dispensed" (*dispensari*) through the pastors of the Church. To say that the gate of life is opened by the Word is, in Calvin's estimation, to say that the key is "put into the hand of the minister of the Word."[153] By way of emphasis Calvin adds, in his exegesis of the *locus classicus* pertaining to the keys, that sins are remitted by the "voice and testimony of men."[154] Indeed, while Christ's promise that those whose sins the apostles remit are indubitably remitted in heaven is hailed by Calvin as the sum of the gospel, he amplifies on this by reminding us that the remitting of sins must not be separated from the *teaching* office.[155] So intransigent is Calvin on this matter that any "key" to remission which is other than the preached Word he describes as "imaginary" in so far as it has been "manufactured magically" from God's Word.[156]

While the keys are conferred upon the Church as a whole, then, the door to the treasure is opened only as the preacher wields the key. Calvin's final, uncompromising word on this matter is that the apostles (and therefore the pastors) remit sin *only* as they preach.[157]

THE HOLY SPIRIT AND PREACHING

Throughout this discussion of preaching there have been references to the work of the Holy Spirit in the relation of preaching to faith. It has been noted in all the above chapters that the natural man, for Calvin, has no capacity for faith; precisely because the natural mind is "dark" faith is not "formed naturally by preaching alone" but only as "heavenly light" operates.[158] The human voice has no inherent power for penetrating men's stone-hard hearts; as a human activity alone preaching is profitless, a dead letter, mere words—in short, incapable of achieving or conferring anything by itself.[159] One sinner does not engraft another sinner into the

---

[152]*Inst.* 4.6.3.

[153]*Comm.* Matt. 16:19.

[154]Ibid.

[155]Ibid.: *a docendi officio.*

[156]*Comm.* Luke 11:52.

[157]*Comm.* John 20:23; cf. *Inst.* 4.11.1.

[158]*Comms.* John 15:27 and Acts 16:14.

[159]*Comms.* Rom. 10:17, Acts 16:14, John 15:27, Acts 26:18.

divine life. Nor is it the case that preaching is a form of "semi-Pelagianism," as though the Holy Spirit were added in order to supply what was insufficient in human endeavor. Rather, God so acts through preaching that the *entire* efficacy depends on his Spirit.[160] Without the Spirit the human voice is not so much inadequate as useless.[161] Indeed, in view of the spiritual condition of both hearer *and* preacher the birth of faith, in response to preaching, is nothing less than divine miracle.[162]

While no preacher can control or presume upon the Holy Spirit, it is equally sinful to doubt the presence of the Spirit to the preaching of the gospel; that is, to suspect that the Spirit is given spasmodically. Confidence in preaching is maintained only as one is certain that the relationship of Spirit to gospel ensures that the preacher's speaking is always the speaking of Jesus Christ himself.[163] The Spirit guarantees that the preached Word will always be a means of grace, Christ's self-declaration, and will never become merely a sign pointing to Jesus Christ (the difficulty then being that of bridging the gap between the preached word and the Word behind it). It is not the case that Spirit and preached word are related statically, as though the Spirit were simply "added to" the preached word (the homiletical equivalent of Nestorianism).[164] Rather, the Spirit is the preached Word in *its* power; the Spirit is the Word "forging" itself into mind and heart. It is never the case that the preached Word is "here" and the Spirit "over there," the two somehow being brought together. The Spirit effects God's never-failing adoption of the preached word, such adoption being necessary because of the sinfulness of the preached word; the preached word becomes the preached Word by grace alone.[165] In short, the Spirit's action is God's rendering the preached word *his* Word without transmuting the former into the latter. The preacher, then, has full confidence that when he utters what is creaturely his congregation hears what is divine.

---

[160]*Comm.* Eph. 5:26.

[161]*Comms.* John 17:3, Acts 16:14, I Thess. 5:24, II Pet. 1:3.

[162]*Comm.* I Cor. 3:6.

[163]*Sermon* I Tim. 1:1-2.

[164]Admittedly, Calvin can say, uncharacteristically, that the minister executes his commission and *then* the inward power of the Holy Spirit is joined to the outward voice (*Comms.* Psalm 105:31 and Acts 10:44; cf. *Sermon* II Tim. 1:1-2).

[165]By "preached word" I mean only the human, audible declaration of the minister; by "preached Word" I mean the human declaration which the Holy Spirit adopts and uses so as to render it the self-declaration of Jesus Christ. In his discussion of Calvin's doctrine of preaching Parker considers the creatureliness of the preached word but not its sinfulness (T. H. L. Parker, *The Oracles of God*).

While the presence of the Holy Spirit never excuses a preacher's laziness or incompetence, that presence does spare him anxiety concerning his "making a case" for the gospel; while the preacher is to spare nothing in applying what has been given him to say, he is *not* to attempt to persuade men himself. "Persuasion," Calvin insists, belongs to that "human wisdom" much valued by those who have lost confidence in the Spirit as the One who facilitates communication of the truth and reality of Jesus Christ.[166] In view of the unintelligibility of the gospel, "communication" is a miracle which the preacher is not called to attempt. The credibility of the declaration of the kingdom does not rest with him; indeed, "the foundation of faith would be frail and unsteady if it rested on human wisdom; and therefore, as preaching is the instrument of faith, so the Holy Spirit makes preaching efficacious."[167]

CONCLUSION

In view of his maintaining both that preaching begets faith and that no spiritual efficacy inheres the preacher, Calvin cautions his readers against either venerating or demeaning the ministry. On the one hand we must be careful of transferring to the ministry what belongs to God alone; on the other hand, God's using the ministry to bestow upon men his reality as Father "makes this name ('father') suitable for ministers."[168] Calvin himself must be allowed the final, succinct word of this discussion:

> "But when Paul calls himself a minister of the Spirit, he does not mean that the grace and power of the Holy Spirit are so bound to his preaching that he could, whenever he wished, breathe out the Spirit along with the words that he spoke. He simply means that Christ has blessed his ministry with his Spirit and so has fulfilled what was prophesied of the gospel. That Christ should grant his power to man's teaching is quite a different thing from that man's teaching prevailing in its own strength alone. And so we are ministers of the Spirit not because we hold him bound or captive (*inclusum et quasi captivum*) and not because at our own whim we can confer his grace upon all or upon whom we please, but because through us Christ enlightens men's minds, renews their hearts, and wholly regenerates them. It is because of this bond and conjunction (*coniunctio et nexus*) between Christ's grace and man's work that a minister is often given credit for what belongs to God alone. For this is done not out of regard for any mere individual but in the

---

[166] *Comm.* I Cor. 2:4.

[167] *Comm.* Eph. 1:13: *ergo sicuti praedicatio instrumentum est fidei, ita spiritus sanctus facit ut praedicatio sit efficax.*

[168] *Comms.* Eph. 5:26 and I Cor. 4:15.

light of the whole dispensation of the gospel, which consists both of the secret power (*arcana virtute*) and the external work of man."[169]

---

[169]*Comm.* II Cor. 3:6: ... *eo non intelligit, gratiam spiritus sancti ac vim suae praedicationi esse alligatam: ut quoties libuerit, una cum voce spiritum e guttere proferat. . . . aliud autem est, Christum adiungere hominis doctrinae suam virtutem, quam hominis doctrinam per se tantum valere.* Cf. *Comm.* I Cor. 3:7.

CHAPTER 8

THE SACRAMENTS AND FAITH

"But what is a sacrament received apart from faith but the most certain ruin of the Church?"[1]

"We have in the sacraments another aid to our faith related to the preaching of the gospel." Calvin amplifies this statement in his longer definition of a sacrament: "it is an outward sign by which the Lord seals on our consciences the promises of his good-will toward us in order to sustain the weakness of our faith; and we in turn attest our piety toward him in the presence of the Lord and of his angels and before men."[2]

That the concept of sacrament is most intimately related to that of faith is evident not only from the use of "faith" in the definition, but also from the mention of "promises," "seal," "good-will," all of which have been discussed earlier. The sacraments, then, are an aid to *faith*, divinely ordained by the ever-compassionate Lord who pities us in our ignorance, dullness and weakness.

Since the purpose of the sacrament is to strengthen faith, and since faith's author and object are the Word of promise, it follows that the sacrament strengthens faith in that it subserves the Word to which it is affixed and of which it is the sign. Indeed, the reader of Calvin must be careful to see that the sacrament does not support (quasi-magically) *my* faith directly, but rather confirms to me and in me the promise; in this manner it strengthens faith. The sacrament subserves faith by subserving the Word of promise which begets faith and which faith embraces. The sacrament adds nothing to the promise; it imports no new content into the Word. Rather, in confirming and sealing the promise itself the sacrament makes it "more evident" and "in a sense" ratifies it.[3]

---

[1] *Inst.* 4.14.14: *certissimum Ecclesiae exitium* (Fr. *la ruyne de L'Eglise*—"most certain" lacking).

[2] *Inst.* 4.14.1.

[3] *Inst.* 4.14.3: *testatiorum*—"more evident" (Battles), "better attestation" (Beveridge); *quodammodo*—"in a sense" (Battles), "in a manner" (Beveridge).

Why does Calvin use such expressions as "more evident" and "in a sense"? "More evident" pertains to the sacrament's (allegedly) being able to bespeak God's mercy with greater assurance to the person doubting his pardon than the (merely) verbal declaration; "in a sense" is Calvin's cautious reference to what he said earlier when discussing faith: that since the Word is both author and object of faith, that Word alone can authenticate faith; that is, faith is self-authenticating as it embraces the Word. However, since the Word can be embraced without the sacrament, and since such "embracing" (faith) presupposes the action of the Holy Spirit sealing the promise on the believer's heart, then the Word of promise ratifies itself. Accordingly, the sacrament can ratify the promise only "in a sense"; it is not that the sacrament ratifies the promise in the face of the promise's inability to ratify itself. Calvin wishes to avoid saying that something material *of itself* can strengthen faith; but neither does he want to say that if the Word can (and does) authenticate itself then the sacrament may be regarded as superfluous. (The latter, of course, would be little short of blasphemy, since God has deemed the sacraments necessary.) The sum of Calvin's teaching on the point is that the sacrament, in its function of ratifying the promise, never supplants the Word as that which ratifies (or better, the Word which ratifies in the power of the Spirit); nor does it ratify the promise in a sense other than that in which the Word (and Spirit) does, the word to which it is affixed.

Since there is an integral relation between the Word and the word of preaching, the Word is heard, understood, and received only where there is the preached word. The latter is not a "formula" which lends efficacy to the elements; it is that which explicates the meaning *for faith* of the visible sign.[4] (It must be remembered that the gospel, for Calvin, is not intelligible to the creature *qua* creature.) Without this preached word the sacrament degenerates into superstition. In other words, without the preached word there is no true sacrament—which is to say that without *preaching* the sacrament cannot confirm faith. The sacraments bespeak the promises—but only insofar as the Word is spoken along with the sacraments and informs them. In other words, the sacrament is the means whereby the Word is "reflected" with greater clarity upon our sin-darkened and doubt-beclouded faith.

---

[4]Cf. *Comm.* Acts 10:37: "And the chief thing in all sacraments is certainly this, that the Word of God, engraved in them, may give its light and its voice clearly to resound. That is all the more reason for detesting that impious profanation which is to be seen in the Papacy, because they have buried preaching and intone the sacraments with a merely magical muttering."

Since there is no faith without understanding (knowledge) —and understanding specifically the Lord's offer of mercy—faith and faith alone understands that what is to be apprehended in the sacraments is the Word (of mercy). Since faith's understanding is faith's knowing reception of Christ's self-communication, to unfaith the sacraments are but "cold and empty figures."[5]

It is most important that the Word be understood as the content of the sacrament, since Calvin is sometimes accused of affirming, in effect, that the believer's faith is the content. The foregoing dispels this notion. Moreover, since faith is precisely what needs strengthening, any device which merely "reflected" weak faith to weak faith would be worse than useless.

While it is certainly true that the Word is the content of the sacrament, Calvin insists equally on the truth that the Word never *inheres* the sacrament.[6] "God never resigns his office to outward symbols."[7] Grace is never enclosed (*includitur*) in a sacrament. God does not infuse himself into the sacrament; the creaturely is never deified, and the creaturely never becomes the object of faith. While sign and reality are not disjoined, they most certainly ever remain distinct.[8]

Distinct though sign and reality are, the reality is not so loosely associated with the elements as to suggest that it is *my* faith which conjoins Word to elements. Calvin argues that Paul, when testifying that the sacraments bring no benefits to unbelievers, indicates that there is no intrinsic efficacy in the sacrament; when Paul speaks of sacraments in relation to believers he speaks in a "telescoped" manner: by "metonymy" (one of Calvin's favorite expressions) the elements are referred to as including the reality.[9]

It is, of course, the Holy Spirit who reveals and fulfils in believers the "reality" to which the sacraments point (that "reality" missed by unbelievers). While the sacraments are indeed seals (that is, they certify that of which they are seals without adding to its content), they cannot perform this operation apart from the activity of the Holy Spirit. Thus Calvin can write that he assigns to the *sacraments* the particular ministry of confirm-

---

[5] *Inst.* 4.14.7.

[6] "Short Treatise on the Lord's Supper"; *Tracts and Treatises*, 185. Cf. *Comm.* II Cor. 3:6 where Calvin denies that the Word so inheres preaching that the preacher can "breathe forth the Spirit along with the utterance of the voice."

[7] *Inst.* 4.4.17: *resignet.*

[8] *Def. Doct. de Sac.* (*Calvini Opera* 9.18): *a rebus signati distincta sunt signa, non tamen disiungi nec separari.*

[9] *Comms.* Gal. 3:27 and I Cor. 4:10.

ing and increasing faith,[10] and then write a few pages after that the *Spirit of God* is the sole author of the confirmation and increase of faith.[11] Obviously, then, the sacraments and the Holy Spirit cannot be a seal in precisely the same sense; the elements are of the creaturely order while the Holy Spirit is God himself, the effectual action of the exalted Christ. Then what is the relation between the two types of seal? Calvin answers, "What increases and confirms faith is precisely the preparation of our minds by (the Holy Spirit's) inward illumination to receive the confirmation extended by the sacraments."[12] The sacraments, even as seals, cannot confirm faith by themselves. The Spirit, who alone can penetrate hearts, move affections and open souls, is he who makes actual the confirmation of the sacraments. Accordingly, Calvin insists on making "such a distinction between Spirit and sacraments that the power to act rests with the former, and the ministry alone is left to the latter—a ministry empty and trifling, apart from the action of the Spirit, but charged with great effect when the Spirit works within and manifests his power."[13] The sacraments strengthen weak faith, then, only as the Holy Spirit enables believers to "see" the Word engraven upon them.

But does not this suggest that the Holy Spirit renders the sacraments effective through begetting faith? Does not Calvin want to indicate that the Holy Spirit strengthens faith by rendering the sacraments effective? It must be remembered that Calvin will not countenance any notion of the Spirit's rendering a sacrament effective apart from the Spirit's rendering effective the Word to which the sacrament points. And "Word-rendered-effective" implies faith. It is the Spirit who renders both Word and sacrament (n.b. the order) effective witnesses to the living God who presses his mercy upon men. The sacraments hold out what the promises first hold out; and the sacraments can be received "properly" (effectively) only as the Word of promise is: through faith. Jesus Christ, the living Word, is the reality or substance of the sacraments.[14] He is offered to us in

---

[10] *Inst.* 4.14.9.

[11] *Inst.* 4.14.10.

[12] Ibid.: *illustrate proponitur.* This latter word means both "set forth" and "promise." Calvin's understanding includes both meanings.

[13] *Inst.* 4.14.9: *itaque sic inter Spiritum sacramentaque partior, ut penes illum agendi virtus resideat, his ministerium dumtaxat relinquatur: idque sine Spiritus actione inane et frivolum* (Fr. *inutiles et vains*): *illo vero intus agente.* It should be noted that in this section of the *Institutes* (4.14.8) Calvin speaks of faith as the proper and entire work of the Holy Spirit.

[14] *Inst.* 4.14.16: *materiam . . . substantiam.*

the word of promise and is received in faith.[15] The sacraments are effective only as through them the Word appears to us in "sharper focus."

Unbelievers who receive the elements certainly have Christ offered to them. However, since they do not participate in Christ ("Yet it is one thing to be offered, another to be received"[16]) they receive no benefit from the sacrament whose substance *is* Christ. While Word and sacraments have the same office, "to offer and set forth Christ to us, and in him the treasures of heavenly grace,"[17] Christ is received in the sacrament only as the Word is received in faith.

BAPTISM

"Baptism was given for the arousing, nourishing, and confirming of our faith."[18]

"Baptism is an appurtenance of faith, and therefore it is later in order; . . . if it be given without faith whose seal it is, it is both a wicked and exceedingly gross sacrilege."[19]

"Baptism is the sign of the initiation by which we are received into the society of the Church, in order that, engrafted in Christ, we may be reckoned among God's children."[20] In explicating the above definition throughout the *Institutes* and the *Commentaries* Calvin returns again and again to what he stated earlier in the discussion concerning sacraments: baptism is of no effect apart from faith; baptism does not infuse remission or renewal; it can but seal the promise; it confirms faith in the Word; apart from faith in the Word there is no adoption of "God's children," and hence baptism of itself cannot confer this reality; from baptism we obtain only as much as we receive in faith; baptism points to and seals believers in the Word (of mercy) illumined by the Holy Spirit and therefore received in faith. Baptism, which is a once and for all event in the life of the believer, while not effecting the irrevocable pardon, nevertheless attests an irrevocable pardon: those whom Christ draws into participation in himself he does not subsequently release or repel.[21]

---

[15] Ibid.: *offertur . . . suscipimus.* (Calvin often uses *apprehendo* for "receive." *Apprehendo* has the force of "seize" rather than merely "catch"—"receive." Calvin wishes to indicate both that the benefit is *given,* and that there must be a human affirmation.)

[16] *Inst.* 4.17.33.

[17] *Inst.* 4.14.17.

[18] *Inst.* 4.15.14.

[19] *Comm.* Acts 8:37.

[20] *Inst.* 4.15.1.

[21] *Inst.* 4.15.3. To be sure, the believer will sin subsequent to baptism, but continued faith-participation will determine his existence: sin is present, but sin is not "lord," and the sinful believer, granted standing in Christ, is no longer "seen" as guilty and condemned.

As expected, Calvin repeats in this section that baptism is not optional, it not being fitting for us to second-guess the Lord who insists that we need it. At the same time, he maintains that the Word or Spirit do not inhere the water of baptism. In fact, this is the error of those who "stop at the outward element, and on that fix their hope of salvation. . . . They do not regard Christ as the only author of all the blessings therein offered for us; they transfer the glory of his death to the water; they tie the secret power of the Spirit to the visible sign."[22] Calvin affirms, on the other hand, that "we ought to acknowledge in baptism a spiritual washing; we ought to embrace therein the testimony of the remission of sin and the pledge of our renovation, yet (says Calvin, returning to the first point) so as to leave to Christ his own honour, and also to the Holy Spirit; so that no part of our salvation should be transferred to the sign . . . the outward sign of itself avails nothing."[23] The reality itself (Christ and his benefits) must never be confused with or collapsed into the sign, for no one should "glory in a naked and dead sign."[24] The water attests that *Christ* is our cleansing. Calvin readily acknowledges that while nearly all persons are baptized, only a few are saved, since these latter did not receive merely the naked sign. Baptism should be received "really and effectually";[25] that is, received in the context and with the content of Word, Spirit, and faith, for the sign "has no efficacy without the Spirit."[26] When baptism is received with the Spirit-empowered faith whose object is the Word, then it is a "seal of the Word."[27]

Again, Calvin insists that the sign is not "empty," in that "God does not sport with us by unmeaning figures, but inwardly accomplishes by his power what he exhibits by the outward sign; and therefore baptism is fitly and truly said to be 'the washing of regeneration.' "[28] In short, "when Paul says that we are washed by baptism, his meaning is that God employs it for declaring to us that we are washed, and at the same time performs what it represents."[29] Calvin notes, similarly, that where Paul speaks of the faithful, he connects the reality and the effect with the outward sign; "for we know that whatever the Lord offers by the visible symbol is

---

[22] *Comm.* I Pet. 3:21.

[23] Ibid. For same idea see *Comm.* Acts 22:16.

[24] Ibid.

[25] Ibid.: *nudo signo.*

[26] *Comm.* Eph. 5:26.

[27] Ibid.

[28] *Comm.* Titus 3:5. For same idea see *Comm.* Acts 22:16.

[29] *Comm.* Eph. 5:26.

confirmed and ratified by their faith."[30] In other words, Calvin always wills to avoid (i) any notion that suggests that there is anything other than the closest association between the symbol and the reality to which it points, and (ii) any notion that the symbol "contains" the efficacy. He is trying to avoid both these errors when he says such things as "the grace of the Spirit shall always be annexed to baptism, unless the impediment be in ourselves."[31] Baptism's "real character" is the uniting together of the "institution of the Lord and the faith of the godly."[32] How careful Calvin is in this matter is evident in his insistence that baptism does indeed assure us of our salvation, "provided that we are ingrafted into Christ *by faith*."[33] Anyone at all may receive the sacrament; believers alone receive the reality with the sacrament. Ingrafting ever remains the function of the Spirit, not of the water as such; the "whole efficacy" of the sign depends on the Spirit (and therefore on faith).[34]

Admittedly, Calvin is at times somewhat unguarded in his discussion and does come close to declaring what he rejects as the error of Rome; for example, "our first regeneration was given to us through baptism alone."[35] Similarly, he occasionally speaks of union with Christ at baptism in a way which suggests that this union is effected through baptism, when he almost everywhere else states that union with Christ is effected only through faith (Holy Spirit), the efficacy of the sacrament of baptism presupposing faith. Almost always, however, Calvin's position is that baptism points us to, confirms us in, and assures us of what Christ presses upon people as the Spirit of Christ creates and maintains faith: "for because we receive Christ's gifts by faith, and baptism is a help to confirm and increase our faith, remission of sins, which is an effect of faith, is annexed unto it as unto the inferior means."[36] Calvin's last word on the topic is, characteristically, that "the true and proper use of the sacrament is to lead us directly to Christ, and to place all our dependence upon him."[37] There is no transmutation of Christ into the symbol.

---

[30] *Comm.* Rom. 6:4 (n.b. here again Calvin speaks of *faith* confirming what the symbol points to, rather than the symbol confirming faith).

[31] *Comm.* Acts 2:38: *impedimentum.*

[32] *Comm.* Rom. 6:4.

[33] *Comm.* Titus 3:5 (italics mine).

[34] *Comm.* Eph. 5:26; see also *Comm.* Titus 3:5 where Calvin maintains that with respect to "the washing of regeneration" Paul is speaking directly (characteristically— *proprie*) about the Holy Spirit while alluding (*alludere*) to baptism.

[35] *Inst.* 4.15.4.

[36] *Comm.* Acts 2:38: *effectus.*

[37] *Comm.* Eph. 5:26.

INFANT BAPTISM

> "Whoever does not have this (that is, Philip's confession of Jesus Christ as Saviour and Redeemer) when he is grown up, in vain does he boast of the baptism of his infancy. For to this end Christ admits infants by baptism, that so soon as the capacity of their age shall suffer, they may addict themselves to be his disciples; that being baptized with the Holy Spirit, they may comprehend, with the understanding of faith, his power which baptism prefigures."[38]

In the 1536 *Institutes* Calvin maintained that the baptism of infants was consistent with his theology of baptism and of sacrament generally in those cases where the candidates for infant baptism had been granted faith and hence had put on Jesus Christ and his benefits. Subsequently, however, he moved away from this contention and attempted to ground infant baptism in the covenant and what the covenant portends for children and their children. Of course, Calvin insisted that scriptural authorization could be found for this practice, and not merely tradition.

Calvin begins his defence of infant baptism by drawing comparisons between infant baptism and circumcision. God promised Abraham forgiveness of sins and instituted circumcision as a sign of remission and mortification. Calvin sees such similarities between the two rites that he says that whatever belongs to circumcision pertains likewise to baptism.[39] Since infants participate in the covenant, why should they be denied the sign of that covenant? "If they grasp the truth, why should they be driven away from the figure?"[40] (Whether, in fact, children do "grasp the truth" Calvin does not tarry to discuss at this point.) Having made a covenant with Abraham, the Lord immediately commanded it to be sealed in infants by an outward sign; and since Christ commanded that the children be brought to him, how can they be denied the symbol of fellowship? The parallelism, in Calvin's mind, is undeniable. (Again, the fact that "fellowship," *societas*, is used elsewhere in conjunction with faith and is virtually a synonym for *participatio* Calvin ignores at this point.) He sums up his statement concerning the appropriateness of infant baptism by saying,

---

[38] *Comm.* Acts 8:37.

[39] *Inst.* 4.16.4. Since this study deals only with the relation of faith to baptism, an exhaustive investigation of Calvin's understanding of baptism is not feasible. Suffice it to say that Calvin's asseveration concerning the relation of baptism to circumcision is pivotal, would bear minute scrutiny, and is problematic. In his exegesis of Col. 2:12 Calvin points out that circumcision made in the heart is the circumcision of Christ, and therefore that which is "outward" is no longer required. Flesh-circumcision foreshadowed the reality of Christ; when the reality is present, the foreshadowing is no longer required. Does not his argument here weaken his relating circumcision to infant baptism? Cf. Chapter Six for Calvin's understanding of the relation between circumcision and faith.

[40] *Inst.* 4.16.5.

"When we pay attention to the purpose for which it (that is, baptism) was instituted, we clearly see that it is just as appropriate to infants as to older persons."[41]

How "clearly" this can be seen, however, is very much in doubt, given Calvin's insistence that Christ and his benefits are granted only to faith. He seems to be aware of this: in a section where he puts forward several different arguments supporting the parallels of infant baptism and circumcision he can suddenly say, "all those who *by faith* receive Christ as author of the blessing are heirs of his promise, and are therefore called children of Abraham."[42] Not surprisingly, Calvin precedes and follows this assertion with other reasons for infant baptism, one of which is that children, "being engrafted into the body of the Church, are somewhat more commended to the other members. Then, when they have grown up, they are greatly spurred to an earnest zeal for worshipping God."[43] Similarly, he can speak of the rite as a "sort of" initiation into the Church, and a sign of spiritual regeneration.[44] What is the force of this "somewhat greater commendation to other Church members"? Can it ever justify the practice of *infant* baptism, in view of what Calvin believes scripture to affirm explicitly about baptism?

Developing yet another argument Calvin insists that the children of Christians are sanctified by their parents. His major support for this notion he finds in I Cor. 7:14, which verse he finds teaching that "the children of the pious are set apart from others by a sort of exclusive privilege, so as to be reckoned holy in the Church."

> In *Comm.* Romans 11:16 he argues that Israel was sanctified through Abraham; that is, the first fruits sanctify the whole lump; the goodness of the juice extends from the roots as far as the branches. Similarly, "posterity hold the same connection with their parents from whom they proceed."
>
> It should be noted that the footnote added by the translator of the Calvin Theological Society edition (1844-1855) suggests that the sanctification of Israel in Abraham was "external and relative, not personal and inward"—the Israelites enjoyed the external privileges of the covenant which God had made with Abraham, but were not thereby renewed individually. The footnote does not support the argument in the text.
>
> However, the distinction between the "external" privileges and the "inward" matter is supported by Calvin in *Comm.* Romans 9:7. Calvin has noted that some of the baptized children of believers do not come to faith; whereupon he answers that "the election of God is not tied to the natural descendants of Abraham, and it is not a thing that is included in the conditions of the

---

[41]*Inst.* 4.16.8.

[42]*inst.* 4.16.12 (italics mine).

[43]*Inst.* 4.16.9: *aliquando.*

[44]*Inst.* 4.16.30: *veluti initiatio.*

covenant."[45] *Some* of Abraham's descendants are "by special privilege elected out of the chosen people, in whom the common adoption becomes efficacious and valid."[46] Physical descent from Abraham does not guarantee salvation; but it does ground circumcision, and by extension, infant baptism. (Calvin never seems to have stated that inclusion in Israel was a matter of birth, while according to John 1:12-13 inclusion in Christ is not.) Calvin wants to say here that circumcision points to God's promise that he will be Israel's God; that is, it points to God's faithfulness. But a sacrament points to God's faithfulness in so far as it points to the Word—which Word is never without its power, the Holy Spirit, whose entire work is the creating and supporting of faith.

Calvin admits that children are by nature children of wrath (Eph. 3:2) and are conceived in sin (Psalm 51:7); hence "it is not as regenerated by the Spirit that believers beget children after the flesh."[47] However, in the case of believers' children this curse of nature is removed by the blessing of the covenant: "those who were by nature unholy are consecrated to God by grace"; since such children are "exempted from the common lot of mankind so as to be set apart for the Lord,"[48] why should they be denied the sign? The difficulty here, of course, is that throughout Book III of the *Institutes* Calvin has insisted that exemption from the common lot of mankind occurs only through faith-participation in the Exempt One.

Calvin returns to the argument that Christ enjoined children to be brought to him, whom he then quickened through making them partakers of himself. In a lengthy exegesis of Matt. 19:13-15 Calvin argues that as Christ receives the children he dedicates them to the Father, pours upon them the Spirit he has at his disposal, grants them participation in himself, and does not dismiss the children without bestowing on them some of the gifts of the Spirit. The children, too young to understand, are renewed according to the capacity of their age; the power which Christ has concealed in them will become fully manifest at the proper time. Calvin states that this passage proves false, *with respect to infants, that adoption is by faith only.* Next he states that the children were renewed to

---

[45]*Comm.* Rom. 9:7: *non alligari Dei electionem carnali Abrahae generationi, neque vero id contineri in foederi conditione. . . .*

[46]Ibid. The same expression is used in *Comm.* Rom. 11:2.

[47]*Comm.* I Cor. 7:14. It should be noted, in this context, that Calvin does *not* refer to infant baptism in texts which mention "households" and which even speak of households coming to faith; e.g., *Comms.* Acts 10:48, Acts 11:44, Acts 16:15, Acts 16:33, I Cor. 1:16, I Cor. 16:15, Heb. 2:13.

[48]Ibid.

the *hope* of salvation. Given their renewal, why should they be denied the sign?[49]

However, since faith is the proper and entire work of the Holy Spirit, can Christ, in Calvin's frame of reference, pour his Spirit upon them without bringing them to faith? What are "some of the gifts of the Spirit" which he bestows upon them? Can they be given gifts but not *the* gift (Holy Spirit and faith)? Why are the children renewed to the *hope* of salvation? Throughout this passage Calvin does not even allude to the argument of I Cor. 7:14. Why not?

Manifesting unease about the above, Calvin states that those infants who are to be saved in infancy are "previously regenerated by the Lord."[50] God sanctified John the Baptist *in utero*—and God can do it with others.[51] Christ, sanctified from infancy, can sanctify anyone from infancy. (Obviously, however, Christ's sanctification was not of faith; everyone else's is.) Moreover, previously to *what* were these infants sanctified who were to be saved? If previous to faith, then Calvin's fulminations against infused righteousness and baptismal regeneration have returned to haunt him. Is he going to say that justification is possible apart from faith? He does maintain that while believers are regenerated only by the Word of God, infants can be regenerated by "God's power"; the Lord can make himself known to them "in any way he pleases."[52] What has happened to the matrix of Word, Spirit, and faith? While the Lord begets faith of hearing "ordinarily," such ordinariness does not restrict him to this way; in addition to the "ordinary" manner of calling there is "another secret means."[53] Indeed, in the context of infant baptism Calvin can speak of the illumination of the Spirit apart from the medium of preaching.[54] Has the Spirit become divorced from the Word?

---

[49]*Comm.* Matt. 19:13-15: *consecrat . . . participationem* (the word Calvin uses everywhere with "faith"). Cf. *Comm.* Mark 2:1-12 where Calvin states that believers "propagate" the grace of God to their children (and grandchildren) before those children are born, even though children are not yet capable of faith.

[50]*Inst.* 4.16.17.

[51]*Inst.* 4.16.17. Oddly, Calvin does not develop his exegesis of Luke 1:15 ("he—John the Baptist—will be filled with the Holy Spirit, even from his mother's womb") to support this point. The force of the exegesis is that the operation of the Spirit in men is free. Calvin's discussion of this point does not substantiate his position concerning infant baptism.

[52]*Inst.* 4.16.18: *virtute.*

[53]*Comm.* Rom. 10:4 and *Inst.* 4.16.19: *ordinarium.*

[54]*Inst.* 4.16.19: *Spiritus illuminatione, nulla intercedente praedicatione.* (The French omits any reference to the illumination of the Spirit; it states that God can give *la foy aux siens . . . sans iamais leur faire ouyr parolle* insofar as he touches them inwardly.)

In yet a different argument Calvin maintains that infants are baptized into a future repentance and faith.[55] The secret working of the Spirit implants the seed of both within them, although repentance and faith are not yet *formed* in them.[56] However, within a few lines Calvin can add that since children receive forgiveness of sins, they should be baptized. Then is remission granted to unfaith, or has the seed issued in fruit: faith, in which case Calvin is returning to the position of the 1536 *Institutes*? Or is Calvin attempting to posit here a distinction between being regenerate (through faith) and being an heir of the covenant? In any case, the discussion as to what accrues to children through baptism pertains only to children of believers; the child of impious parentage is "reckoned as alien to the fellowship of the covenant until he is joined to God through faith."[57]

It would appear that on the subject of infant baptism Calvin's notion of the relations among the Word of promise, faith, and sacraments as seals of that faith has broken down. Calvin has lost sight of what he insisted upon in the chapter on justification; that while God does indeed perform what he promises, the promise-performance is established only in faith.

THE LORD'S SUPPER

"Christ is the only food of our soul."[58]

"The reality of the sacrament is that which is connected with the sign."[59]

The chief purpose of the Supper, as sacrament, is the strengthening of our faith; hence the Supper is "a special assurance that we are being helped by our God."[60] Since faith is the means by which everything that is Christ's becomes ours (as he himself becomes ours), the Supper bolsters

---

[55]*Comm.* Acts 8:37. See quotation at the beginning of this chapter.

[56]*Inst.* 4.16.20.

[57]*Inst.* 4.16.22. The difference in the situation of the children of believers and those of unbelievers, with respect to infant baptism, ultimately points to the relation between election and faith. E. Grislis ("Calvin's Doctrine of Baptism," *Church History*, Vol. 31, 1962) maintains that the tensions in Calvin's exposition of infant baptism can be resolved only through a restatemenc of Calvin's doctrine of election. J.D.Benoît ("Calvin et le Baptème des Enfants," *Revue d'Histoire et de Philosophie Religieuses*, 1937) argues, on the other hand, that the practice of infant baptism and its relation to election indicate that "God saves and sanctifies whom he will."

[58]*Inst.* 4.17.1; cf. "Short Treatise on the Lord's Supper," *Tracts and Treatises*, 166.

[59]*Comm.* Matt. 26:26: *veritas*.

[60]*Sermon* Titus 1:5-6.

our faith as through it we are enabled to "conclude assuredly" that what is his has indeed become ours efficaciously.[61]

Calvin insists that Christ is received in the reality of his death and resurrection, that such reception effects our remission and renewal, that such reception is through faith, and that understanding (knowledge) is part of that faith: "we do not eat Christ duly and unto salvation unless he is crucified (and) we in living experience grasp the efficacy of his death."[62]

Again, Calvin associates very closely the reality (Christ) and the sign which points to it; the bread is "as bread for the spiritual life of the soul . . . when being offered to us to eat, it makes us sharers in him by faith."[63] When the sign is shown, the reality itself is "shown," or else God is a deceiver. And unless the reality were given with the sign, faith would not pertain to it. The consecration of the elements (wherein Christ appoints an earthly and corruptible sign for a spiritual use) can take place *only* if "his command and promise are distinctly heard for the edification of *faith*."[64] In other words, while Christ's body must be received (Christ himself not being dissociated from his body and blood; that is, "Jesus Christ" is not a disembodied spectre or spirit), that body (Christ himself) is *never* transmitted by the mouth; rather, the elements are a sacrament only to those persons who hear the Word in faith.[65]

At the same time Calvin stresses that the action of eating and drinking helps the communicant realize that Christ is not received by "mere knowledge"; faith is not merely "understanding and imagination"; the knowledge of faith is not that of an "intellectualism"; *notitia* and *assensus* do not of themselves constitute faith. Christ does not make himself ours because we happen to understand certain concepts.

The action of eating reminds the communicant that Christ must be "embraced" and not simply be viewed "from afar"; Calvin again reminds

---

[61] *Inst.* 4.17.4: *certo.* Since Christ's benefits cannot be separated from Christ himself, Calvin insists that in the Supper Christ himself is received—deity and humanity, body and blood. However, in criticizing the Lutherans Calvin denies that Christ's "flesh" is received where that flesh is the sort that a butcher handles. Calvin repudiates as well the Lutheran notion of the ubiquity of Christ's body on the grounds that it renders Christ's humanity unreal.

[62] *Inst.* 4.17.4: *neque enim Christo, rite et salutariter* (Fr. *avec fruict*) *vescimur nisi crucifixio, dum efficaciam mortis eius vivo senso apprehendimus.* Beveridge's translation is weaker: "We do not eat Christ duly and savingly unless as crucified, while with lively apprehension we perceive the efficacy of his death."

[63] *Inst.* 4.17.5: *nobis autem porrigi ut vescamur, quum fide nos facit eius participes.* (The French is lacking entirely.) Beveridge: "*he* extends it to us for food when *he* makes us partakers of it by faith" (italics mine).

[64] *Comm.* Matt. 26:26 (italics mine).

[65] *Inst.* 4.17.15.

his reader that there is no eating of *Christ* apart from faith. Apart from faith, the elements alone are consumed. In his discussion of the pertinent passages in the Fourth Gospel, Calvin insists that Christ *alone* is our life. and hence Christ's command to "eat" is his exhorting us to faith, "which alone enables us to enjoy this bread, so as to derive life from it."[66] Since faith alone is the life of the soul, all that nourishes and assists faith is compared to food[67] or, changing the metaphor, faith is the God-ordained manner of eating the flesh of Christ; the holy Supper is a seal and confirmation of God's ordination.[68] Calvin's final word on this is that "it is mockery to dream of any manner of eating the flesh of Christ without faith, since *faith alone* is the mouth so to speak, and the stomach of the soul."[69] The purpose of the Supper is to point us to Christ, who is God's self-offering for us and to us and the life of our lives.

While all communicants are "offered" and "shown" the signified reality, believers alone receive its "benefit,"[70] since believers alone receive in faith the one who *is* the benefit; which is to say that the Holy Spirit (whose entire work is faith) gives Christ to the believer: without the Holy Spirit, Christ is not received at all. The faithful embrace Christ in the Supper, not because Christ inheres the elements, but because the Holy Spirit binds believers to Christ.[71] Indeed, with respect to the Supper Calvin accuses the Schoolmen of being little concerned with true faith, by which alone we attain fellowship with Christ.[72]

----

[66] *Comm.* John 6:51; cf. "Short Treatise on the Lord's Supper," *Tracts and Treatises*,

[67] *Comm.* John 6:27.

[68] *Comm.* John 6:55.

[69] *Comm.* John 6:56 (italics mine).

[70] *Inst.* 4.17.11: *cum fructu* (lacking in French).

[71] Calvin denies that Christ is "enclosed" (*inclusum*) in the elements. On this ground he rejects the Lutheran notion that all communicants receive Christ, unbelievers receiving him to their detriment. Christ is life, and as such cannot be received to anyone's detriment.

The Holy Spirit overcomes the spatial separation between Christ and believers— something that believers "experience" rather than understand: *experior magis quam intelligam* (*Inst.* 4.17.32).

K. McDonnell fails to understand Calvin at this point. He writes, "To say that we receive Christ substantially in faith can be quite orthodox. But it is quite something else to say that union with Christ in faith and union with Christ in the Eucharist take place in the same way. To this degree his doctrine of union with Christ in the Eucharist wants a sacramental realism. Instead of explaining the very real sacramental efficacy by means of instrumental causality, he explained it by the role he assigns to the Holy Spirit" (*John Calvin, the Church, and the Eucharist*, 375). "Instrumental causality" is precisely what Calvin wishes to avoid by means of speaking of the function of the Holy Spirit. Christ is no less "truly present" in the Eucharist in virtue of the Spirit's activity.

[72] *Inst.* 4.17.13: *vera fide.*

To conclude: the "right attitude," the "worthiness" to bring to the sacrament, "consists chiefly in faith, which reposes all things in Christ, but nothing in ourselves."[73] By means of the bread and wine Christ intended nothing else than that our faith remain fixed on him *alone*.[74]

---

[73]*Inst.* 4.17.42.

[74]*Comm.* Matt. 26:27.

CHAPTER 9

A CRITICISM OF THE DISCUSSIONS OF WALTER STUERMANN AND EMILE DOUMERGUE CONCERNING CALVIN'S UNDERSTANDING OF FAITH

WALTER STUERMANN

W. E. Stuermann, in his doctoral dissertation, *Calvin's Concept of Faith* (Tulsa, 1952), attempts to indicate the role of faith in virtually every aspect of Calvin's theology; hence he discusses creation, fall, natural theology, Scripture, justification, sanctification, prayer, Christian freedom, the Church (preaching, sacraments and doctrine) and meditation on the future life. Although its breadth is commendable, his treatment often overlooks the coherence and therefore at times the profundity of Calvin's thought. Since the present work examines the same aspect of Calvin's thought as did Stuermann's, it is perhaps necessary to indicate where Stuermann's work is deficient and why the author of this study believed that this area of Calvin's thought still called for explication.

Nowhere in his book does Stuermann discuss election and its relation to faith, even though Calvin states frequently that election is the sole cause of faith. Not surprisingly, then, Stuermann fails to indicate clearly that the "mirror" of election, Jesus Christ, in the power of his own Spirit, is the author and object of faith. When election (Jesus Christ) is not recognized as the *prius* of faith, faith inevitably comes to be understood as "something in itself which saves"; the Spirit ceases to be the Spirit of Christ alone; the nature and function of Scripture are misapprehended;

and the eschatological dimension of Calvin's theology is unappreciated. In the remainder of this section I shall attempt to expound these criticisms.[1]

Stuermann speaks of faith as "the means for the apprehension of abiding values" (374) indicating in the context no understanding of Jesus Christ as that reality which creates the faith to which faith is directed. Similarly, he maintains that faith is the answer given to the question, "How can I be saved?" where his discussion contains no reference at all to the "Lord Jesus Christ" in whom one is to believe (36). In other words, he blurs the distinction between δια πιστιν and δια πιστεω. Indeed, because he fails to appreciate Jesus Christ as the "whence" and "whither" of faith he finds no difficulty in saying, "with faith comes an impetus to flee to the mercy of God" (58), not realizing that the "impetus" is mercy drawing man to itself. For Stuermann, mercy does not create faith nor does faith embrace mercy. Failing to appreciate that mercy alone can act positively upon man who deserves nothing, and failing to discern that as a spiritual corpse fallen man is incapable of raising himself, Stuermann speaks of "the tremendous responsibility" which the fallen creature has to "rise again to life with God" (60). While he does say that the Trinity is the "multi-personal Spirit which initiates faith," he yet fails to understand the centrality of Jesus Christ as *Deus erga nos*, as the One who *acts* in the power of his Spirit on the sinner's behalf; for this reason Stuermann maintains that faith "must first look to the Holy Spirit, the immediate minister of religious life, then through the Spirit to Christ, and finally through Christ the mediator to God himself" (70). (Throughout Chapter One of his book he uses "God himself" to mean "God unmediated," the annihilating One. What he means on page 70 is uncertain.) In a protracted statement Stuermann maintains, without any reference to Jesus Christ at all, that "the highly personal and esoteric nature of faith is also indicated by Calvin's insistence that faith is a secret work of the Spirit in the human mind and heart, and that it is intimately connected with pious affections and a personal confidence in God's good will toward us" (95). But nowhere does he indicate that God's good will is mercy; "good will" suggests little more than kindly indulgence. Similarly, he argues that since confidence must be "in" something "on the basis" of something, then "the Spirit, by *illuminatio* and *obsignatio* delivers the mind from confusion and the will from bondage to sin, and directs them to God. Then after the renewal and redirection of the will, it can exhibit a trust or confidence in

---

[1] Hereafter in this chapter the numbers in parentheses indicate the page number of the work discussed.

God" (107). For Stuermann the Spirit redirects the will so as to facilitate trust in God—without any reference to Jesus Christ as the mercy in whom the mercy-renewed will is allowed to stand before God. Despite Calvin's frequent use of expressions such as "put on Christ," "fellowship with Christ" and "participation in Christ," Stuermann can speak of obedience as being conformed to the divine will (without any discussion of Jesus Christ as that will) and as being given a "new spiritual life" (111). To whom is obedience rendered? What motivates one to render it?

Stuermann does not discern Calvin's understanding of the relation between Jesus Christ and gospel; he speaks of the gospel as a "further mediating agent" which "stands between the faithful subject and the triune God" (70). In what sense is the gospel a *further* mediating agent? To what is it "further"? If the gospel stands between the believer and the triune God, then what is its relationship to Jesus Christ, who is, everywhere in Calvin, the sole mediator? Just as Stuermann says little about Jesus Christ he says little about the living Word, preferring to identify the Word with scripture. In one of the few places where he plainly does *not* intend Word to mean "Scripture" but gospel, he argues that the "divine intention to save men is expressed in Christ and the Word" (69). What is the force of "expressed"? Is not the divine intention known only as God *acts* to save men? He then adds that the Holy Spirit is "the divine agent" (again, no reference to Jesus Christ) by which *God* initiates faith and keeps it fixed on its "objects" (69). Why does faith have two objects (Christ and the Word)? Failure to relate Jesus Christ and gospel adequately suggests failure to relate both to preaching adequately. And indeed Stuermann is vague and inaccurate in his discussion of the role of preaching in the genesis and nurture of faith: "inspiration and the preaching of the Church" he maintains to be the "dual sources" of faith (318), as though inspiration and preaching were two "ingredients" without logical or theological connection. A few pages later he states that faith is produced when preaching is "done under the auspices of the visible Church" (322). However, his omission of any discussion of the "keys," of the "treasure" which has been "deposited" in the Church, and of the nature of the authority of the Church leaves the reader with no interpretation of "auspices"; thus the reader is left without any indication of the manner in which the preaching of the Church is authoritative and brings forth faith.

When Stuermann does consider the relationship of Jesus Christ to faith he does not recognize Jesus Christ as constitutive of faith; rather, he asserts that the revelation of the promises in God's Word (that is, Scripture) "confirms and supports the personal experience of believers" (93); these promises are the "external criterion" of assurance (there being no discussion of Jesus Christ as the One who bestows himself upon men and enables them to *know* it). "Jesus Christ" is connected to the promises in God's Word, and hence has some significance for faith, but the connection and the significance are not clearly articulated: at best, Jesus Christ illustrates or confirms a situation or an experience which the Christ-less Spirit has brought about. Moreover, while Stuermann is correct in discerning some connection between the promises and faith, he does not understand that Jesus Christ, as mercy, is *the* promise; when he considers the relationship of faith to the promises, in his discussion of meditation on the future life, he states, "Now a promise is the declaration of the future achievement of what is not yet possessed. Thus, when it is said that faith relies with confidence upon the divine promises, we have expressed the inevitability with which faith is drawn toward the future and the unswerving contemplation of last things which is indigenous to it" (353). For Calvin, however, meditation on the future life is related to promise in that believers know that the mercy which constitutes their Christian life now will never vanish. In short, Stuermann does not know what the promise is in Calvin's thought, and hence does not understand the relation of promise to faith.

While the "first principle" of Calvin's epistemology, argues Stuermann, is "personal relationship" (again there is no mention of Jesus Christ as one of the persons in the relationship), the "second principle" is conformity to *Scripture* (123). Stuermann does not appear to appreciate the function of scripture in the genesis of faith, nor, consequently, the nature of the authority of scripture. Whereas for Calvin, Jesus Christ, as *sermo Dei*, is that Word which creates faith, Stuermann speaks instead of Scripture as the "congealed" form of the Word of God (presumably, Jesus Christ is the "uncongealed" form) to which men must resort "if they require authentic information about God" (144)—that is, "heavenly information" (146). As a "repository of wisdom" (159) scripture is the "Spirit's means of ministering to the human soul" (154, 157). Not surprisingly Stuermann insists that *Scripture* is "the complement of faith" (151, 153). The matter is not rendered any clearer or more accurate with his suggestion that both Scripture and faith are "dual aspects of the one process of acquiring knowledge and salvation" (151). That faith which "directs itself" to scripture finds there the "benevolence" of God (Stuermann does not indicate that Jesus Christ *is* that benevolence) as well as the "will of God" (164). (For Stuermann "will of God" is not mercy but claim alone.) Indeed, unbelievers, discerning only the claim, fear God's "vindictive" power (214). In saying this Stuermann is ignoring Calvin's tireless repetition of the truth that the gospel, God's unambiguous mercy, is only life-giving and becomes death-dealing only "accidentally" as unbelievers "make it so."

Because he is unaware of Calvin's concentration upon Jesus Christ as *the* eternal God (*Comms*. John 1:1 and I John 1:1) Stuermann fails to recognize that for the reformer Jesus Christ is the substance of the God-given law. Thus, in considering the third use of the law, he does not apprehend the law as that obedience enjoined by Jesus Christ as he conforms to himself those who are in him; instead, Stuermann maintains that obedience-in-faith is "the attempts on the part of the faithful to make their conduct conform to God's specifications" (283) as they strive after "perfection" (289); indeed, through the law the believer serves God "in a life which is a mean between an exuberant lustfulness and a stifling asceticism" (262). Any discussion of Jesus Christ and the law is conspicuously absent.

Inasmuch as Stuermann fails to understand Jesus Christ as he who bestows faith as he acts in the power of his Spirit, he fails to understand the Spirit as the Spirit of Christ only and as having no other task than that of binding men to him and him to them. Rather, in Stuermann's understanding the Spirit is a "power" which God visits upon persons in order to grant them "faith" (even though it is never clearly stated that faith can be only faith in Jesus Christ). Thus Stuermann can say that faith is "a gift of God which comes through the secret work of the Spirit in the soul of men" (317), or that it is the role of the Spirit to convey and support the gift of faith (69), without indicating that faith is the act of Jesus Christ giving himself so as to effect the reception of himself, all in his own power. Earlier it was indicated that Stuermann did not appreciate the relation of Jesus Christ, gospel and preaching; he reflects this lack of understanding when he comes to speak of the Spirit: "the work of the Spirit on the mind and heart is simultaneous with the reception of the preached Word" (81). Simultaneity is but a temporal relation; there is lacking a discussion of the logical (theological) relation of Spirit and preached Word, and of course of Spirit and preached Word to Jesus Christ.

This misapprehension Stuermann reflects again and again; for example, in order to elect a man to salvation God "gives him faith by the secret inspiration of the Spirit" (329); faith is "initiated and supported by the secret work of the Spirit" (322); faith is "an instrument for the self-disclosure of God, administered and governed by the Spirit" (93). The principal point is omitted. Similarly, Stuermann speaks of assurance as "a personally apprehended certainty ministered to the human mind and heart by the Spirit" (94), without indicating that believers are granted assurance only as they are assured *of Jesus Christ* who comes only to make them his. Stuermann fails to indicate that Calvin relates the "inner" testimony of the Spirit to Jesus Christ and to Scripture by declaring that this Spirit is Christ in present power illumining the apostolic witness to himself as he bestows himself upon men; Stuermann can only say that the inner testimony "denotes also the reformatory and confirmatory work of the Spirit in the human heart"; similarly, the testimony of the Spirit is "a particular application of the broader distinction of the Spirit's mastery of all of life" (101). Whereas for Calvin *vivificatio* refers to the believer's aspiring to "work out" (Phil. 2:15) that new life which has become his (eschatologically) in virtue of Jesus Christ's having become his, Stuermann maintains that *vivificatio* "refers first of all to that change brought about by the Spirit in the soul" (217).

The misapprehension in the above arises from Stuermann's failure to understand the Spirit as the power in which Jesus Christ acts to bestow himself upon men; his saying, then, that the Spirit "ministers a work of God to the soul" (98) and that "the Spirit and faith are instruments of salvation" (225) is understandable, but it is a departure from Calvin's way of putting the matter. For Calvin, the Spirit is never a "power" which bestows faith or grants assurance apart from the Word.

Inasmuch as Stuermann fails to represent properly the place of Calvin's understanding of election, mercy and the Spirit in the creation of faith, he fails to take seriously Calvin's insistence that faith is but an "empty vessel," the Spirit-facilitated receiving of Jesus Christ. Grace disappears, and there is now predicated of faith what properly pertains to grace. Thus Stuermann can speak of faith (albeit from the "human perspective") as the "basis" of salvation (4); God offers faith as the "condition" for reconciliation (23); faith "goes before" (before what?) as the "condition" for insertion into the Church (329); faith is the "condition" for efficacious partaking of the Lord's Supper (343); faith "brings the requisite condition" for in it God "undertakes to reveal himself clearly and certainly to man" (140). Stuermann's interpretation of Calvin's concept of faith reaches its culmination when he argues that "faith institutes a new relationship to God" (26). This would be acceptable only if Stuermann were employing the word "faith" metonymically. It is clear that he is not. Thus, it is necessary to state that for Calvin, Jesus Christ (Word, grace) institutes the new relationship with God; moreover, faith *is* this relationship. While for Calvin, Jesus Christ (grace) is the mediator who bridges the abyss between God and man brought about by sin, Stuermann speaks of faith as "the device of God used for this purpose" (47). Faith is no longer the joyful recognition of and grateful reception of what God has done; faith is now the "doer." Again, Stuermann reverses the relation of grace and faith: "in the personal religious history of an individual, he is first given faith. With this faith he acquires a knowledge of God's nature and will" (49); "by faith the Spirit leads us into the light of the gospel" (70); faith "brings" felicity (124); it is faith which illumines minds and makes hearts "amenable to receive heavenly information" (146). The same confusion of faith with grace is evident in his saying that the Church "arises from faith and the Word" (156). (Does the Word merely confirm that faith which is logically prior to it?) It is faith (not grace) which "effects regeneration" and "effects a mystical union with Christ" (167); faith is the foundation of repentance (203); forgiveness of sins is granted solely on account of faith (208); faith gives the elect hope and consolation (251).

While Stuermann insists that it is faith which "brings," "does," "effects," even "saves" (101), the reader is left unsure as to what exactly faith does bring, in view of the paucity of reference to Jesus Christ as the object of faith. The unsureness is magnified as the reader learns that faith brings "the achievement of the chief good(s) of man," and "furthermore" brings a mystical union with Christ (374). What are the chief goods of man? How can these be brought unless Jesus Christ is brought? And if faith brings them, what is the force of "furthermore"? Stuermann nowhere indicates an understanding of faith as the act of Jesus Christ creating human capacity for receiving him even as he presses himself upon men and women.

It appears that Stuermann often counters the "flow" of Calvin's thought. For instance, Stuermann reverses Calvin's understanding of the relation of soteriology and epistemology; for Calvin soteriology precedes epistemology: epistemology is an implication of soteriology. Stuermann everywhere suggests that intelligibility precedes soteriology: God imparts knowledge, and in virtue of man's acquiring that knowledge, salvation is bestowed. That this is clearly Stuermann's view of Calvin's thought is indicated where he maintains that, according to Calvin, "knowledge and salvation" are given in faith (2); and where he contends that he is interpreting Calvin by placing in apposition to "whatever knowledge is given to man", "whatever religious insights and loyalties are realized by him" (3). While Calvin insists that Jesus Christ appears to remedy the defilement of sin, Stuermann argues that "Christ becomes man and God not only to give a clear and certain knowledge of God, but also to hide his majesty" (13). While Stuermann does admit that knowledge and "participation in the saving effects of faith" (no mention is made of participation in Jesus Christ) occur simultaneously, he does not indicate logical (soteriological) priority (64). Hence the reader finds inappropriate in a thesis concerning Calvin's notion of faith assertions such as, "faith is the instrument for the acquisition of knowledge" (72) and "from the human perspective . . . faith must first appear as the instrument whereby the various parts of true wisdom become clear and certain to man" (72). Stuermann spends a considerable part of one chapter indicating how Calvin's understanding of faith is a means of moving beyond the nominalist/realist and the rationalist/empiricist controversies in the theory of knowledge, including a note informing the reader that the distinctively human modes of description and manipulation "are relative to the type of nervous system and perceptive mechanisms which the human body has for dealing with the world" (78). This has nothing at all to do with that knowledge which Calvin maintains to be integral to faith. Equally inappropriate as an interpretation of Calvin is Stuermann's contention that the knowledge appropriate to faith is one which "goes far beyond what can be achieved by the exercise of the intellect. It is equivalent to an intuitive perception of God himself" (150).

Stuermann also counters the "flow" of Calvin's thought in speaking of the Word of God as the complement of faith (46) and of faith as that by which man can "avail himself of God's self-disclosure" (138). This misunderstanding of Calvin by Stuermann is well illustrated in the following:

> "First, there is an inner illumination of the mind and a sealing action on the heart. This is interpreted by Calvin as a personal acquaintance with God, marked by certainty, clarity, vividness, and pious affections. This personal relationship to God, which transcends man's ordinary powers of comprehension, is what the term *fides* refers to. Second, *inseparably correlated* with this subjective aspect of the Spirit's work, there is an objective aspect, the Spirit's ministry to the soul through the written Word. Faith discovers that the Word has been efficacious in its generation." (160; italics his.)

For Calvin, illumination and sealing are always a consequent of the Word's going forth in its own power.

Calvin speaks of faith as fellowship with Christ, participation in Christ, engrafting into Christ, or union with Christ. Stuermann discusses this aspect of Calvin's theology in terms of an *unio mystica*, but does not succeed in relating adequately this term to Calvin's understanding. For Calvin faith *is* union with Christ; Stuermann, on the other hand, states that faith includes a mystical union (45, 180) or effects a mystical union (94, 184, 324); that the mystical union is the ground of justification (187, 191). Nowhere does Stuermann indicate how these three usages of *unio mystica* are related. The reader is not helped upon being informed that the mystical union is the "inhabitation of the soul by the spirit of Christ" (196). (Note the lower-case "s.") What is the spirit of Christ, and how is its inhabiting the soul related to justification? How can the mystical union be "the bond between faith and repentance" (218) if it is but an aspect of faith? For Calvin believers are justified in that they have fellowship with (are united to) the righteous One, a perfect fellowship in the *eschaton*, which perfect relationship is at present imputed to them. Stuermann fails to understand this and hence asks why imputation of Christ's righteousness is necessary (that is, why believers must be given a standing not in themselves but in Jesus Christ) if faith *already* effects a union with Christ; and if such an imputation is in order, what the mystical union adds to the situation (182). Stuermann does not understand the relation of Jesus Christ the righteous One, imputation, and faith as union with that One; rather he thinks fellowship with the righteous One and the mystical union to be distinct. His uncertainty is made evident in his saying, "the phrase *eius participatione sumus iusti*, which Calvin uses, seems to imply an intimate mystical relation between Christ and the human soul" (191).

In so far as Stuermann does not recognize Jesus Christ to be the author and object of faith he fails to perceive the eschatological dimension in Calvin's understanding of faith. God acts in Jesus Christ to bring to the fulness of righteousness (that is, right relation with him) his chosen. This full or total righteousness is first of all present in Jesus Christ. It is present now in God's chosen by the imputation of final righteousness and thus the believer is already *totus iustus* as well as *totus peccator*. However, believers believe and await the fulfilment of the day of the Lord when they will only be wholly righteous, the wholly sinful being removed from them then. Because Stuermann does not comprehend this emphasis in Calvin he fails to see that the justified man is the man given standing in the eschatological One; instead he describes the justified man as one whom God "reputes" just—without referring to Jesus Christ (173). His uncertainty and confusion are reflected in his saying, "the fact that Christ dwells in the creature by faith may be the reason that God looks upon the creature *as if* Christ's righteousness were his" (186; italics his). Stuermann manifests the same lack of understanding of eschatology in his discussion of repentance, where he fails to discern that the believer's repentance is his aspiration to live ("live out") that which he is (eschatologically) in virtue of Christ's having become his, even though the "arrears" of sin remain with him. Having misunderstood Calvin at this point Stuermann suggests that the reformer maintains that "a part of the unregenerated man remains under the power of death and Satan" (210), and elsewhere that repentance is but partial because of the "unreclaimed portion of the soul" (242). Which part of the regenerated man remains under the power of death? which portion of the soul? Stuermann never understands repentance as "Christ is my king now," but as "an increasing participation of the spirit of Christ" (221), since the restoration of life is "not once for all" (226)—this against Calvin's assertion that it *is* eschatologically! Again, Stuermann misses the eschatological dimension in Calvin because he misses the determinative place of Jesus Christ. Thus he can speak of repentance as conversion ("basically an inner transformation effected by the Spirit"—389) and never mention the One who is the new, true Man. Because he does not recognize Jesus Christ and participation in him as the truth and reality of the believer's existence, Stuermann thinks that that truth and reality is the partial "improvement" in character which the Holy Spirit has effected.

While this reader of Stuermann's book does not wish to engage in pedantic fault-finding or in magnifying unnecessarily the weaker parts of the book, nonetheless he is driven to conclude that some of Stuermann's interpretation of Calvin is not merely unusual but simply incorrect. This assessment, severe though it is, cannot be withheld in virtue of his assertion, for instance, that the written Word is the object of faith (158). Again, Stuermann contradicts, rather than explicates, Calvin when he insists that if faith is an "empty vessel" or "nothing in itself" then it is ineffective; that while faith certainly "brings a man empty before God" it is inadmissible to conclude that "faith in itself is nothing" (54). Rather, faith is "a 'something' originated by the creator" (54). If faith were not this "something" then it could not "convey positive saving benefits" (54). However, Stuermann never indicates what the "something" is and how the "something" yet remains an empty vessel. Calvin's point, of course, is that while faith is a genuine human affirmation, faith does not contribute anything to justification, sanctification, and so forth; that there does not inhere man a human qualification for fellowship with Jesus Christ. Faith is "nothing in itself" in that the life of faith is not the admixture of "something" and Jesus Christ; rather, faith is the action of Jesus Christ creating his own receptivity. Stuermann's remark, "It is we who are empty, not faith" (56) suggests that faith is something which is added to man, or a *tertium quid* between God and man. This reader's assessment of Stuermann is confirmed when the latter argues that "faith is 'something' of a divine nature through which the benefits of Christ are communicated to us and a new spiritual life is our possession" (56). " 'Something' of a divine nature" is not Calvin's expression and appears to be unrelated to anything which is. Stuermann continues his argument, contending that "if all that could be said about faith is that it conducts a man before God destitute of every virtue, it would be no instrument of redemption" (56). Has he confused himself by his use of "instrument"? Even if not, why would faith not be an "instrument of redemption" if it "did" as little as Stuermann suggests? Indeed, why is it not an instrument of redemption *only* if it is but an empty vessel? (It should be noted that Calvin does not speak of faith as "conducting a man before God".)

Stuermann does not correctly represent Calvin where he maintains that Calvin spoke of God as revealing himself "in faith," "in nature," and "in Scripture" (127). "In" is used equivocally; to say that God reveals himself "in faith" and "in Scripture" is to commit a category error. Similarly, Stuermann speaks of God's self-disclosure "in nature, in scripture, and even in himself" (139). He does not realize that revelation is always *by* God *of* God; revelation "in Scripture" is not other than revelation "in himself." Indeed this is why Stuermann does not understand the nature of the authority of scripture in Calvin's thought; according to Calvin God authenticates scripture to us as he authenticates himself to us through scripture. Stuermann does not grasp Calvin's argument; instead, he thinks that Calvin affirms that scripture is authoritative in so far as it is a repository of edifying "heavenly information." Thus Stuermann urges us, according to his understanding of Calvin, "to direct our attention to those portions of Scripture which conduce to edification" (130). Again, his confusion and uncertainty are reflected in his weak statement, "it seems that Calvin conceives Scripture to stand in a different and special relation to faith than that between nature and faith" (142).

Stuermann has not grasped what Calvin means by "knowledge" when he faults Calvin for using the word in instances where that knowledge is not publicly verifiable ("the public availability of the reputed event"— 372), adding, "One may be sentimental about the approach to God through personal experience and feel in part the significance of what Calvin has to say about faith as knowledge, but the seriousness of this criticism cannot be shrugged off" (372). So far from being "serious" his "criticism" and indeed the interpretation of Calvin upon which he bases his "criticism" is at a remove from "serious" examination of Calvin's thought. His errors were foreshadowed in the early part of his book when he suggested that all "celestial" knowledge *must* be relative since even "terrestrial" knowledge is rendered relative by man's not apprehending all pertinent sense-data and by the peculiarity of his nervous system (33). Similarly this reader can only conclude that Stuermann is far from Calvin's theology when he maintains that faith is "the common denominator by which the divine and human persons can be shown to be commensurate" (36). For Calvin, faith has nothing to do with demonstration; and God and man are *never* "commensurate." Furthermore, faith is *not* that which "makes the human creature amenable for the reception of a knowledge of God" (36).

In short, Stuermann has failed to grasp Calvin's notion of faith and its relation to the determinative aspects of his theology: Jesus Christ, Holy Spirit, and eschatology. In places Stuermann's interpretation of Calvin is unbalanced; in places it is simply wrong.

EMILE DOUMERGUE

Since the work of E. Doumergue has stood for many decades (over fifty years) as the principal exposition of Calvin's thought it is fitting that this study include a brief examination of Doumergue's work. As a major Calvin scholar, Doumergue (*Jean Calvin:* Geneva, Slatkine Reprints, 1970), of course, presents Calvin's understanding much more accurately and impressively than Stuermann. In Doumergue's work we see expounded the major points: faith is entirely the work of Jesus Christ (Vol. 4: p. 240); faith is not mere credulity (4: 243); faith is always imperfect (4: 246); while faith is ever man's putting on of Jesus Christ, man puts on Christ only in the power of the Holy Spirit (4: 240). In short, Doumergue does not commit the serious errors of Stuermann with respect to the nature of faith, the function of the Holy Spirit, the object of faith, the role of the Scriptures, et al.

A major disappointment in Doumergue's presentation, however, is that he devotes little space to an exposition of several very important areas of Calvin's thought; for example, his exposition of the third use of the law receives only one-half page; the first use, three-quarters of a page; the Holy Spirit, two pages; "justification by faith," one-half page. Because Doumergue seeks to offer a comprehensive view of Calvin, his presentation of specific points in doctrine is often brief and his critical remarks briefer still. In expounding an aspect of Calvin's thought Doumergue usually makes a statement requiring no more than two lines and then adduces several quotations from Calvin to support his statement. As a result the reader is often offered a catena of Calvin citations rather than an articulation of Calvin's understanding. In addition, Doumergue's comments which preface the quotations do not always reflect precisely the nuances of Calvin's thought; the presentation tends to be truer to Calvin when Calvin is quoted than when he is discussed; for example, in the presentation of the relation of judgment to justification, Doumergue states that *faith* is man's only refuge, and then quotes Calvin to the effect that the refuge of the unrighteous is his "embracing" the Righteous One himself (4: 267). Again, Doumergue discusses the peace which justification and assurance bring to the conscience as an instance of Christian mysticism (4: 269); the quotation from Calvin he brings forward, however, does not suggest that consciences are assuaged because of mystical awe, but because the believer hears and receives God's promise of pardon, wherein he is assured that God is propitious. Calvin's argument simply does not depend on the peculiarities of mysticism as a religious genus.

The same passing over of the finer distinctions in Calvin's thought is evident in Doumergue's discussion of the law. Here he does not state plainly that Jesus Christ is the substance of the law (although he does allude to it when he notes that both Old and New Testaments speak of redemption and the Redeemer [4:199] and when he speaks of the "continuity of revelation"—[4:201]): that the condemnatory function of the first use of the law is but "accidental"; that law and letter are distinguished sharply; that the second use of the law is a "school" for the obedience of faith; that the third use of the law is the action of Jesus Christ whereby he conforms believers to himself. Indeed, Doumergue's statement of the third use of the law is weak: "A servant who desires to serve his master well and to please him in everything needs to familiarize himself with the customs (*moeurs*) of his master, in order to adapt himself to them" (4: 193). While Doumergue does present lucidly an aspect of Calvin's understanding, namely, that the law is necessary in order to bridle the believer's proclivity to sin, he does not expound the law as that by which Jesus Christ gives "shape" to the lives of those who have become his. At the beginning of his discussion of law Doumergue quotes Calvin as saying that God's gracious act of liberation is the ground of his claim upon Israel's obedience, but Doumergue himself does not appear to give due notice to Calvin's statement; he does not amplify it or integrate it into his presentation of the law; nowhere does Doumergue discuss the believer's motive (gratitude) for obeying the law (4: 181-83).

Doumergue appears to miss a fundamental point in his understanding of Calvin throughout his discussion of justification by faith and its relation to sanctification. Calvin maintains that justification and sanctification are not directly related to each other; that is, they are not related as objective aspect to subjective aspect, nor does one ground the other. Rather, justification and sanctification are related to each other in so far as they are two aspects of the one work of Christ. While one is never present without the other (since Christ cannot be divided), neither does one effect the other. Doumergue, however, does ground sanctification in justification; the former is an aspect of the latter; indeed, Doumergue's table of contents informs the reader that sanctification is an *element* of justification (4: 483). Throughout his *Commentaries* Calvin states again and again that the sum of the gospel is justification *plus* sanctification or regeneration or newness of life; one is not to be collapsed into the other. Doumergue's failure to discern the distinction between and the relation of justification and sanctification lends a moralistic aspect to his consideration of the topic; sanctification is a "moral element" in justification (4: 271); the inexorability of divine judgment puts a question to men "on religious and moral grounds, above all" (4: 267). While the reader is aware of what Doumergue means in this context (that is, he has not completely falsified Calvin's understanding), he is yet disturbed by the vocabulary in view of Calvin's insistence that "religion" and "morality" are activities of *fallen* man and are not manifestations of faith.

The confusion of sanctification and justification is likely related to Doumergue's overlooking the eschatological dimension of Calvin's thought. Doumergue maintains that the first element of justification is imputation (of Christ's righteousness) while the second element is regeneration. For Calvin, a man is "seen" either in Christ or in himself; to be "seen" in Christ is to be given standing outside himself; that is, to have Christ's standing imputed to him and his sins not imputed. This is an eschatological reality since the believer continues to sin. Doumergue, overlooking the eschatological dimension, adds regeneration to justification in order not to render justification empty or artificial or specious. When Doumergue speaks of the "immediate results" of justification he mentions the preservation of God's honour and the assuaging of troubled consciences (4: 268), but he does not speak of new standing in Christ. And when Doumergue discusses sanctification he does not speak of the effectual Kingship of Jesus Christ in whose Kingly power the believer is enabled to (begin to) "live out" his new existence; instead he speaks of that "moral" conduct which contradicts the accusation that free justification encourages antinomianism (4: 271). In attempting to protect Calvin from this accusation Doumergue argues that sanctification is a *psychological* consequence of faith in Jesus Christ (4: 270). This line of misinterpretation arises from his confusion of sanctification with justification and his overlooking of the eschatological rootage of both "benefits."

Doumergue refers several times to good works as "proof" of salvation or of election (4: 284-85). However, the appeal to good works is an aspect of his doctrine of election which Calvin did not magnify, and which indeed appears as a surd element in his theology: as long as believers remain sinners, and as long as their works require justification (a point which Doumergue does not mention) then how can an appeal to their works confirm anything but believers' sinfulness? Calvin maintains, in *Comm.* Col. 3:3, that the sanctification of believers is discerned only by faith; sanctification is "nowhere evident" to the "senses," including the senses of believers themselves. Hence the reader must regard Doumergue's insistence that "good works are proof of faith, of salvation, of election" (4: 284) in the theology of Calvin as insufficiently critical.

While Doumergue does state, as was indicated at the beginning of this critique, that faith is the work of Jesus Christ, his discussion of faith contains little reference to Jesus Christ as the author and object. Faith is said to admit one to the *status justificationis*, but faith is not considered at length as the Christ-facilitated embracing of the Son himself. Most conspicuously absent is a forceful reference to the fact that Christ as sheer *mercy* is the author of faith.

Doumergue does discuss adequately and accurately Calvin's understanding of election in terms of the disqualification of merit, in terms of the assurance of salvation Calvin reckoned it would bring to believers, and in terms of Calvin's prohibiting speculation concerning the decrees. Similarly, Doumergue notes perceptively the shift in the location of Calvin's articulation of the doctrine from the context of Providence (1539 *Institutes*) to the context of participation in Christ (1559 *Institutes*). When he remarks that predestination is not the foundation of Calvin's theology but the "key block" which sustains the edifice (4: 357), presumably he means that Jesus Christ *is* the foundation of Calvin's theology and that the "key block" is the sovereign power of God whereby he engrafts into Christ those who are, of themselves, wholly incapable of fellowship with him.

Doumergue did not, however, indicate either the great strengths or the great weaknesses of Calvin's doctrine. The strength of Calvin's presentation is his insistence, in many places throughout the *Commentaries*, that Jesus Christ is the sole, definitive Word and act of God; that the "whole God" is found in him; that in him God appears "essentially"; that in the Son are hid *all* the treasures and the wisdom of God; that in him alone God is known truly; in brief, that election to life is the *one* decree of Father and Son. The weakness of Calvin's presentation is his insistence upon the "secret counsel," that will of God which contradicts mercy. (Doumergue states without any explication that the mystery of God's secret counsel is a "mystery of justice"—4: 387.) In brief, the weakness, as indicated in Chapter Four, occurs as Calvin shifts the focus from *voluntas* to *arbitrio*. Inasmuch as Doumergue does not indicate Calvin's strengths and weaknesses in this doctrine he does not comment critically on the difficulties in Calvin's presentation. Thus, Doumergue defends Calvin's notion that the Word is the mirror and confirmation of election, but does not indicate that that Word is relativized by a "secret" word alongside it (4: 370). Similarly, Doumergue argues that predestination is not an invitation to speculation but rather a postulate of one's reflection upon experience (4: 358), without mentioning the pitfall which awaits the inferring of theological verities from empirical observation. Indeed, Calvin often warns his reader against ever departing from the Word as the foundation for all correct theological knowledge. In various places Doumergue states that faith is "proof" of election (4:371, 398); however, to assert this unqualifiedly may be to urge faith to instrospect in order to gain assurance, whereas Calvin usually qualifies this "proof" by the additional comment that faith gains assurance only as it looks away from itself to Jesus Christ. Finally Doumergue avoids the discussion of the reprobate and the difficulties concerning reprobation by speaking of election as if it were synonymous with predestination (4: 369). Predestination and election, however, are not synonymous. A contemporary reader cannot so evade the issue, and thus it was discussed above in Chapter Four.

In his discussion of the Church Doumergue mentions both the marks of the Church and Calvin's insistence on an ordained ministry, but he does not elaborate upon why that ministry is necessary or how the marks of the Church are related to the functions of the ministry (5: 39). Nor does he elaborate on the relation of preaching to Jesus Christ (his entire discussion of preaching occupies only one-quarter page) beyond saying that by the Spirit, God acts through his Word and by the selfsame Spirit God acts through his ministers (5: 39); nor does he elaborate on the manner in which preaching is constitutive of the Church. While Doumergue does state that the Word is the authority of the Church (5: 58) he does not indicate *how* the authority of the Word, that is, the prophetic-apostolic authority, and the authority of the Church are related. Also lacking is a discussion of the "keys." Content to say that for Calvin the ministry is of the *esse* of the Church, Doumergue adds, without explanation or comment, "No ministry, no Church" (5: 96, 98).

Doumergue's discussion of the sacraments, and especially of the Lord's Supper, has surely earned the acclaim of being an accurate reflection of Calvin's understanding. Nonetheless, the reader is somewhat surprised at the brevity of his discussion of the function of the Holy Spirit (one-quarter page). The subsequent paucity of reference to the Holy Spirit most likely accounts for his insistence that in entering the area of the sacraments we are entering fully (*en plein*) the domain of Calvin's mysticism (5: 329); that baptism is a "realistic mysticism" (*mysticisme réaliste*—5: 330); that Calvin's doctrine of the sacraments is a "mean" between a "gross and magical realism" and a "cold and empty symbol" (5: 335). Here Doumergue employed a vocabulary which is largely foreign to Calvin; Calvin's understanding of the Holy Spirit obviates any need to speak of his notion of the sacraments as a mean between grossness and emptiness.

In attempting to strengthen Calvin's argument for infant baptism Doumergue brings forward considerations which Calvin does not mention; for instance, Doumergue insists that the way in which the question of whether or not to baptize infants was answered determined whether the Reformation would give rise to a Church or a sect (5: 336); that to repudiate infant baptism is to deny that the Church is a society which rears children in grace, and to promote division in the Church (5: 337). (Doumergue never indicated why these consequences would arise from the repudiation of infant baptism.)

Finally, the reader is puzzled by Doumergue's inclusion in a theological discussion of extra-theological considerations which Calvin never mentions. Doumergue maintains that Calvin's "heteronomy" (that is, Calvin's rejection of faith as a human work) is "the most creative human autonomy which the world has ever seen" (4: 240). Similarly, Doumergue defends the *theological* understanding of predestination on the grounds that the highest civilization is found in those countries which affirm it in its purity; Arminianism is incapable of attaining a "truly elevated degree" of civilization (5: 414). Philosophical determinism (the genus of which Calvin's doctrine of predestination is a species) is to be valued in that it "guarantees its adherents a remarkable moral vigour;" viz., the absoluteness of a "general order" (5: 391). Ultimately, do these assessments have anything to do with Calvin's theology?

BIBLIOGRAPHY

SOURCES

Calvin J. *Calvini Opera*, Vols. 1-59 (*Corpus Reformatorum*, Vols. 29-87.) Ed. G. Baum, E. Cunitz, E. Reuss.

_____ . *Concerning the Eternal Predestination of God*. Trans. J. K. S. Reid. London: James Clarke and Co.

_____ . *Deux Congrégations et Exposition du Catéchisme*. Ed. R. Peter. Paris: Presses Universitaires de France, 1964.

_____ . *Institutes of the Christian Religion*. Trans. F. L. Battles. Philadelphia: Westminster Press, 1960.

_____ . *Institutes of the Christian Religion*. Trans. H. Beveridge. Grand Rapids: Eerdmans, n.d.

_____ . *Instruction in Faith* (1537). Trans. P. T. Fuhrmann. Philadelphia: Westminster Press, 1950.

BOOKS

Barth, K. *Calvin*. München: C. Kaiser, 1936.

_____ . *Calvinfeier*. München: C. Kaiser, 1936.

_____ . *The Faith of the Church*. Trans. G. Vahanian. New York: Meridian Books, 1958.

_____ . *Die Kirche und die Kirchen*. München: C. Kaiser, 1935.

_____ . *Das Problem der Natürlichen Theologie bei Calvin*. München: C. Kaiser, 1935.

Berkouwer, G. C. *Calvin and the Church*. Amsterdam: Vrije Universiteit, 1959.

Biéler, A. *The Social Humanism of Calvin*. Trans. P. T. Fuhrmann. Richmond: John Knox Press, 1964.

Bohatec, J. *Calvin und das Recht*. Darmstadt: Scientia Verlag Aalen, 1971.

_____ . *Calvins Lehre von Staat und Kirche*. Darmstadt: Scientia Verlag Aalen, 1961.

Boisset, J. *Calvin et la Souveraineté de Dieu*. Paris: Editions Seghers, 1969.

Bolsec, J. H. *Vies de Jean Calvin et de Théodore de Bèze*. Génève, 1835.

Bossert, A. *Calvin*. Paris: Hachette, 1906.

Bratt, J. H. *The Life and Teachings of John Calvin*. Grand Rapids: Baker Book House, 1958.

Breen, Q. *John Calvin: A Study in French Humanism.* Grand Rapids: Eerdmans, 1931.

Bretschneider, K. G. *Calvin et l'Eglise de Génèe.* Trad. G. de Felice. Génève: J. J. Paschoud, 1822.

Cadier, J. *The Man God Mastered.* Trans. O. R. Johnston. London: Inter-Varsity Fellowship, 1960.

Cairns, D. *The Image of God in Man.* London: Collins, 1973.

Cornut, X. *L'Académie de Calvin: Extrait de la Grande Revue de ler Février 1902.* Génève: H. George, 1902.

Crawford, D. J. *God in Human History.* Diss. Knox College, Toronto, 1967.

Cubine, M. V. *Calvin's Doctrine of the Work of the Holy Spirit.* Ann Arbor: University Microfilms, 1955.

Dakin, Z. *Calvinism.* London: Duckworth, 1940.

Davies, R. E. *The Problem of Authority in the Continental Reformers.* London: Epworth Press, 1946.

Doumergue, E. *L'Art et le Sentiment dans l'Oeuvre de Calvin.* Geneva: Slatkine Reprints, 1970.

———. *Le Caractère de Calvin: L'Homme, le Système, l'Eglise, l'Etat.* Geneva: Slatkine Reprints, 1970.

———. *Jean Calvin, les Hommes et les Choses de son Temps.* Lausanne: G. Bridel, 1899-1927.

Dowey, E. A. *The Knowledge of God in Calvin's Theology.* New York: Columbia University Press, 1952.

Duffield, G. E., ed. *John Calvin.* Appleford, Abingdon (Berks.): Sutton Courtenay Press, 1966.

Farris, A. L. *John Hus, Churchman, Patriot and Martyr* and *John Calvin: Obedient Servant,* n.d.

Favré-Dorsaz, A. *Calvin et Loyola, Deux Réformés.* Paris: Editions Universitaires, 1951.

Fläto, L. "How Does Sinful Man Come to a Knowledge of God? A Comparison of Luther and Calvin." Diss. Wycliffe College, Toronto, 1951.

Forstman, H. J. *Word and Spirit.* Stanford: Stanford University Press, 1962.

Friethoff, C. *Die Prädestinationslehre bei Thomas von Aquin und Calvin.* Freiburg: St. Paulus-Druckerei, 1926.

Gagnebin, B., ed. *A la Rencontre de Jean Calvin.* Génève: George, 1964. (Textes et documents de Jean Calvin.)

Ganoczy, A. *Calvin, Théologien de l'Eglise et du Ministère.* Paris: Editions du Cerf, 1964.

———. *Le Jeune Calvin: Génèse et Evolution de sa Vocation Réformatrice.* Wiesbaden: F. Steiner, 1966.

Gauthiez, P. *Etudes sur le Seizième Siècle.* Paris: Leceve, Oudin, 1893.

Gentle, S. W. "The Significance of the Law for John Calvin." Diss. Knox College Toronto, 1964.

Grass, H. *Die Abendmahlslehre bei Luther und Calvin.* Gütersloh: C. Bertelsmann, 1954.

Gutersohn, V. *Calvin als Mensch, Mann der Kirche und Politiker.* St. Gallen: Schweizerischer CVJM Verlag, 1945.

Hall, B. *John Calvin: Humanist and Theologian.* London: Historical Association, 1956.

Hall, C. A. *With the Spirit's Sword: The Drama of Spiritual Warfare in the Theology of John Calvin.* Richmond: John Knox Press, 1970.

Harkness, G. E. *John Calvin, the Man and His Ethics.* New York: Holt, 1931.

Hauck, W. A. *Vorsehung und Freiheit nach Calvin, ein Evangelisches Glaubenszeugries.* Gütersloh: C. Bertelsmann, 1947.

————. *Was Sagt Uns Heutigen Calvin? Die Schuldfrage im Spiegel der Christliche Lehre von Sünde und Erbsünde.* Heidelberg: Jedermann Verlag, 1946.

Hoogland, M. P. *Calvin's Perspective on the Exaltation of Christ in Comparison with the Post-Reformation Doctrine of the Two States.* Kampen: J. H. Kok, 1966.

Hunter, A. M. *The Teaching of Calvin.* London: James Clark, 1950.

Imbart de la Tour, P. *Les Origines de la Réforme, Tome IV.* Paris: Firmin-Didot, 1935.

Jacobs, P. *Prädestination und Verantwortlichkeit bei Calvin.* Darmstadt: Wissenschaftliche Buchgesellschaft, 1968.

Jansen, J. F. *Calvin's Doctrine of the Work of Christ.* London: J. Clark, 1956.

Jones, J. M. "The Problem of Faith and Reason in the Thought of John Calvin." Diss. Duke, 1942.

Kolfhaus, W. *Christusgemeinschaft bei Johannes Calvin.* Neukirchen: Buchhandlung des Erziehungsvereins Neukirchen Kr. Moers, 1949.

————. *Vom Christlichen Leben nach Johannes Calvin.* Ansbach: Erziehungsvereins Neukirchen Kr. Moers, 1949.

Lamorte, A. *Réflexions à propos des Doctrines de la Prédestination et du Baptème chez Calvin.* Paris: Librairie Protestante, 1959.

Lechner, J. M. *Le Christianisme Social de Jean Calvin.* Génève: Labor et Fides, 1953.

Leith, J. H. "Creation and Redemption: Law and Gospel in the Theology of John Calvin." In *Marburg Revisited: A Re-examination of Lutheran and Reformed Traditions.* Ed. C. Empie and J. I. McCord. Minneapolis, 1966.

Lobstein, P. *La Connaissance Religieuse d'après Calvin.* Paris: Fischbacher, 1909.

McDonnell, K. *John Calvin, the Church and the Eucharist.* Princeton: Princeton University Press, 1967.

McKenzie, P. R. "The Invisibility of the Church for Luther and Calvin." Diss. Edinburgh, 1953.

Milner, B. C. *Calvin's Doctrine of the Church.* Leiden: Brill, 1970.

Mülhaupt, E., ed. *Der Psalter auf der Kanzel Calvins, Bisher Unbekannte Psalmenpredigten.* Neukirchen: Neukirchen Verlag, 1959.

Neeser, M. *Le Dieu de Calvin d'après l'Institution de la Religion Chrétienne.* Neuchâtel: Secrétariat de l'Université, 1956.

Niesel, W. *The Theology of Calvin.* Trans. H. Knight. London: Lutterworth Press, 1956.

Nixon, L. *John Calvin's Teachings on Human Reason* New York: Exposition Press, 1963.

Parker, T. H. L. *Calvin's Doctrine of the Knowledge of God.* Grand Rapids: Eerdmans, 1959.

————. *Calvin's New Testament Commentaries.* London: SCM Press, 1971.

Quistorp, H. *Calvin's Doctrine of the Last Things.* Trans. H. Knight. Richmond: John Knox Press, 1965.

Reuter, K. *Das Grundverständnis der Theologie Calvins.* Neukirchen: Neukirchen des Erziehungsvereins, 1963.

Richard, L. J. *The Spirituality of John Calvin.* Atlanta: John Knox Press, 1974.

Rilliet, J. H. *Calvin.* Paris: Fayard, 1963.

Rolston, H. *John Calvin versus the Westminster Confession.* Richmond: John Knox Press, 1972.

Schmidt, A. M. *Calvin and the Calvinistic Tradition.* Trans. R. S. Wallace. London: Longmans, 1960.

Sebestyen, P. "The Object of Faith in the Theology of Calvin." Diss. Chicago, 1963.

Senarclens, J. de. *Heirs of the Reformation.* London: SCM Press, 1963.

———. *De la Vraie Eglise, selon Jean Calvin.* Génève: Editions Labor et Fides, 1965.

Stob, H., ed., *Justification and Sanctification.* n.p., 1965.

Stuermann, W. E. *A Critical Study of Calvin's Concept of Faith.* Tulsa, 1952.

Tholuck, A. *Calvin as an Interpreter of the Holy Scriptures.* Trans. Woods. Edinburgh: Calvin Translation Society, 1854.

Torrance, T. F. *Calvin's Doctrine of Man.* London: Lutterworth Press, 1949.

Walker, W. *John Calvin, the Organizer of Reformed Protestantism.* New York: Schocken Books, 1969.

Wallace, R. S. *Calvin's Doctrine of the Christian Life.* London: Oliver and Boyd, 1959.

———. *Calvin's Doctrine of the Word and Sacrament.* London: Oliver and Boyd, 1953.

Warfield, B. B. *Calvin and Augustine.* Philadelphia: Presbyterian and Reformed Publishing, 1956.

———. "Calvin's Doctrine of the Knowledge of God," In W. P Armstrong's *Calvin and the Reformation.* New York: Fleming H. Revell, 1909.

Wendel, F. *Calvin: The Origins and Development of His Religious Thought.* Trans. P. Mairet. London: Collins, 1963.

Willis, E. D. *Calvin's Catholic Christology.* Leiden: E. J. Brill, 1966.

JOURNAL ARTICLES

Battenhouse, R. W. "Doctrine of Man in Calvin and in Renaissance Platonism," *Journal of Historical Ideas,* 9 (Oct. 1948), 447-71.

Benôit, J. D. "Calvin et le Baptème des Enfants," *Revue d'Histoire et de Philosophie Religieuses,* (1937), 457-73.

Berkeley, D. "A Vulgar Error Touching Calvin's Doctrine of Total Depravity," *Notes and Queries for Readers, Writers, Collectors and Librarians,* 14 (1951), 293-95.

Bray, J. S. "Value of Works in the Theology of Calvin and Beza," *Sixteenth Century Journal,* (October 1973), 77-86.

Brouwer, A. R. "Calvin's Doctrine of Children in the Covenant. Foundation for Christian Education," *Reformed Review,* 18 (Jan. 1965), 17-29.

Bulman, J. M. "The Place of Knowledge in Calvin's View of Faith," *Review and Expositor,* 50 (1953), 323-29.

Casteel, T. W. "Calvin and Trent: Calvin's Reaction to the Council of Trent in the Context of His Conciliar Thought," *Harvard Theological Review,* 63 (June 1970), 91-117.

Coates, Thomas. "Calvin's Doctrine of Justification," *Concordia Theological Monthly*, 34 (1963), 325-34.

Courvoisier, J. "La Dialectique dans l'Ecclésiologie de Calvin," *Revue d'Histoire et de Philosophie Religieuses*, 44:4 (1964), 267-422.

Crawford, J. R. "Calvin and the Priesthood of All Believers," *Scottish Journal of Theology*, 21 (Jan. 1968), 145-56.

Dakin, A. "Calvin's Doctrine of Baptism," *Baptist Quarterly*, 9 160-64.

Dankbaar, W. F. "L'Office des Docteurs chez Calvin," *Revue d'Histoire et de Philosophie Religieuses*, 44:4 (1964), 267-422.

Edwards, C. E. "Calvin on Infant Salvation," Bibliotheca Sacra, 88 (July 1931), 316-28.

Emerson, E. H. "Calvin and Covenant Theology," *Church History*, 25 (June 1956), 136-44.

Farris, A. L. "Calvin and the Laity," *Canadian Journal of Theology*, 11 (Jan. 1965), 54-67.

Fuhrmann, Paul T. "Calvin the Expositor of Scripture," *Interpretation*, 6 (1952), 188-209.

Geocaris, K. "Image of Man: The Perspectives of Calvin and Freud," *Interpretation*, 14 (Jan. 1960), 28-42.

George, A. R. "The Theology of Calvin," *Expository Times*, 63:12 (1951-52), 375-89.

Gerrish, B. A. "Biblical Authority and the Continental Reformation," *Scottish Journal of Theology*, 10 (Dec. 1957), 337-60.

———. "John Calvin and the Meaning of the Reformation," *McCormick Quarterly*, 21 (Nov. 1967), 114-22.

———. "John Calvin and the Reformed Doctrine of the Lord's Supper," *McCormick Quarterly*, 22 (Jan. 1969), 85-98.

———. "The Lord's Supper in the Reformed Confessions," *Theology Today*, 23:2, 224-43.

———. "To the Unknown God: Luther and Calvin on the Hiddenness of God," *Journal of Religion*, (July 1973), 263-92.

Gordh, G. "Calvin's Conception of Faith," *Review and Expositor*, No. 51 (1954), 207-15.

Grensted, L. W. "The Theology of Calvin," *Catholic Quarterly Review*, 155 (1954), 406-407.

Grislis, E. "Calvin's Doctrine of Baptism," *Church History*, 31 (Mar. 1962), 46-65.

Hesselink, I. J. "Development and Purpose of Calvin's Institutes," *Reformed Review*, 28 (1970), 136-42.

———. "Charismatic Movement and the Reformed Tradition," *Reformed Review*, 28 (1975), 147-56.

Hesselink, John R. "The Catholic Character of Calvin's Life and Work," *Reformed Review*, 19 (1965), 13-19.

Hoekema, Anthony, "The Covenant of Grace in Calvin's Teaching," *Calvin Theological Journal*, 2 (1967), 133-61.

Huizinga, A. V. C. P. "Calvinistic View of Church and State," *Bibliotheca Sacra*, 83 (Apr. 1926), 174-84.

Hunt, R. N. C. "Calvin's Theory of Church and State," *Church Quarterly Review*, 108 (Apr. 1929), 56-71.

Johnson, George. "Calvinism and Ethics," *Evangelical Quarterly*, 5 (1933), 82-93.

Johnson, T. C. "John Calvin and the Bible," *Evangelical Quarterly*, 4 (1932), 257-66.

Jong, P. Y. de. "Calvin's Contribution to Christian Education," *Calvin Theological Journal*, 2 (Nov. 1967), 162-201.

Keesecker, W. F. "John Calvin's Mirror," *Theology Today*, 17 (Oct. 1960), 288-89.

Lang, A. "The Sources of Calvin's Institutes," *Evangelical Quarterly*, 8 (1936), 130-41.

Lehmann, Paul. "The Reformers' Use of the Bible," *Theology Today*, 3 (1946), 328-44.

Leith, J. H. "John Calvin—Theologian of the Bible," *Interpretation*, 25 (July 1971), 329-44.

Marcel, D. C. "Relation between Justification and Sanctification in Calvin's Thought," *Evangelical Quarterly*, 27 (July-Sept. 1955), 132-45.

Marshall, I. H. "Sanctification in the Teaching of J. Wesley and J. Calvin," *Evangelical Quarterly*, 34 (1962), 75-82.

Matheson, J. G. "Calvin's Doctrine of the Christian Life," *Scottish Journal of Theology*, 2 (1949), 48-56.

McDonnell, K. "Ecclesiology of John Calvin and Vatican II," *Religion in Life*, 36 (Winter 1957), 542-56.

McLelland, J. C. "Calvin and Philosophy," *Canadian Journal of Theology*, 11 (Jan. 1965), 42-53.

McNeill, J. T. "Calvin as an Ecumenical Churchman," *Church History*, 32 (Dec. 1963), 379-91.

_____. "Natural Law in the Teaching of the Reformers," *Journal of Religion*, 26 (1946), 168-82.

_____. "Significance of the Word for Calvin," *Church History*, 28 (June 1959), 131-46.

_____. "The Church in Sixteenth Century Reformed Theology," *Journal of Religion*, 22 (1942), 252-69.

_____. "The Doctrine of the Ministry in Reformed Theology," *Church History*, 12 (1943), 77-97.

Meyer, B. "Calvin's Eucharistic Doctrine, 1536-1539," *Journal of Ecumenical Studies*, 4 (1967), 47-65.

Meyer, J. R. "Mysterium Fidei and the Later Calvin," *Scottish Journal of Theology*, (Nov. 1972), 392-411.

Oberman, H. A. "Extra Dimension in the Theology of Calvin," *Journal of Ecclesiastical History*, 21 (Jan. 1970), 53-64.

Partee, C. "Calvin and Determinism," *Christian Scholar's Review*, No. 5 (1975), 123-28.

_____. "Calvin and Experience," *Scottish Journal of Theology*, 27 (May 1973), 169-81.

_____. "Soul in Plato, Platonism, and Calvin," *Scottish Journal of Theology*, 22 (Sept. 1969), 278-96.

Parker, T. D. "Interpretation of Scripture: A Comparison of Calvin and Luther on Galatians," *Interpretation*, 17 (Jan. 1963), 61-75.

Parker, T. H. L. "Calvin's Concept of Revelation," *Scottish Journal of Theology*, 2 (1949), 29-47.

_____. "The Approach to Calvin," *Evangelical Quarterly*, 16 (1944), 165-72.

Parratt, J. K. "Witness of the Holy Spirit: Calvin, the Puritans and St. Paul," *Evangelical Quarterly*, 41 (July-Sept. 1969), 161-68.

Pauck, W. "Calvin's Institutes of the Christian Religion," *Church History,* 15 (Mar. 1946), 17-37.

Pelkonen, J. P. "The Teaching of John Calvin on the Nature and Function of the Conscience," *Lutheran Quarterly,* 21 (Feb. 1969), 24-88.

Peter, J. F. "Ministry in the Early Church as Seen by John Calvin," *Evangelical Quarterly,* 35 (1963), 68-78.

―――――. "The Place of Tradition in Reformed Theology," *Scottish Journal of Theology,* 18 (1965), 294-307.

Petry, Ray C. "Calvin's Conception of the 'Communio Sanctorum,'" *Church History,* 5 (1936), 227-38.

Peyer, E. de. "Calvin's Doctrine of Divine Providence," *Evangelical Quarterly,* 10 (1938), 30-45.

Priest, R. C. "Was Calvin a Biblical Literalist?" *Scottish Journal of Theology,* 20 (Sept. 1967), 312-28.

Prins, R. "The Image of God in Adam and the Restoration of Man in Jesus Christ: A Study in Calvin," *Scottish Journal of Theology,* 25 (1972), 32-44.

Pruett, G. E. "Protestant Doctrine of the Eucharistic Presence," *Calvin Theological Journal,* (Nov. 1975), 142-74.

Pruyser, P. W. "Calvin's View of Man: A Psychological Commentary," *Theology Today,* 26 (Apr. 1969), 51-68.

Räcke, G. "Gesetz und Evangelium bei Calvin," *Theologische Literaturzeitung,* 80:3 (1955), 179.

Rakow, M. "Christ's Descent into Hell: Calvin's Interpretation," *Religion in Life,* (Summer 1974), 218-26.

Ray, R. "Witness and the Word," *Canadian Journal of Theology,* 15 (Jan. 1969), 14-23.

Reardon, P. H. "Calvin on Providence: The Development of an Insight," *Scottish Journal of Theology,* 6 (1975), 517-34.

Richard, L. J. "John Calvin and the Role of the Church in the Spiritual Life," *Journal of Ecumenical Studies,* 2 (1974), 477-500.

Rolston, H. "Responsible Man in Reformed Theology: Calvin versus the Westminster Confession," *Scottish Journal of Theology,* 23 (May 1970), 129-56.

Rott, J. "Documents Strasbourgeois concernant Calvin," *Revue d'Histoire et de Philosophie Religieuses,* 44:4 (1964), 267-422.

Santmire, H. P. "Justification in Calvin's 1540 Romans Commentary," *Church History,* 33 (Sept. 1964), 294-313.

Saxer, E. "Reformierte Tauflehre in der Krise?" *Theologische Zeitschrift,* (Mar.-Apr. 1975), 95-107.

Smith, Samuel D. "John Calvin and Worldly Religion," *Lutheran Theological Quarterly,* 3:3 (1968), 65-74.

Smits, Luchese. "L'Autorité de S. Augustin, dans l'Institution Chrétienne de Jean Calvin," *Revue d'Histoire Ecclésiastique,* 45 (1950), 670-78.

Torrance, T. F. "Knowledge of God and Speech about Him According to John Calvin," *Revue d'Histoire et de Philosophie Religieuses,* 44:4 (1964), 267-422.

Tylenda, J. N. "Calvin and Christ's Presence in the Supper: True or Real," *Scottish Journal of Theology,* 27 (Feb. 1974), 65-75.

_____ . "Calvin's Understanding of the Communication of Properties," *Westminster Theological Journal,* (Fall 1975), 54-65.

_____ . "Christ the Mediator: Calvin versus Stancaro," *Calvin Theological Journal,* (Apr. 1973), 5-16.

_____ . "Controversy on Christ the Mediator: Calvin's Second Reply to Stancaro," *Calvin Theological Journal,* (Nov. 1973), 131-45.

Walker, C. S. M. "Calvin and the Church," *Scottish Journal of Theology,* 16 (1963), 371-89.

Warfield, B. B. "Calvin's Doctrine of Creation," *Princeton Theological Review,* 14 190-225.

Weber, O. "Compétence de l'Eglise et Compétence de l'Etat d'après les Ordonnances Ecclésiastiques de 1561," *Revue d'Histoire et de Philosophie Religieuses,* 44:4 (1964), 267-422.

Wyneken, K. H. "Calvin and Anabaptism," *Concordia Theological Monthly,* 36 (May 1965), 18-29.

Zimmerman, J. A. K. "Christian Life in Luther and Calvin," *Lutheran Quarterly,* 16 (Apr. 1964), 272-301.